Annie's *Favorite* Home Decor Projects™

Annie's Attic®

Editorial Director . . . . Andy Ashley

Production and Photography Director . . Ange Van Arman

Design Manager . . . . Marilyn Shelton

Design Staff . . . . Mickie Akins, Alice Vaughan &
Elizabeth Ann White

Senior Editor . . . . Janet Tipton Perrin

Project Editor . . . . Donna Scott

Editorial Staff . . . . Shirley Brown, Liz Field,
Skeeter Gilson, Nina Marsh & Shelly Riley

Photography Manager . . . . Scott Campbell

Photography Staff . . Tammy Coquat-Payne & Martha Coquat

Book Design & Production Manager . . . . . Diane Simpson

Production . . . . Joanne Gonzalez

Color Specialist . . . . Betty Holmes

Production Coordinator . . . . Glenda Chamberlain

Library of Congress Cataloging-in-Publication Data
ISBN: 0-9655269-6-8
First Printing: 1999
Library of Congress Catalog Card Number: 99-73065
Published and Distributed by Annie's Attic, LLC, Big Sandy, Texas 75755;
www.anniesattic.com
Printed in the United States of America

Table of Contents

Dear Friends,

Our home is our haven—a place that we can return to that is safe, secure and reflects the very essence of our being, our likes and dislikes, and all that we hold dear.

This concept, often called "nesting," is more important in the hectic, fast-paced world that we live than it has ever been before. It is vital to our very well being that we have a place to rest, relax and recharge our creative side.

Personally, I can think of no better way to accomplish these "Three R's" than with the art that we all know and love—crochet!

I would suggest that we use this art to surround ourselves with one-of-a-kind creations that are decorator pieces in their own right, and that give our guests a glimpse at our personalities.

That is why I personally chose the unique offerings that you'll find in the pages of this beautifully-designed book. There are almost 100 designs in eight chapters—all conveniently arranged so you can easily locate the perfect project for every room of your home!

There are even chapters devoted exclusively to afghan designs and projects perfect for decorating your holiday home—you couldn't ask for more!

Annie

Pretty Parlor

Dress up your salon in style with the dozen dainty and delicate designs in this chapter. Choose from decorator accessories, including an Irish-crochet embellished wall clock; an elegant rose filet crochet armchair set, a lovely and lacy luncheon cloth, a Victorian-style floral wreath, beautiful bead-trimmed tassels, and a coordinating pillow, doily and coaster set. When you fill your surroundings with these timeless crochet treasures, it's almost as if you've been transported to a time of ease and elegance that we can only dream of today!

Irish Wall Clock

by Colleen Sullivan

Finished Size: 11" diameter × 1" thick.

Materials:
- ❑ Size 10 crochet cotton thread:
    - 660 yds. green
    - 330 yds. white
- ❑ Styrofoam® circles:
    - 10"diameter × 1" thick
    - 6"diameter × ½" thick
- ❑ Quartz clock movement
- ❑ 6"-diameter self adhesive clock face with hands
- ❑ 12" square green felt
- ❑ 8 pearl 4mm beads
- ❑ Fabric stiffener
- ❑ Plastic food wrap
- ❑ Rust-proof straight pins
- ❑ Glue gun and glue stick
- ❑ Craft glue
- ❑ Nos. 2 and 8 steel crochet hooks or hook needed to obtain gauge

Gauge: No. 2 hook and two strands, 12 sc = 2"; 11 sc rows = 2".

Basic Stitches: Ch, sl st, sc, dc.

Notes: *Hold two strands of thread together as one throughout unless otherwise stated.*
Use No. 2 hook throughout unless otherwise stated.
Work in continuous rnds; do not join or turn unless otherwise stated. Mark first st of each rnd.

Clock Cover

Rnd 1: With green, ch 8, sl st in first ch to form ring, ch 1, 16 sc in ring. *(16 sc made)*
Rnd 2: (Sc in next st, 2 sc in next st) around. *(24)*
Rnd 3: (Sc in next 2 sts, 2 sc in next st) around. *(32)*
Rnd 4: (Sc in next 3 sts, 2 sc in next st) around. *(40)*
Rnd 5: (Sc in next 4 sts, 2 sc in next st) around. *(48)*
Rnd 6: (Sc in next 5 sts, 2 sc in next st) around. *(56)*
Rnd 7: (Sc in next 6 sts, 2 sc in next st) around. *(64)*
Rnd 8: (Sc in next 7 sts, 2 sc in next st) around. *(72)*
Rnd 9: (Sc in next 8 sts, 2 sc in next st) around. *(80)*
Rnd 10: (Sc in next 9 sts, 2 sc in next st) around. *(88)*
Rnd 11: (Sc in next 10 sts, 2 sc in next st) around. *(96)*
Rnd 12: (Sc in next 11 sts, 2 sc in next st) around. *(104)*
Rnd 13: (Sc in next 12 sts, 2 sc in next st) around. *(112)*
Rnd 14: (Sc in next 13 sts, 2 sc in next st) around. *(120)*
Rnd 15: Sc in each st around, join with sl st in **back lp** *(see Stitch Guide)* of first sc.
Rnd 16: Working this rnd in **back lps**, ch 1, sc in each st around, join with sl st in **both lps** of first sc.
Rnd 17: Ch 1, sc in each st around, join.
Rnd 18: Ch 1, sc in each st around, **turn, do not join.**
Rnd 19: Working this rnd in **back lps**, (sc in next 14 sts, 2 sc in next st) around, **turn.** *(128)*
Rnd 20: (Sc in next 15 sts, 2 sc in next st) around. *(136)*
Rnd 21: (Sc in next 16 sts, 2 sc in next st) around. *(144)*
Rnd 22: (Sc in next 17 sts, 2 sc in next st) around. *(152)*
Rnd 23: (Sc in next 18 sts, 2 sc in next st) around. *(160)*
Rnd 24: (Sc in next 19 sts, 2 sc in next st) around. *(168)*
Rnd 25: (Sc in next 20 sts, 2 sc in next st) around. *(176)*
Rnd 26: (Sc in next 21 sts, 2 sc in next st) around. *(184)*
Rnd 27: (Sc in next 22 sts, 2 sc in next st) around. *(192)*
Rnds 28–29: Sc in each st around.
Rnd 30: Working this rnd in **back lps,** sc in each st around.
Rnds 31–34: Sc in each st around.
Rnd 35: Sc in each st around, join with sl st in **back lp** of first sc.
Rnd 36: Working this rnd in **back lps,** (sc in next 6 sts, sc next 2 sts tog) around, join with sl st in first sc. *(168)*
Rnds 37–38: Ch 1, sc in each st around, join. At end of last rnd, fasten off.
Rnd 39: For **trim,** with right side of work facing you, working in **remaining lps** of rnd 35, join green with sl st in first st, sl st in each st around, join with sl st in first sl st. Fasten off.
Rnd 40: For **trim,** with right side of work facing you, working in **remaining lps** of rnd 15, join green with sl st in first st, sl st in each st around, join. Fasten off.
Rnd 41: For **edging,** with wrong side of work facing you, working in **remaining lps** of rnd 29, join green with sc in first st, sc in each st around, join with sl st in first sc, **turn.** *(192)*
Rnd 42: (Ch 5, dc) in first st, skip next st, sc

continued on page 13

Floral Set

by Elizabeth Ann White

Finished Sizes: Armrest is 8¼" × 9¼". Headrest is 15" × 20".

Materials:
- ❏ 350 yds. white size 10 crochet cotton thread
- ❏ No. 6 steel hook or hook needed to obtain gauge

Gauge: 7 mesh = 2"; 4 mesh rows = 1".

Basic Stitches: Ch, sl st, sc, dc, tr.

Special Stitches: For **mesh,** ch 2, skip next 2 dc, dc in next dc **or** ch 2, skip next 2 chs, dc in next dc or ch.

For **beginning block (beg block),** ch 3, dc in next 3 dc **or** ch 3, 2 dc in first ch sp, dc in next dc.

For **beginning increase (beg inc),** ch 5, dc in fourth ch from hook, dc in next ch, dc in next dc.

For **end increase (end inc),** tr in same st as last dc made, tr in first lp in side of last tr *(see illustration),* tr in first lp in side of last tr made.

For **block,** dc in next 3 dc **or** 2 dc in next ch sp, dc in next dc.

For **double block,** 5 dc in next double mesh.

For **double mesh,** ch 5, skip next sc, dc in next dc.

For **lacet,** ch 3, skip next 2 dc **or** 2 chs, sc in next dc **or** ch, ch 3, skip next 2 dc **or** 2 chs, dc in next dc.

Note: *See Special Stitches for working pattern instructions.*

continued on page 12

▨ = Beg Block, Block

☐ = Mesh

☐ = Double Mesh

▨ = Double Block

⧖ = Lacet

X = Beg or End Inc

— = Sl St Across Sts

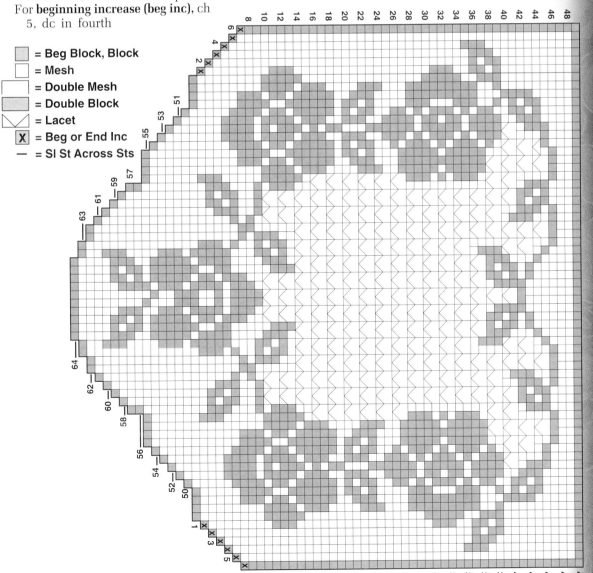

Luncheon Cloth

Finished Size: 24¾" square.

Materials:
- ❑ 2,000 yds. white size 30 crochet cotton thread
- ❑ No. 12 steel hook or hook needed to obtain gauges

Gauges: Large Motif is 2¾" across; rnds 1–3 are 1¾" across. Small Motif is ½" across.

Basic Stitches: Ch, sl st, sc, dc.

Special Stitches: For **beginning shell (beg shell)**, sl st in next 2 sts, (sl st, ch 3, 2 dc, ch 2, 3 dc) in first ch sp.
For **shell,** (3 dc, ch 2, 3 dc) in next ch sp.
For **double picot (dp),** (sc, ch 5, sc, ch 5, sc) in ch sp of next shell.
For **joining double picot (jdp),** sc in next shell, ch 2; working on Motif specified, sl st in first ch sp of corresponding dp at rectangle or X *(see joining illustration)*, ch 2, sc in same shell on this Motif, ch 2; working in same Motif as last sl st, sl st in second ch sp of corresponding dp, ch 2, sc in same shell on this Motif.
For **long sc (lsc),** working over ch sp of last row, sc in ch sp on second row below.

First Row
First Large Motif
Rnd 1: Ch 8, sl st in first ch to form ring, ch 3, 24 dc in ring, join with sl st in top of ch-3. *(25 dc made)*
Rnd 2: Ch 4, skip next st, (dc in next st, ch 1) around, join with sl st in third ch of ch-4. *(24 dc, 24 ch sps)*
Rnd 3: Ch 3, 2 dc in first ch sp, (dc in next st, 2 dc in next ch sp) around, join. *(72 dc)*
Rnd 4: Ch 1, sc in first st, ch 6, skip next 5 sts, (sc in next st, ch 6, skip next 5 sts) around, join with sl st in first sc. *(12 sc, 12 ch sps)*
Rnd 5: Ch 1, 10 sc in each ch sp around, join. *(120 sc)*
Rnd 6: Sl st in next 3 sts, (sl st, ch 3, 2 dc) in next st, ch 2, 3 dc in next st, ch 6, (skip next 8 sts, 3 dc in next st, ch 2, 3 dc in next st, ch 6) around to last 5 sts, skip last 5 sts, join with sl st in top of ch-3. *(72 dc, 12 ch-2 sps, 12 ch-6 sps)*
Rnd 7: Beg shell *(see Special Stitches)*, *ch 5, skip next 3 sts, skip next ch-6 sp, skip next 3 sts, **shell** *(see Special Stitches)*; repeat from * 10 more times, ch 5, skip next 3 sts, skip last ch-6 sp, join. *(12 shells, 12 ch-5 sps)*
Rnd 8: Sl st in next 2 sts, ch 1, **dp** *(see Special Stitches)*, *ch 5, **lsc** *(see Special Stitches)*, ch 5, dp; repeat from * 10 more times, ch 5, lsc, ch 5, join with sl st in first sc. Fasten off.

Second Large Motif
Rnds 1–7: Repeat rnds 1–7 of First Large Motif.
Rnd 8: Sl st in next 2 sts, dp, (ch 5, lsc, ch 5, dp) 9 times, ch 5, lsc, ch 5, *jdp *(see Special Stitches)* on last Motif, ch 5, lsc, ch 5; repeat from *, join with sl st in first sc. Fasten off.
Repeat Second Large Motif 7 more times.

continued on page 12

Luncheon Cloth

continued from page 11

Second Row
First Large Motif

Working on bottom of First Large Motif on First Row *(see illustration)*, repeat Second Large Motif of First Row.

Second Large Motif
Rnds 1–7: Repeat rnds 1–7 of First Large Motif on First Row.

Rnd 8: Sl st in next 2 sts, dp, (ch 5, lsc, ch 5, dp) 6 times, ch 5, lsc, ch 5, (jdp on last Motif, ch 5, lsc, ch 5) 2 times, dp, ch 5, lsc, ch 5, (jdp on Motif above, ch 5, lsc, ch 5) 2 times, join with sl st in first sc. Fasten off.

Repeat Second Large Motif of Second Row 7 more times.

Next Rows
Work Second Row 7 more times.

Small Motif
Rnd 1: Ch 8, sl st in first ch to form ring, ch 3, 16 dc in ring, join with sl st in top of ch-3. *(17 dc made)*

Rnd 2: Ch 4, skip next st, (dc in next st, ch 1) around, join with sl st in third ch of ch-4. *(16 dc, 16 ch sps)*

Rnd 3: Ch 3, 2 dc in first ch sp, (dc in next st, 2 dc in next ch sp) around, join. *(48 dc)*

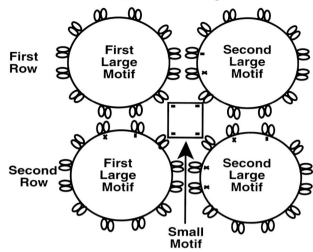

☐ = First Joining of Motif
☒ = Next Joinings

First Row — First Large Motif, Second Large Motif

Second Row — First Large Motif, Second Large Motif

Small Motif

Rnd 4: Ch 1, sc in first st, (ch 5, sc in next st) 2 times, *[ch 4, skip next 3 sts, sc in next st, ch 2; working on one Large Motif, sl st in first ch sp of corresponding dp *(see square on joining illustration)*, ch 2, sc in next st, ch 4, skip next 3 sts], sc in next st, (ch 5, sc in next st) 2 times; repeat from * 2 more times; repeat between [ ], join with sl st in first sc. Fasten off.

Work one Small Motif in each sp between Large Motifs. ⚷

Floral Set

continued from page 9

Armrest (make 2)
Row 1: Ch 87, dc in fourth ch from hook, dc in each ch across, turn. *(85 dc made)*

Row 2: Beg block, 26 mesh, block, turn.

Rows 3–40: Beg block, work across according to graph on this page, turn. At end of last row, fasten off.

Headrest
Row 1: Ch 165, dc in fourth ch from hook, dc in next 11 chs, (ch 2, skip next 2 chs, dc in next ch) 17 times, (dc in next 3 chs, ch 2, skip next 2 chs, dc in next ch) 2 times, dc in next 12 chs, (ch 2, skip next 2 chs, dc in next 4 chs) 2 times, (ch 2, skip next 2 chs, dc in next ch) 17 times, dc in last 12 chs, turn. *(87 dc made)*

Row 2: Beg inc, work across according to graph on page 9, end inc, turn.

Rows 3–49: Work across according to graph, turn. At end of last row, fasten off.

Row 50: Working on opposite side of starting ch on row 1, skip first 12 chs, join with sl st in next ch, ch 3, work across according to

graph leaving remaining chs unworked, turn.

Rows 51–64: Work across according to graph, turn. At end of last row, fasten off. ⚷

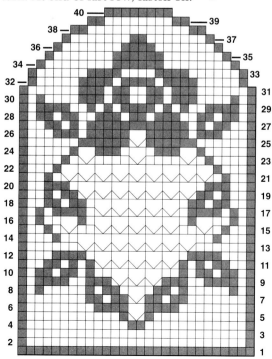

☒ = Beg Block, Block
☐ = Mesh
☐ = Double Mesh
▨ = Double Block
◹ = Lacet
X = Beg or End Inc
— = Sl St Across Sts

in next st, skip next st, *(dc, ch 2, dc) in next st, skip next st, sc in next st, skip next st; repeat from * around, join with sl st in third ch of ch-5. *(48 ch sps)*

Rnd 43: Ch 1, 5 sc in each ch sp around, join with sl st in first sc. Fasten off.

Rose (make 4)

Rnd 1: With No. 8 hook and single strand of white, ch 3, 9 dc in third ch from hook, join with sl st in top of ch-3. *(10 dc made)*

Rnd 2: Ch 1, sc in each st around, join with sl st in first sc.

Rnd 3: Ch 1, sc in first st, ch 3, skip next st, (sc in next st, ch 3, skip next st) around, join. *(5 ch sps)*

Rnd 4: For **petals**, (sl st, ch 2, 4 dc, ch 2, sl st) in each ch sp around, join with sl st in first sl st. *(5 petals)*

Rnd 5: Working behind petals, ch 1, (sc in next skipped st of rnd 2, ch 4) around, join with sl st in first sc. *(5 ch sps)*

Rnd 6: For **petals**, (sl st, ch 2, 6 dc, ch 2, sl st) in each ch sp around. *(5 petals)*

Rnd 7: Working behind petals, ch 2, (sc in bottom two strands of third dc of next petal, ch 6) around, join with sl st in first sc. *(5 ch sps)*

Rnd 8: For **petals**, (sl st, ch 2, 8 dc, ch 2, sl st) in each ch sp around, join with sl st in first sl st. Fasten off.

Leaf (make 8)

Row 1: With No. 8 hook and single strand of white, ch 15, sc in second ch from hook, sc in next 12 chs, (sc, ch 3, sc) in last ch; working in remaining lps on opposite side of starting ch, sc in next 11 chs leaving last 2 chs unworked, turn. *(26 sc, 1 ch sp made)*

Rows 2–6: Working these rows in **back lps**, ch 1, sc in each st across to ch-3 sp, (sc, ch 3, sc) in ch-3 sp, sc in each st across leaving last 2 sts unworked, turn.

Row 7: Working in **back lps**, ch 1, sc in each st across to ch-3 sp, sl st in ch-3 sp leaving remaining sts unworked. Fasten off.

Small Flower (make 8)

Rnd 1: With No. 8 hook and single strand of white, ch 2, 5 sc in second ch from hook, join with sl st in first sc. *(5 sc made)*

Rnd 2: For **petals**, (ch 2, 3 dc, ch 2, sl st) in first st, (sl st, ch 2, 3 dc, ch 2, sl st) in each st around, join with sl st in joining sl st of rnd 1. Fasten off.

Lace Edging

Rnd 1: With No. 8 hook and single strand white, ch 160, sl st in first ch to form ring, ch 1, sc in each ch around, join with sl st in first sc. *(160 sc made)*

Rnd 2: Ch 1, sc in first st, *(ch 4, sl st in third ch from hook—*picot made*) 2 times, ch 1, skip next 4 sts, sc in next st; repeat from * 30 more times, (ch 4, sl st in third ch from hook) 2 times, ch 1, skip last 4 sts, join. *(96 ch sps)*

Rnd 3: Sl st in next ch sp and in next picot, ch 1, sc in next ch sp between picots, (ch 5, sl st in third ch from hook) 2 times, *ch 2, skip next 2 ch sps, sc in next ch sp between picots, (ch 5, sl st in third ch from hook) 2 times; repeat from * around, ch 2, join.

Rnd 4: Sl st in next ch sp and in next picot, ch 1, sc in next ch sp between picots, (ch 6, sl st in third ch from hook) 2 times, *ch 3, skip next 2 ch sps, sc in next ch sp between picots, (ch 6, sl st in third ch from hook) 2 times; repeat from * around, ch 3, join.

Rnd 5: Sl st in next ch sp and in next picot, ch 1, sc in next ch sp between picots, (ch 5, sl st in third ch from hook) 3 times, *ch 2, skip next 2 ch sps, sc in next ch sp between picots, (ch 5, sl st in third ch from hook) 3 times; repeat from * around, ch 2, join. Fasten off.

Clock Base

For **back**, using clock movement as pattern, cut center out of 10" styrofoam® circle.

For **front**, using glue gun, center and glue 6" styrofoam® circle to opposite side of 10" styrofoam® circle.

Assembly

Apply fabric stiffener to Clock Cover and Lace Edging according to manufacturer's instructions.

Place dampened Clock Cover over Clock Base; pin to shape. Remove pins when completely dry.

Place Lace Edging on a flat surface covered with plastic wrap; pin to shape. Remove plastic wrap and pins when completely dry.

Using back of Clock Base as pattern, cut piece from felt; cut out center to match opening in styrofoam® circle. Using craft glue, glue felt to back of styrofoam® with inside edges of felt over edges at opening. Let dry completely.

Place clock movement inside opening at back of Clock Base, pushing stem through styrofoam® pieces.

Place clock face over front of Clock Base; fasten hands to stem according to manufacturer's instructions.

With glue gun, glue Lace Edging to Clock Cover on Clock Base. Arrange and glue Roses, Leaves and Small Flowers over Lace Edging *(see photo)*. Glue one pearl bead to center of each Small Flower.

Victorian Wreath

An Original by Annie

Finished Size: 12" wreath.

Materials:
- ❑ Worsted yarn:
  - 3½ oz. white
  - 2½ oz. each of assorted pinks and reds for roses
  - 2 oz. green
- ❑ 10 yds. blue 1½" ribbon
- ❑ 12" Styrofoam® ring
- ❑ Low-temp hot glue
- ❑ Two 6" pieces 22-gauge floral wire
- ❑ Small-head straight pins
- ❑ T-pins
- ❑ Tapestry needle
- ❑ F and H hooks or hooks needed to obtain gauges

Gauge: H hook, 4 sts = 1"; ttr is 1½" tall. F hook, 5 sts = 1".

Basic Stitches: Ch, sl st, sc, dc, tr.

Special Stitch: For **triple treble cluster (ttr cluster)**, *yo 4 times, insert hook in st, yo, pull loop through, (yo, pull through 2 lps on hook) 4 times, leaving last lps on hook; working in same st, repeat from * for number of ttr called for in cluster, yo and pull through all lps on hook.

Eyelet Lace

Rnd 1: For **foundation chain on inner edge,** with H hook and white, (ch 3, dc in third ch from hook) 32 times, join with sl st in ch at base of first dc, **do not turn or fasten off.**

Rnd 2: For **foundation chain on outer edge,** ch 11, tr in fourth ch from hook, ch 4, tr in fourth ch from hook, skip ch at base of last dc on inner edge, *work a **2-ttr cluster** (see Special Stitch) in ch at base of next dc (see illustration), (ch 4, tr in fourth ch from hook) 2 times, skip ch at base of next dc on inner edge; repeat from * around, join with sl st in ch at base of first tr on outer edge.

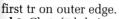

Rnd 3: Ch 1, (7 hdc in next ch-4 sp, ch 1) around, join with sl st in top of ch-1.

Rnd 4: Sl st in each st across to center st of first 7-dc group, sc in center dc, ch 2, (dc, ch 5, dc) in next ch-1 sp, ch 2, *sc in center st of next 7-dc group, ch 2, (dc, ch 5, dc) in next ch-1 sp,

ch 2; repeat from * around, join with sl st in first sc.

Rnd 5: Ch 1, sc in first sc, 9 dc in next ch-5 sp, (sc in next sc, 9 dc in next ch-5 sp) around, join with sl st in first sc. Fasten off.

Rnd 6: Working in foundation chain on inner edge, with white, join with sc in first ch-3 sp, 4 sc in same ch sp, 5 sc in each ch-3 sp around, join with sl st in first sc. Fasten off.

For **ch-9 back lps,** working on wrong side of Lace, with H hook and white, join with sl st in top of any 2-ttr cluster, ch 9, (sl st in top of next 2-ttr cluster, ch 9) around, join with sl st in top of first 2-ttr cluster. Fasten off.

Repeat on opposite edge of Lace, working into bottom of 2-ttr clusters.

Irish Rose (make 2 of assorted colors)

Rnd 1: With F hook and yarn, make **slip ring** (see Stitch Guide), ch 3, 9 dc in ring, pull end tightly to close ring, join with sl st in top of ch-3. (10 dc made)

Rnd 2: Ch 1, sc in each st around, join with sl st in first sc.

Rnd 3: Ch 3, skip next st, (sc in next st, ch 2, skip next st) around, sc in joining sl st of rnd 2. (5 ch sps)

Rnd 4: For **petals,** (sl st, ch 2, 4 dc, ch 2, sl st) in each ch sp around. (5 petals)

Rnd 5: Working behind petals, ch 1, (sc in **back lp**—see Stitch Guide—of next skipped sc on rnd 2, ch 4) around, join with sl st in first sc. (5 ch sps)

Rnd 6: For **petals,** (sl st, ch 2, 7 dc, ch 2, sl st) in each ch sp around. (5 petals)

Rnd 7: Ch 2, *working behind next petal between 2 center dc (see illustration), sc around ch sp, ch 5; repeat from * around, join. (5 ch sps)

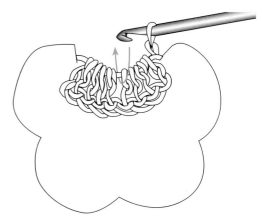

continued on page 24

Parlor Perk-Up

by Donna Jones

Finished Sizes: Pillow is 15" square including Ruffles. Doily is 12½" square. Coaster is 4¾" square.

Materials:
- ❏ Worsted yarn:
    - 7 oz. rose
    - 3 oz. white
- ❏ 600 yds. white size 10 crochet cotton thread
- ❏ Polyester fiberfill or 14" square pillow form
- ❏ Bobby pins for markers
- ❏ Embroidery needle
- ❏ G hook and No. 5 steel hook or hooks needed to obtain gauges

Gauges: G hook and worsted yarn, rnd 6 of Pillow is 4" square. **No. 5 steel hook and crochet thread,** rnd 7 of Doily is 4¼" across.

Basic Stitches: Ch, sl st, sc, hdc, dc, tr.

Special Stitches: For **triple treble crochet (ttr),** yo 4 times, yo, insert hook in st, yo, pull through st, (yo, pull through 2 lps on hook) 5 times.
For **shell,** (3 dc, ch 2, 3 dc) in next ch sp.
For **beginning (beg) shell,** (sl st, ch 5, 3 dc) in first ch sp.
For **end shell,** 2 dc in first ch sp, join with sl st in third ch of ch-5 *(beg shell and end shell form one complete shell).*
For **V st,** (dc, ch 1, dc) in next ch sp unless otherwise stated.
To **join,** sl st in st or ch indicated unless otherwise stated.

Doily

Rnd 1: With No. 5 steel hook and crochet cotton thread, ch 4, sl st in first ch to form ring, ch 1, 8 sc in ring, **join** *(see Special Stitches)* in first sc. *(8 sc made)*

Rnd 2: Ch 1, (sc, ch 12) 2 times in each of next 7 sts, (sc, ch 12, sc) in last st, ch 6, **ttr** *(see Special Stitches)* in first sc to form joining ch lp. *(16 ch lps made)*

Rnd 3: Ch 1, sc in joining ch lp, ch 3, (sc in next ch lp, ch 3) around, join in first sc. *(16 sc, 16 ch sps)*

Rnd 4: Ch 1, sc in each st and 3 sc in each ch sp around, join. *(64 sc)*

Rnd 5: (Ch 5, 3 dc) in first st *(half of first shell made),* ch 1, skip next 3 sts, dc in next st, ch 1, skip next 3 sts, *(3 dc, ch 3, 3 dc) in next st *(next shell made),* ch 1, skip next 3 sts, dc in next st, ch 1, skip next 3 sts; repeat from * around, 2 dc in same st as ch 5 *(this completes first shell),* join in third ch of ch-5. *(8 shells, 8 dc)*

Rnd 6: Beg shell *(see Special Stitches),* ch 2, skip next ch sp, **V st** in next st, ch 2, skip next ch sp, **(shell,** ch 2, skip next ch sp, V st in next st, ch 2, skip next ch sp) around, **end shell.** *(8 shells, 8 V sts)*

Rnd 7: Beg shell, ch 3, skip next ch sp, V st, ch 3, skip next ch sp, (shell, ch 3, skip next ch sp, V st, ch 3, skip next ch sp) around, end shell.

Rnd 8: Beg shell, ch 4, skip next ch sp, V st, ch 4, skip next ch sp, (shell, ch 4, skip next ch sp, V st, ch 4, skip next ch sp) around, end shell.

Rnd 9: Beg shell, ch 5, skip next ch sp, V st, ch 5, skip next ch sp, (shell, ch 5, skip next ch sp, V st, ch 5, skip next ch sp) around, end shell.

Rnd 10: Beg shell, ch 5, skip next ch sp, (dc, ch 1, dc, ch 1, dc) in next ch sp, ch 5, skip next ch sp, *shell, ch 5, skip next ch sp, (dc, ch 1, dc, ch 1, dc) in next ch sp, ch 5, skip next ch sp; repeat from * around, end shell. *(8 shells, 16 ch-1 sps)*

Rnd 11: Beg shell, ch 5, skip next ch sp, V st, ch 2, V st, ch 5, skip next ch sp, (shell, ch 5, skip next ch sp, V st, ch 2, V st, ch 5, skip next ch sp) around, end shell. *(8 shells, 16 V sts, 8 ch-2 sps)*

Rnd 12: Beg shell, *[skip next V st; for **fan,** (ttr, ch 7, sc) in next ch-2 sp, (ch 12, sc) 5 times in same ch-2 sp, (ch 7, ttr) in same ch-2 sp *(fan made),* shell in next shell, ch 5, V st in next V st, ch 3, skip next ch-2 sp, V st in next V st, ch 5], shell in next shell; repeat from * 2 more times; repeat between [ ], end shell. *(4 fans, 8 V sts, 8 shells)*

Rnd 13: Beg shell, *[ch 3, (sc in next ch lp on fan, ch 3) 7 times, shell in next shell, ch 5, (V st in next V st, ch 5) 2 times]; shell in next shell; repeat from * 2 more times; repeat between [ ], end shell. *(32 ch-3 sps, 8 V sts, 8 shells)*

Rnd 14: Beg shell, *[ch 5, skip next ch-3 sp; working across fan, 3 sc in next ch sp, (sc in next sc, 3 sc in next ch sp) 5 times, ch 5, shell in next shell, ch 5, V st in next V st, ch 7, V st in next V st, ch 5], shell in next shell; repeat from * 2 more times; repeat between [ ], end shell. *(92 sc, 4 ch-7 sps, 8 V sts, 8 shells)*

Rnd 15: Beg shell, *[ch 5, skip next ch sp and next 3 sc, V st in next sc, (ch 3, skip next 3 sc, V st in next sc) 4 times, ch 5, shell in next shell, ch 5, V st in next V st, ch 3, V st in fourth ch of next ch-7, ch 3, V st in next V st, ch 5], shell in next shell; repeat from * 2 more times; repeat between [ ], end shell. *(32 V sts, 8 shells)*

Rnd 16: Beg shell, *[ch 5, V st in next V st, (ch 3, V st in next V st) 4 times, ch 5, shell in next shell, ch 5, dc in next V st; for **fan,** (ttr, ch 7, sc) in next V st, (ch 12, sc) 5 times in same V st, (ch 7, ttr) in same V st *(fan made),* dc in next V st, ch 5], shell in next shell; repeat from * 2

continued on page 23

Tassel Trimmings

by Carolyn Christmas

Basic Instructions

Finished Sizes: Tassels range in size from 5½" to 7" long, excluding Cord.

Basic Materials:
- ❑ Rayon crochet thread *(see individual patterns for colors and amounts)*
- ❑ 2-yd. scrap of crochet cotton thread or pearl cotton
- ❑ Two 1-yd. lengths of embroidery floss to match Tassel and Cord
- ❑ 5" × 7" piece thin smooth-surfaced wood, heavy-duty corrugated cardboard or old hardback book cover (**do not** use light-weight cardboard, as it will buckle from the weight and tension of the thread wraps)
- ❑ Masking tape
- ❑ Pencil
- ❑ 2 kitchen or dining chairs
- ❑ Scissors
- ❑ Large-eyed sharp-pointed embroidery needle

Basic Twisted Cord

1: Place backs of chairs three times as far apart as you want the final length of Cord to be *(for 24" and 27" Cords in this set, the chairs were 2 yds. and 2½ yds. apart)*. If chair backs do not have spindles, turn chairs upside down and use legs for the next step.

2: Holding all rayon thread strands needed *(see individual pattern for amounts and colors)* together as one, tie to one spindle or leg of one chair; bring strands across to other chair and around one spindle or leg *(see Twisted Cord Illustration below)*; continue wrapping the number of times listed in individual pattern and end at same point where you began. Cut ends. Untie first end of rayon thread strands from spindle and tie it to last end of rayon thread strands.

3: Remove one end of loops from one chair and place pencil through loops; keeping strands taut, turn pencil clockwise, twisting thread about 100 times or until it begins to twist back on itself when tension is released.

4: Being careful not to let twisted thread kink or escape your grasp, hold pencil in one hand and grasp center of twisted thread with other hand, bringing end with pencil across to match end on chair; release center fold and carefully allow twisted thread to twist back on itself. Holding twisted thread firmly to keep it from unwinding, remove ends from pencil and chair; holding these ends together, tie a large overhand knot about 4" from ends.

5: To make knot secure, thread needle with one length of matching color embroidery floss and sew through the knot several times. Secure ends and trim excess.

6: Trim ends past knot leaving at least 2" *(if hiding knot inside Tassel—see Step 1 of Basic Finishing on page 20—trim ends closer)*. For **rayon thread only,** straighten by wetting these ends, squeeze out excess water and let dry.

Basic Tassel

1: Cut a 20" strand from 2-yd. scrap of crochet cotton thread or pearl cotton. Fold 20" strand in half and tape it across the top edge of wood, cardboard or book cover *(see Tassel Illustration 1)*. Fold remainder of thread or pearl cotton in half and thread ends opposite of the fold through needle.

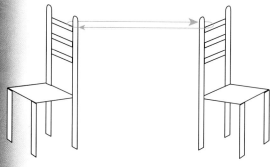

2: Using one strand for **small** Tassel, two strands for **medium** Tassel, or three strands for **large** Tassel *(see amounts and colors stated in individual patterns)*, wrap entire amount of rayon thread for desired size around the 7" length of wood, cardboard or book cover.

3: Remove tape from top edge and tie the loose ends of the thread in a knot as tightly as possible around end of rayon thread lps *(see Tassel Illustration 2)*. Holding the tied end of rayon lps firmly with one hand, cut opposite end of lps with scissors.

4: Holding rayon strands at tied end, smooth strands down. Pick up needle threaded with crochet cotton thread and wrap thread around rayon

continued on page 20

Tassel Trimmings

continued from page 18

strands about 1" to 1½" from knot at top *(see Tassel Illustration 3)*, run needle through fold in crochet cotton and pull tight. Wrap crochet cotton tightly around rayon strands several times and run needle under the wraps two times to secure *(see Tassel Illustration 4)*. Clip off excess crochet cotton.

5: To **straighten strands of rayon thread Tassel only,** wet loose strands of Tassel up to crochet cotton wraps *(do not wet top section of Tassel)* by holding strands under running water or dipping strands in bowl of water. Squeeze *(do not wring)* out excess water by hand, then roll Tassel in a dry towel to sponge out as much water as possible. Using crochet cotton ends at top, tie Tassel to a towel bar or bottom of clothes hanger; allow Tassel to hang until dry, shaking periodically as it dries.

3.

4.

Basic Finishing

1: Going from top to bottom, insert the unknotted end of Twisted Cord *(for a different finished look on Cord, the knotted end on the small and medium sizes can be used here instead to hide it inside the Tassel)* through center of rnd 1 on Tassel Cap *(made in individual pattern)*, push Tassel Cap up on Cord several inches.

2: Being careful not to cut strands of Tassel, cut crochet cotton thread wraps from neck of Tassel and divide ends of Tassel so that crochet cotton thread tied at top is visible on underside *(see Tassel Illustration 5)*.

3: Separate twist in unknotted end of Cord and make an opening large enough to slip over half of Tassel strands; place Tassel strands through opening *(see Tassel Illustration 5)* and slide end of Cord up to top of Tassel.

4: Fold remaining length of matching color embroidery floss in

5.

half and thread ends opposite fold through needle; wrap thread around neck of Tassel in same manner as step 4 of Tassel. Remove crochet thread used to tie top of Tassel.

5: Slide Tassel Cap down Cord and over top of Tassel. Floss wrapped around neck of Tassel may need to be repositioned up or down slightly to be hidden behind rnds of Cap.

6: If desired, tie a knot in Cord at top of Tassel Cap. Trim bottom ends of Tassel to desired length. ☞

Red & Green

Materials:
- ❑ Rayon crochet thread or size 10 crochet cotton:
    - 200 yds. green *(for Tassel)*
    - 100 yds. red *(for 27" Cord and Cap)*
    - 60 yds. white *(for Cord)*
- ❑ 7 small red ribbon roses with leaves
- ❑ Craft glue
- ❑ No. 7 steel hook or hook needed to obtain gauge

Gauge: 8 chs or sts = 1"; 2 sc rows and 1 dc row = ½"; rnds 1–3 are 1¼" across.

Basic Stitches: Ch, sl st, sc, dc.

Tassel Cap

Rnd 1: With red, ch 10, sl st in first ch to form ring, ch 1, 16 sc in ring, join with sl st in first sc. *(16 sc made)*

Rnd 2: (Ch 3, dc) in first st, ch 1, skip next st, (2 dc in next st, ch 1, skip next st) around, join with sl st in top of ch-3. *(16 dc, 8 ch sps)*

Rnd 3: Ch 1, sc in first 2 sts, 2 sc in next ch sp, (sc in next 2 sts, 2 sc in next ch sp) around, join. *(32 sc)*

Rnd 4: Ch 3, dc in next st, ch 2, skip next 2 sts, (dc in next 2 sts, ch 2, skip next 2 sts) around, join. *(16 dc, 8 ch sps)*

Rnds 5–6: Repeat rnds 3 and 4.

Rnd 7: Repeat rnd 3.

Rnd 8: Ch 3, dc in next st, ch 1, skip next 2 sts, (dc in next 2 sts, ch 1, skip next 2 sts) around, join.

Rnd 9: Ch 1, sc in first 2 sts, sc in next ch sp, (sc in next 2 sts, sc in next ch sp) around, join. *(24 sc)*

Rnds 10–11: Ch 1, sc in each st around, join. At end of last rnd, fasten off.

Twisted Cord & Tassel

Hold one strand red and one strand white together as one; wrapping multicolor strand around chair spindles 10 times, work Basic Twisted Cord instructions on page 18.

With two balls green, work Basic Tassel instructions for medium size on pages 18 and 20.

Finishing

Work Basic Finishing instructions on this page.

Glue ribbon roses around bottom of Tassel Cap. ☞

Green & Black

Materials:
- ❑ Rayon crochet thread or size 10 crochet cotton thread:
    - 300 yds. green *(for Tassel, 27" Cord and Cap)*
    - 200 yds. black *(for Tassel)*
- ❑ 8 opaque black 10mm round faceted beads
- ❑ 8 gold washed 10mm large-hole disks
- ❑ 9 regular metal paper clips
- ❑ 8 medium-sized metal washers
- ❑ Craft glue
- ❑ No. 7 steel hook or hook needed to obtain gauge

Gauge: 8 chs or sts = 1"; rnds 1–2 are 1⅛" across.

Basic Stitches: Ch, sl st, sc, dc.

Tassel Cap

Rnd 1: With green, ch 10, sl st in first ch to form ring, ch 1, 16 sc in ring, join with sl st in first sc. *(16 sc made)*

Rnd 2: (Ch 3, dc) in first st, 2 dc in each st around, join with sl st in top of ch-3. *(32 dc)*

Rnds 3–6: Ch 3, dc in each st around, join.

Rnd 7: Ch 3, dc in next st, dc next 2 sts tog, (dc in next 2 sts, dc next 2 sts tog) around, join. *(24)*

Rnd 8: Ch 3, dc in each st around, join.

Rnd 9: Ch 3, dc in next 2 sts, ch 3, (dc in next 3 sts, ch 3) around, join. *(24 dc, 8 ch sps)*

Rnd 10: Ch 3, dc in next 2 sts, ch 3, skip next ch sp, (dc in next 3 sts, ch 3, skip next ch sp) around, join.

Rnd 11: Ch 2, dc next 2 sts tog; for **picot**, ch 3, sl st in **front lp and left bar** *(see Stitch Guide)* of last st made *(picot made)*; ch 3, (sc, ch 12, sc) in next ch sp, ch 3, *dc next 3 dc tog, picot, ch 3, (sc, ch 12, sc) in next ch sp, ch 3; repeat from * around, join with sl st in top of first dc. Fasten off.

To **straighten ch-12 lps,** dampen lps with water; bend each paper clip into an S-shaped hook. Using one paper clip, hang Tassel Cap from a towel bar or bottom of a clothes hanger. Using paper clips, hook a washer onto each lp; allow washers to hang from lps for several hours or overnight. Remove clips and washers when lps are no longer curled.

Twisted Cord & Tassel

Wrapping green around chair spindles 25 times, work Basic Twisted Cord instructions on page 16.

With one ball green and two balls black, work Basic Tassel instructions for large size on pages 18 and 20.

Finishing

Work Basic Finishing instructions on page 20.

To attach beads to each ch-12 lp on last rnd of Tassel Cap, thread needle with a piece of scrap thread; run needle through beads in the following order: one black round and one gold disk. Being careful not to let beads slide off, run needle through ch-12 lp and back through beads *(see illustration);* holding both ends of scrap thread, pull ch-12 lp through beads. Remove scrap thread and apply a tiny drop of glue to end of ch-12 lp and opening of bottom bead, securing end of lp inside bead. ☞

White & Wine

Materials:
- ❑ Rayon crochet thread or size 10 crochet cotton thread:
    - 300 yds. white *(for Tassel)*
    - 100 yds. wine *(for 27" Cord and Cap)*
- ❑ 17 yds. white size 5 pearl cotton
- ❑ 10 yds. gold metallic thread
- ❑ 8 gold washed 7 mm large-hole round beads
- ❑ 17 regular metal paper clips
- ❑ 16 medium-sized metal washers
- ❑ Craft glue
- ❑ No. 7 steel hook or hook needed to obtain gauge

Gauge: 8 chs or sts = 1"; rnds 1–2 are 1" across.

Basic Stitches: Ch, sl st, sc, dc.

Tassel Cap

Rnd 1: With wine, ch 10, sl st in first ch to form ring, ch 1, 16 sc in ring, join with sl st in first sc. *(16 sc made)*

Rnd 2: Ch 1, sc in first st, (ch 4, skip next st, sc in next st) around to last st, ch 1, skip last st, join with dc in first sc. *(Joining ch sp made—8 sc, 8 ch sps)*

Rnds 3–6: Ch 1, sc in joining ch sp, (ch 5, sc in next ch sp) around, ch 2, join with dc in first sc.

Rnd 7: Ch 1, sc in joining ch sp, (ch 4, sc in next ch sp) around, ch 4, join with sl st in first sc.

Rnd 8: Sl st in first ch sp, ch 1, 4 sc in each ch sp around, join. *(32 sc)*

Rnds 9–10: Ch 1, sc in each st around, join.

Rnd 11: Ch 1, sc in first 4 sts, ch 15, (sc in next 4 sts, ch 15) around, join. *(32 sc, 8 ch sps)*

Rnd 12: Ch 1, sc in first 2 sts, ch 60; (holding ch-15 of last rnd behind sts as you work, sc in next 4 sts, ch 60) around to last 2 sts, sc in last 2 sts, join. Fasten off.

To **straighten ch lps,** dampen lps with water; bend each paper clip into an S-shaped hook. Using one paper clip, hang Tassel Cap from a towel bar or bottom of a clothes hanger. Using

continued on page 22

paper clips, hook a washer onto each lp; allow washers to hang from lps for several hours or overnight. Remove clips and washers when lps are no longer curled.

Twisted Cord & Tassel

Wrapping remainder of wine thread around chair spindles, work Basic Twisted Cord instructions on page 18.

With 3 balls white thread, work Basic Tassel instructions for large size on pages 18 and 20.

Finishing

Work Basic Finishing instructions on page 20.

For each **Mini-Tassel** *(make 8)*, from white pearl cotton, cut 25 pieces, each 3" long; place center of all strands held together at center of one long ch lp on last rnd of Tassel Cap and fold in half over ch lp. Thread doubled strand of gold metallic thread on needle and wrap tightly around strands ¼" from fold eight times, forming a ¼" band; run needle behind wraps to secure and trim end.

To attach one gold bead to each short ch lp on last rnd of Tassel Cap, thread needle with a piece of scrap thread; run needle through bead, through ch lp and back through bead *(see illustration);* holding both ends of scrap thread, pull ch lp through bead. Remove scrap thread and apply a tiny drop of glue to end of ch lp and opening of bottom bead, securing end of lp inside bead. ✏

Red & Cream

Materials:

❑ Rayon crochet thread or size 10 crochet cotton thread:
    400 yds. red *(for Tassel and 27" Cord)*
    200 yds. cream *(for Cord and Cap)*
❑ 5 ruby 19 × 8.5mm elongated bicone beads
❑ 5 gold washed 6mm round sand beads
❑ 11 regular metal paper clips
❑ 10 medium-sized metal washers
❑ Craft glue
❑ No. 7 steel hook or hook needed to obtain gauge

Gauge: 8 chs or sts = 1"; 4 dc rnds = 1"; rnds 1–2 are 1⅛" across.

Basic Stitches: Ch, sl st, sc, dc.

Tassel Cap

Rnd 1: With cream, ch 10, sl st in first ch to form ring, ch 1, 20 sc in ring, join with sl st in first sc. *(20 sc made)*

Rnd 2: Ch 4 *(counts as first dc and ch-1),* (dc in next st, ch 1) around, join with sl st in third ch of ch-4. *(20 dc, 20 ch sps)*

Rnds 3–6: Ch 4, (dc in next dc, ch 1) around, join.

Rnds 7–8: Ch 3, dc in each dc around, join with sl st in top of ch-3. *(20 dc)*

Rnd 9: Ch 4, (dc in next st, ch 1) around, join with sl st in third ch of ch-4. *(20 dc, 20 ch sps)*

Rnd 10: Ch 4, (dc in next dc, ch 1) around, join.

Rnd 11: Ch 1, sc in first st, *[ch 3, sl st in third ch from hook, ch 15, sl st in third ch from hook, sc in same st as last sc, skip next ch sp, next dc and next ch sp, (dc, ch 1, dc, ch 1, dc, ch 3, sl st in third ch from hook, ch 25, sl st in third ch from hook, dc, ch 1, dc, ch 1, dc) in next dc, skip next ch sp, next dc and next ch sp], sc in next dc; repeat from * 3 more times; repeat between [ ], join with sl st in first sc. Fasten off.

To **straighten ch lps,** dampen lps with water; bend each paper clip into an S-shaped hook. Using one paper clip, hang Tassel Cap from a towel bar or bottom of a clothes hanger. Using paper clips, hook a washer onto each lp; allow washers to hang from lps for several hours or overnight. Remove clips and washers when lps are no longer curled.

Twisted Cord & Tassel

Hold two strands red and four strands cream together as one; wrapping multicolor strand around chair spindles ten times, work Basic Twisted Cord instructions on page 18.

With three balls red, work Basic Tassel instructions for large size on pages 18 and 20.

Finishing

Work Basic Finishing instructions on page 20.

To attach one red bead to each long ch lp on last rnd of Tassel Cap, thread needle with a piece of scrap thread; run needle through bead, through ch lp and back through bead *(see illustration).* Holding both ends of scrap thread, pull ch lp through bead. Remove scrap thread and apply a tiny drop of glue to end of ch lp and opening of bottom bead, securing end of lp inside bead. Repeat, attaching one gold bead to each short ch lp. ✏

more times; repeat between [ ], end shell. *(4 fans, 20 V sts, 8 shells)*

Rnd 17: Beg shell, *[ch 5, V st in next V st, (ch 3, V st in next V st) 4 times, ch 5, shell in next shell, ch 5, skip next ch sp; working across fan, sc in next ch lp, (ch 3, sc in next ch lp) 6 times, ch 5], shell in next shell; repeat from * 2 more times; repeat between [ ], end shell. *(24 ch-3 sps, 20 V sts, 8 shells)*

Rnd 18: Beg shell, *[ch 5, V st in next V st, (ch 3, V st in next V st) 4 times, ch 5, shell in next shell, ch 5, skip next ch-5 sp, 3 sc in next ch-3 sp, (sc in next sc, 3 sc in next ch-3 sp) 5 times, ch 5], shell in next shell; repeat from * 2 more times; repeat between [ ], end shell. *(92 sc, 20 V sts, 8 shells)*

Rnd 19: Beg shell, *[ch 5, V st in next V st, (ch 3, V st in next V st) 4 times, ch 5, shell in next shell, ch 5, skip next ch-5 sp and next 3 sc, (V st in next sc, ch 3, skip next 3 sc) 2 times, (dc, ch 1, dc, ch 1, dc) in next sc, (ch 3, skip next 3 sc, V st in next sc) 2 times, **turn; for corner,** ch 1, **mark** last ch-1 made, sl st in next V st, ch 6, V st in next V st, ch 3, skip next ch sp, V st in next ch-1 sp, ch 1, V st in next ch-1 sp, (ch 3, V st in next V st) 2 times, **turn,** ch 1, **mark** last ch-1 made, sl st in V st, (ch 3, V st in next V st) 2 times, ch 1, V st in next ch-1 sp, ch 1, (V st in next V st, ch 3) 2 times, sl st in fourth ch of ch-6, ch 4, sl st in next marked ch-1, ch 5], shell in next shell; repeat from * 2 more times; repeat between [ ], end shell.

Rnd 20: Beg shell, *[ch 3, V st in third ch of next ch-5, (ch 3, V st in next V st) 5 times, ch 3, V st in third ch of next ch-5, ch 3, shell in next shell, ch 3, V st in next marked ch-1, (ch 3, V st in next V st) 5 times, ch 3, V st in second ch of next ch-4, ch 3], shell in next shell; repeat from * 2 more times; repeat between [ ], end shell.

Rnd 21: Beg shell, shell in each V st and in each shell around, end shell. Fasten off.

Pillow Side (make 2)

Rnd 1: With G hook and rose, ch 4, sl st in first ch to form ring, ch 1, 12 sc in ring, **join** *(see Special Stitches)* in first sc. *(12 sc made)*

Rnd 2: Ch 1, 2 sc in each st around, join. *(24)*

Rnd 3: (Ch 3—*counts as first dc,* dc) in first st, dc in next st, (2 dc in next st, dc in next st) around, join in top of ch-3. *(36 dc)*

Rnd 4: Ch 1, sc in each st around, join.

Rnd 5: (Ch 3, dc) in first st, dc in next 8 sts, (3 dc in next st, dc in next 8 sts) around, dc in same st as ch-3, join. *(44)*

Note: *Center st of each 3-st group is corner st.*

Rnd 6: Ch 1, 2 sc in first st, sc in each st around with 3 sc in each corner st, sc in same st as ch-1, join. *(52 sc)*

Rnd 7: (Ch 3, dc) in first st, dc in each st around with 3 dc in each corner st, dc in same st as ch-3, join. *(60 dc)*

Rnds 8–22: Repeat rnds 6 and 7 alternately, ending with rnd 6. *(At end of last rnd, 180)*

Rnd 23: For Ruffle, working this rnd in **front lps** *(see Stitch Guide),* ch 1, sc in first st, (ch 4, sc in next st) around, ch 2, dc in first sc to form joining ch sp.

Rnd 24: Ch 1, sc in joining ch sp, (ch 4, sc in next ch sp) around, ch 2, dc in first sc to form joining ch sp.

Rnd 25: Ch 1, sc in joining ch sp, ch 5, (sc in next ch sp, ch 5) around, join in first sc. Fasten off.

Pillow Top

Work same as Doily.

Matching corners, sew Pillow Top centered on one Pillow Side.

Assembly & Center Ruffle

Rnd 1: Matching sts and corners, hold Sides wrong sides together; working this rnd in **back lps** *(see Stitch Guide)* of rnd 22 on both pieces, with G hook, join rose with sc in any st, sc in each st around with 2 sc in each corner st, inserting fiberfill or pillow form before closing, join in first sc. Fasten off.

Rnd 2: For **Center Ruffle,** join white yarn with sc in any st, (ch 4, sc in next st) around, ch 2, dc in first sc to form joining ch sp.

Rnd 3: Ch 1, sc in joining ch sp, ch 5, (sc in next ch sp, ch 5) around, join in first sc. Fasten off.

Small Front Button

With G hook and rose, leaving 10" end, ch 2, 6 sc in second ch from hook, join in first sc. Fasten off.

Large Back Button

Rnd 1: With G hook and rose, ch 4, 11 dc in fourth ch from hook, join in **back lp** of top ch of ch-4. *(12 sts made)*

Rnd 2: Ch 2, **dc back post (dc bp,** *see Stitch Guide)* around next st, (dc bp next 2 sts tog) 5 times, skip ch 2, join in top of first dc. Leaving 10" end, fasten off.

Finishing

Run 10" end of Small Front Button from back to front to back through center of Button, then through center of Pillow from front to back.

Weave 10" end of Large Back Button through tops of sts on rnd 2, stuff Button with about 30" of rose, pull 10" end tight and secure; run 10" end from back to front through center of Button, then back through Button to back.

Pulling snug to indent Pillow, tie 10" ends of both Buttons together on back of Pillow. Hide ends on inside.

Coaster Bottom

Rnd 1: With G hook and rose, ch 4, sl st in first ch to form ring, ch 1, 12 sc in ring, **join** *(see*

continued on page 24

Parlor Perk-Up

continued from page 23

Special Stitches) in first sc. (12 sc made)

Rnd 2: Ch 1, 2 sc in each st around, join. (24)

Rnd 3: (Ch 3, dc) in first st, dc in next 5 sts, (3 dc in next st, dc in next 5 sts) 3 times, dc in same st as ch-3, join. (32 dc)

Rnd 4: Ch 1, 2 sc in first st, sc in each st around with 3 sc in center st of each 3-dc group at corner, sc in same st as first sc, join in first sc. (40 sc)

Rnd 5: (Ch 3, dc) in first st, dc in each st around with 3 dc in second sc of each 3-sc group, dc in same st as ch-3, join in top of ch-3. (48 dc)

Rnd 6: Ch 1, sc in first st; for **picot**, ch 3, sl st in **front lp and left bar** (see Stitch Guide) of last sc made (picot made); *(ch 1, skip next st, sc in next st, picot) 5 times, ch 1, sc in next st, picot, (ch 1, skip next st, sc in next st, picot) 6 times, ch 1*, sc in next st, picot; repeat between first and second *, join in first sc. Fasten off.

Coaster Top

Rnd 1: With No. 5 steel hook and crochet cotton thread, ch 4, sl st in first ch to form ring, ch 1, 8 sc in ring, **join** (see Special Stitches) in first sc. (8 sc made)

Rnd 2: Ch 1, (sc, ch 12) 2 times in each of first 7 sts, (sc, ch 12, sc) in last st, ch 6, ttr in first sc to form joining ch lp. (16 ch lps made)

Rnd 3: Ch 1, sc in joining ch lp, ch 3, (sc in next ch lp, ch 3) around, join in first sc. (16 sc, 16 ch sps)

Rnd 4: Ch 1, sc in each st and 3 sc in each ch sp around, join. (64 sc)

Rnd 5: Beg shell in first st, (*ch 3, skip next 3 sts, hdc in next st, ch 3, skip next 3 sts, sc in next st, ch 3, skip next 3 sts, hdc in next st, ch 3, skip next 3 sts*, shell in next st) 3 times; repeat between first and second *, end shell. (16 ch-3 sps, 4 shells)

Rnd 6: Beg shell, (*ch 3, sc in next ch sp, ch 4, dc next 2 ch sps tog, ch 4, sc in next ch sp, ch 3*, shell in next shell) 3 times; repeat between first and second *, end shell.

Rnd 7: Ch 1, sc in ch sp of beg shell, ch 4, (sc, ch 4) in each ch sp and in each shell around, join in first sc. Fasten off.

Finishing

With right sides of both pieces facing you, matching shells on Top to corners on Bottom, sew Top centered on Bottom. ⚷

Victorian Wreath

continued from page 14

Rnd 8: For **petals**, (sl st, ch 2, 10 dc, ch 2, sl st) in each ch sp around. Fasten off.

Large Rose (make 5 of assorted colors)

Row 1: With F hook and yarn, ch 24, sc in sixth ch from hook, (ch 3, skip next ch, sc in next ch) across, turn. (10 ch sps made)

Row 2: Ch 1, (sc, ch 2, 3 dc, ch 2, sc) in first ch sp, (sc, ch 2, 4 dc, ch 2, sc) in each of next 3 ch sps, (sc, ch 2, 5 dc, ch 2, sc) in each of next 4 ch sps, (sc, ch 2, 6 dc, ch 2, sc) in each of last 2 ch sps. Fasten off.

Beginning with first petal of row 2, roll strand of petals and tack on back side to hold shape.

Medium Rose (make 7 of assorted colors)

Row 1: With F hook and yarn, ch 24, sc in sixth ch from hook, (ch 3, skip next ch, sc in next ch) across, turn. (10 ch sps made)

Row 2: Ch 1, (5 sc, sl st) in first 5 ch sps, (6 sc, sl st) in last 5 ch sps. Fasten off.

Beginning with first petal of row 2, roll strand of petals and tack on back side to hold shape.

Large 3-Leaf Spray (make 6)

With F hook and green yarn, beginning at bottom of stem, ch 16, **do not fasten off.**

Row 1: For **first leaf**, 6 tr in fifth ch from hook, turn. (7 tr made)

Row 2: Ch 3, (dc next 2 sts tog) 2 times, dc in next st leaving last st unworked, turn. (4 dc)

Row 3: Ch 1, skip first st, sc next 2 sts tog leaving last st unworked, **do not turn;** for **tip of leaf**, ch 3, sc in third ch from hook; working down side of leaf, ch 1, sl st in top of st at end of row 2, ch 2, sl st in top of st at end of row 1, ch 4, sl st in same ch as 6 tr of row 1, **do not turn or fasten off.**

For **second leaf**, ch 9, repeat rows 1–3 of first leaf; sl st in next 4 chs below second leaf, **do not fasten off.**

For **third leaf**, ch 5, repeat rows 1–3 of first leaf; sl st in each ch across stem. Fasten off.

Finishing

Pinning ends of ribbon in place with small-head pins, wrap Styrofoam® ring with ribbon overlapping edges of ribbon enough to cover ring.

Place Eyelet Lace on covered ring with inner edge on inside of ring. With white, lace ch-9 back lps together on back of ring, drawing lps together tightly.

With remaining ribbon, make a 6" bow (see photo).

Glue or pin Roses and Leaf Sprays to front of Wreath as desired (see photo). Glue or pin bow at center top on inner edge of Wreath. ⚷

Dining Decor

*Do you remember when dining was
something that the family did together
on a regular basis? Would you like to
make those all-too-infrequent family
times truly memorable experiences?
Look no further than the projects in this
chapter for one-of-a-kind creations that
are sure to make your meals occasions
to remember for years to come!
Whether your taste runs toward elegant
lace tablecloths or tiny trimmings;
place mats made with special stitches or
miniature mats to dress up your dishes;
rag baskets or runners for buffets or
sideboards, we've chosen a sampling of
favorites to serve your family!*

Grape Basket

An Original by Annie

General Instructions

Read Before Starting: These quick and easy baskets can be made using strips cut from fabric scraps, old clothing or sheets you no longer use or material you bought and never used. One color or print fabric or a combination of solids or prints can be used to create just the right accent for any decor.

To make the strips, cut or tear along the longest measurement of a fabric piece. The width of the strips for each basket is listed in the individual instructions.

"To Iron Or Not To Iron." To maintain a consistent color as you are crocheting strips from fabric that has a noticeable difference between the right and wrong side, iron them in half lengthwise with wrong sides together beforehand so the same side of the fabric is always showing as you work. Un-ironed strips from this type fabric will create a variance of colors due to both sides showing as they are worked. Strips with a similar shade of color on both sides do not need to be ironed before crocheting.

Joining the strips can be done several different ways. The length of the strips and the finished look will determine which one to use.

The **"no-sew" method** allows strips to be added as you work without any sewing and hides the ends inside the knot. Hide the knots on the wrong side of the work when crocheting.

The **hand-sewn method** works best when a smooth finish is needed on both sides of the piece. Keep a threaded sewing needle handy as you work; when you reach the end of a strip, add a new one by holding the ends right sides together, then sew a ¼" seam, using a small running stitch *(see illustration).* Very short strips can be machine-sewn end-to-end forming longer strips. Joining a mixture of fabric odds and ends will give a multicolored or variegated effect to the designs. This joining is used for the handle.

Fold end over and snip to within ½" of edge; repeat on end of strip to be added.	**With right sides up, lap end of new strip over last strip, matching slits.**	**Pull other end of new strip through overlapped slits, bottom to top.**	**Pull strips until ends are hidden inside knot.**
			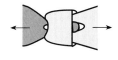

Read Before Starting: Use hand-sewn method for this basket.

Finished Size: 11½" tall.

Materials:
- ❏ Tear or cut main color (MC) fabric into 70 yds. of 5"-wide strips *(equivalent to 8 yds. of 45"-wide fabric)*
- ❏ Scraps of fabric for desired bow *(equivalent to 1⅛ yds. of fabric),* leaf and grape colors *(equivalent to ½ and ⅛ yd. of fabrics)*
- ❏ Sewing thread and needle
- ❏ Polyester fiberfill
- ❏ Craft or hot glue
- ❏ S bulky hook

Basket
Note: *Work this piece in* **back loops** *only (see Stitch Guide).*

Rnd 1: With MC 5"-wide strips, make a slip ring *(see Stitch Guide),* ch 1, 6 sc in ring, **do not join rnds.** *(7 sc made) Ch 1 counts as a st.*

Rnd 2: 2 sc in ch 1, 2 sc in next 6 sts. *(14)*

Rnd 3: (Sc in next st, 2 sc in next st) 7 times. *(21)*

Rnd 4: (Sc in next 2 sts, 2 sc in next st) 7 times. *(28)*

Rnds 5-8: Sc in each st around.

Rnd 9: Sl st in each st around, sl st in **both lps** of next st. **Do not fasten off.** Turn Basket inside out so side with remaining **front lps** is on inside.

Handle
With MC, ch 19, skip next 13 sts on last rnd of Basket, sl st in next st; sl st in each of 19 chs on Handle, sl st in next st on Basket; ch 1, sl st in remaining lps of 19 chs down other side of Handle. Fasten off. Pull end through to inside of Basket.

continued on page 31

Mini Mats

by Deborah Levy-Hamburg

Flower Motif

Finished Size: 5" square.

Materials:
- ❏ Small amounts each yellow, blue, lt. green, peach and purple cotton sport yarn
- ❏ No. 0 steel hook or hook needed to obtain gauge

Gauge: Rnds 1–3 = 3½" diameter.

Basic Stitches: Ch, sl st, sc, hdc, dc, tr.

Mat

Rnd 1: With yellow, ch 6, sl st in first ch to form ring, ch 1, 16 sc in ring, join with sl st in first sc. Fasten off. *(16 sc made)*

Rnd 2: Join blue with sc in first st, sc in next 2 sts, (sc, ch 9, sc) in next st *(petal base made),* *sc in next 3 sts, (sc, ch 9, sc) in next st; repeat from * around, join. *(20 sc)*

Rnd 3: Ch 1, sc in first st, skip next 2 sts, (2 hdc, 17 dc, 2 hdc) in next ch sp *(petal made),* *skip next 2 sts, sc in next st, (2 hdc, 17 dc, 2 hdc) in next ch sp; repeat from * around, join. Fasten off. *(4 petals)*

Rnd 4: Join lt. green with (sc, ch 9, sc) in sc between first two petals; working behind petals, ch 5, *(sc, ch 9, sc) in sc between next two petals, ch 5; repeat from * around, join.

Rnd 5: Ch 1, sc in first st, (2 hdc, 17 dc, 2 hdc) in next ch-9 sp, sc in next st, 5 sc in next ch-5 sp, *sc in next st, (2 hdc, 17 dc, 2 hdc) in next ch-9 sp, sc in next st, 5 sc in next ch-5 sp; repeat from * around, join.

Rnd 6: Ch 1, sc in first st, ch 9; working behind petal, sc in next sc, ch 5, skip next 5 sts, *sc in next sc, ch 9; working behind petal, sc in next sc, ch 5, skip next 5 sts; repeat from * around, join. Fasten off.

Rnd 7: Join peach with (sc, hdc, 2 dc, 15 tr, 2 dc, hdc, sc) in first ch-9 sp, (sc, hdc, 6 dc, hdc, sc) in next ch-5 sp, *(sc, hdc, 2 dc, 15 tr, 2 dc, hdc, sc) in next ch-9 sp, (sc, hdc, 6 dc, hdc, sc) in next ch-5 sp; repeat from * around, join. Fasten off.

Rnd 8: Join purple with sl st in first st, ch 3, dc in each st around, join with sl st in top of ch-3. Fasten off. ✎

Flower Shell

Finished Size: 6" across.

Materials:
- ❏ Small amounts each peach, white and variegated cotton sport yarn
- ❏ No. 0 steel hook or hook needed to obtain gauge

Gauge: Rnd 1 = 1½" diameter.

Basic Stitches: Ch, sl st, sc, dc.

Mat

Rnd 1: With peach, ch 4, sl st in first ch to form ring, ch 3, 23 dc in ring, join with sl st in top of ch-3. Fasten off. *(24 dc made)*

Rnd 2: Join white with (sl st, ch 5, dc) in first st, skip next 2 sts, *(dc, ch 2, dc) in next st, skip next 2 sts; repeat from * around, join with sl st in third ch of ch-5.

Rnd 3: (Sl st, ch 3, 2 dc, ch 1, 3 dc) in first ch sp *(first shell made),* (3 dc, ch 1, 3 dc) in each ch sp around, join. Fasten off. *(8 shells)*

Rnd 4: Join variegated with (sl st, ch 3, 8 dc) in ch sp of first shell, sc in sp between shells, (9 dc in ch sp of next shell, sc in sp between shells) around, join. Fasten off. *(8 dc groups, 8 sc)*

Rnd 5: Join white with (sl st, ch 5, dc) in first sc, ch 3, dc in **back strands** of center dc of next dc group *(see illustration),* ch 3, *(dc, ch 2, dc) in next sc, ch 3, dc in back strands of center dc of 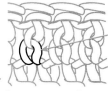 next dc group, ch 3; repeat from * around, join with sl st in third ch of ch-5.

Rnd 6: (Sl st, ch 3, 11 dc) in first ch sp, sc in each of next 2 ch-3 sps, (12 dc in next ch sp, sc in each of next 2 ch-3 sps) around, join. Fasten off.

Rnd 7: Join peach with sc in first st, sc in next 12 sts, **double crochet front post** *(fp—see Stitch Guide)* around next dc on rnd 5, (sc in next 14 sts, fp around next dc on rnd 5) around, join. Fasten off. ✎

Nantucket Ruffle

Finished Size: 5½" diameter.

Materials:
- ❏ Small amounts each white, blue and variegated cotton sport yarn
- ❏ No. 0 steel hook or hook needed to obtain gauge

Gauge: Rnds 1–2 = 2" diameter.

Basic Stitches: Ch, sl st, sc, dc.

Mat

Rnd 1: With white, ch 4, sl st in first ch to form ring, ch 3, 11 dc in ring, join with sl st in top of ch-3. Fasten off. *(12 dc made)*

continued on page 30

Mini Mats

continued from page 29

Rnd 2: Join blue with (sl st, ch 3, dc) in sp between first 2 sts, 2 dc in sp between next 2 sts around, join. Fasten off. *(24)*

Rnd 3: Join white with (sl st, ch 3, 3 dc) in sp between first 2 sts *(dc group made),* skip next 2 sts, (4 dc in sp between next 2 sts, skip next 2 sts) around, join. Fasten off. *(12 dc groups)*

Rnd 4: Join blue with (sl st, ch 3, 4 dc) in sp between center sts of first dc group, 5 dc between center sts of each dc group around, join. Fasten off.

Rnd 5: Join white with (sl st, ch 3, 5 dc) in sp between next 2 dc groups, 6 dc in sp between next 2 dc groups around, join. Fasten off.

Rnd 6: Join variegated with (sl st, ch 3, 9 dc) in sp between first 2 dc groups, 10 dc in sp between next 2 dc groups around, join. Fasten off.

Rnd 7: Join blue with sc in sp between first 2 sts, (ch 3, sc in sp between next 2 sts) 8 times, ch 3, skip next 2 sts, *sc in next st, (ch 3, sc in sp between next 2 sts) 8 times, ch 3, skip next 2 sts; repeat from * around, join. Fasten off.

Peppermint Lace

Finished Size: 5½" diameter.

Materials:
- ❑ Small amounts each dk. pink and white cotton sport yarn
- ❑ No. 0 steel hook or hook needed to obtain gauge

Gauge: Rnds 1–3 = 2" diameter.

Basic Stitches: Ch, sl st, sc, dc.

Mat

Rnd 1: With white, ch 8, sl st in first ch to form ring, ch 3, 15 dc in ring, join with sl st in top of ch-3. Fasten off. *(16 dc made)*

Rnd 2: Join dk. pink with (sl st, ch 3, dc) in sp between first 2 sts, 2 dc between each st around, join. Fasten off. *(32)*

Rnd 3: Join white with (sl st, ch 3, dc) in sp between first 2 sts, dc in sp between next 2 sts, (2 dc in sp between next 2 sts, dc in sp between next 2 sts) around, join. Fasten off. *(48)*

Rnd 4: Join dk. pink with sc in first st, sc in each st around, join with sl st in first sc. *(48 sc)*

Rnd 5: Ch 3, (yo, insert hook in same st, yo, pull through st, yo, pull through 2 lps on hook) 2 times, yo, pull through all 3 lps on hook, ch 3, skip next st, *yo, insert hook in next st, yo, pull through st, yo, pull through 2 lps on hook, (yo, insert hook in same st, yo, pull through st, yo, pull through 2 lps on hook) 2 times, yo, pull through all 3 lps on hook, ch 3; repeat from * around, join with sl st in top of ch-3.

Rnd 6: (Sl st, ch 3, 2 dc, ch 5, 3 dc) in first ch sp, sc in next ch sp, *(3 dc, ch 5, 3 dc) in next ch sp, sc in next ch sp; repeat from * around, join. Fasten off.

Purple Popcorn

Finished Size: 5" diameter.

Materials:
- ❑ Small amounts each dk. peach and purple cotton sport yarn
- ❑ No. 0 steel hook or hook needed to obtain gauge

Gauge: Rnd 1 = 2" diameter.

Basic Stitches: Ch, sl st, sc, dc, tr.

Mat

Rnd 1: With purple, ch 8, sl st in first ch to form ring, ch 4, 3 tr in ring, drop lp from hook, insert hook in top of ch 4, pull dropped lp through st *(popcorn made),* ch 3, *4 tr in ring, drop lp from hook, insert hook in top of first tr of group, pull dropped lp through st *(popcorn made),* ch 3; repeat from * 8 more times, join with sl st in top of first popcorn. Fasten off. *(10 popcorn made)*

Rnd 2: Join dk. peach with sl st in first ch sp; for **beginning shell (beg shell), (ch 3, dc, ch 1, 2 dc) in same ch sp;** for **shell, (2 dc, ch 1, 2 dc) in next ch sp;** shell in each ch sp around, join with sl st in top of ch-3. Fasten off. *(10 shells)*

Rnd 3: Join purple with sl st in ch sp of first shell, beg shell, dc in sp between shells, (shell in ch sp of next shell, dc in sp between shells) around, join. Fasten off. *(10 shells, 10 dc)*

Rnd 4: Join dk. peach with sl st in ch sp of first shell, beg shell, ch 1, dc in sp between shell and next dc, ch 1, dc in sp between dc and next shell, (shell in ch sp of next shell, ch 1, dc in sp between shell and next dc, ch 1, dc in sp between dc and next shell) around, join.

Rnd 5: Working in sps between sts, ch 1, sc in first 14 sps, 2 sc in next sp, (sc in next 14 sps, 2 sc in next sp) 3 times, join with sl st in first sc. *(64)*

Rnd 6: Ch 6, (tr in next st, ch 2) around, join with sl st in fourth ch of ch-6. Fasten off.

Rnd 7: Join purple with (sc, 4 dc, sc) in first ch sp *(petal made),* (sc, 4 dc, sc) in next 7 ch sps; **for flower, drop lp from hook, insert hook between fifth and sixth petals back from dropped lp, pick up lp, pull through;** *(sc, 4 dc, sc) in next 8 ch sps, work flower; repeat from * 6 more times, join with sl st in first sc. Fasten off.

Treetop Motif

Finished Size: 4¾" diameter.

Materials:
- ❑ Small amounts each rose and lt. green cotton sport yarn
- ❑ No. 0 steel hook or hook needed to obtain gauge

Gauge: Rnds 1–2 = 1¾" diameter.

Basic Stitches: Ch, sl st, sc, dc, tr.

Mat

Rnd 1: With rose, ch 4, sl st in first ch to form ring, ch 4 *(counts as first dc and ch-1)*, (dc, ch 1) 9 times in ring, join with sl st in third ch of ch-4. *(10 dc, 10 ch sps made)*

Rnd 2: (Sl st, ch 3, 2 dc) in first ch sp, 3 dc in each ch sp around, join with sl st in top of ch-3. Fasten off. *(10 dc groups)*

Rnd 3: Join lt. green with (sl st, ch 6, dc) in center st of first dc group, **treble crochet front post** *(fp—see Stitch Guide)* around next st on rnd 1, *(dc, ch 3, dc) in center st of next dc group, fp around next st on rnd 1; repeat from * around,

join with sl st in third ch of ch-6. Fasten off.

Rnd 4: Join rose with (sl st, ch 3, 4 dc) in first ch sp, fp around next fp, (5 dc in next ch sp, fp around next fp) around, join. Fasten off. *(10 dc groups)*

Rnd 5: Join lt. green with (sl st, ch 6, dc, ch 3, dc) in center st of first dc group, fp around next fp, *(dc, ch 3, dc, ch 3, dc) in center st of next dc group, fp around next fp; repeat from * around, join with sl st in third ch of ch-6.

Rnd 6: (Sl st, ch 3, 2 dc) in first ch sp, dc in next st, 3 dc in next ch sp, fp around next fp, (3 dc in next ch sp, dc in next st, 3 dc in next ch sp, fp around next fp) around, join. Fasten off. ⚷

Grape Basket

continued from page 26

Leaves & Grape Clusters

From leaf color fabric, cut four pieces 5" × 11" for Large Leaves, two pieces 4½" × 9" for Medium Leaves and three pieces 3½" × 7" for Small Leaves. Fold triangle with right sides together *(see illustration 1)*. Allowing ¼" for seam, sew straight edge, leaving curved bottom edge open *(see illustration 2)*. Turn right side out. Run gathering thread along curved bottom edge, pull tightly to gather *(see illustration 3)*. Secure gathering thread.

For each Grape *(make 51)*, cut a 1¾" circle from grape color fabric. Run gathering thread around edge of circle, place small ball of fiberfill in center and pull thread tightly to close. Secure gathering thread.

For each Cluster, tack Grapes together according to diagrams.

Arrange and glue or tack Leaves and Grape Clusters to one side of Handle and Basket *(see photo)*.

Bow

For bow loops, cut 5" × 38" piece from bow color fabric. Fold piece into a 7½" triple-loop bow, making each layer ½" shorter than the bottom *(see folding illustration)*. Cut a 2" × 3" piece and fold in a 1"-wide strip; wrap around loops, gathering middle to about 1¼". Glue or tack ends on back of loops.

For streamers, cut two 5" × 9" pieces from bow color fabric. Gather one end of each tightly and secure gathering thread. Trim other ends as shown in photo. Glue or tack gathered ends to back of Bow.

Glue or tack Bow to other side of Basket at bottom of Handle. ⚷

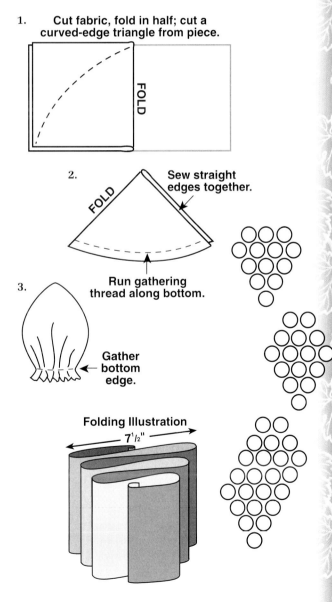

1. Cut fabric, fold in half; cut a curved-edge triangle from piece.

FOLD

2. FOLD — Sew straight edges together.

Run gathering thread along bottom.

3. Gather bottom edge.

Folding Illustration

7½"

Bellflower Tablecloth

by Gloria Coombes

Finished Size: Approximately 45" square.

Materials:
- ❑ 3,000 yds. size 10 crochet cotton thread
- ❑ No. 9 steel hook or hook needed to obtain gauge

Gauge: One Motif is 4¾" square.

Basic Stitches: Ch, sl st, sc, dc, tr.

Special Stitches: For **cluster (cl)**, yo 2 times, insert hook in ch sp or st, (yo, pull through 2 lps on hook) 2 times, *yo 2 times, insert hook in same ch sp or st, (yo, pull through 2 lps on hook) 2 times; repeat from * one more time, yo, pull through all 4 lps on hook.
For **side joining**, (ch 1, sl st in corresponding picot of previous Motif, ch 1, complete picot on Motif being worked.
For **corner joining**, (ch 2, sl st in corner picot on previous Motif, ch 2, complete corner picot on Motif being worked.

First Motif

Rnd 1: Ch 6, sl st in first ch to form ring, ch 5, (dc in ring, ch 2) 7 times, join with sl st in third ch of ch-5. *(8 ch sps made)*

Rnd 2: Ch 1, sc in first st, 3 sc in next ch sp, (sc in next st, 3 sc in next ch sp) around, join with sl st in first sc. *(32 sc)*

Rnd 3: Ch 1, sc in first st, (ch 5, skip next 3 sts, sc in next st) 7 times, join with ch 2, tr in first sc *(counts as ch sp)*. *(8 ch sps)*

Rnd 4: Ch 1, sc in first ch sp, ch 5, (tr, ch 5, tr) in next ch sp, ch 5, *sc in third ch of next ch sp, ch 5, (tr, ch 5, tr) in next ch sp, ch 5; repeat from * around, join with sl st in first sc.

Rnd 5: Ch 4, 2 tr in same st, ch 5, skip next ch sp, tr in next ch sp, (ch 1, tr) 5 times in same ch sp as last tr, ch 5, *3 tr in next sc, ch 5, skip next ch sp, tr in next ch sp, (ch 1, tr) 5 times in same ch sp as last tr, ch 5; repeat from * around, join with sl st in top of ch-4.

Rnd 6: Ch 4, tr in same st, ch 3, skip next tr, 2 tr in next tr, ch 5, **cl** *(see Special Stitches)* in next ch-1 sp, (ch 2, cl in next ch-1 sp) 4 times, ch 5, *2 tr in next tr, ch 3, skip next tr, 2 tr in next tr, ch 5, cl in next ch-1 sp, (ch 2, cl in next ch-1 sp) 4 times, ch 5; repeat from * around, join.

Rnd 7: Ch 4, tr in same st, tr in next tr, ch 4, tr in next tr, 2 tr in next tr, ch 6, cl in next ch-2 sp, (ch 3, cl in next ch-2 sp) 3 times, ch 6, *2 tr in next tr, tr in next tr, ch 4, tr in next tr, 2 tr in next tr, ch 6, cl in next ch-2 sp, (ch 3, cl in next ch-2 sp) 3 times, ch 6; repeat from * around, join.

Rnd 8: Ch 4, tr in next 2 tr, ch 5, tr in next 3 tr, ch 7, cl in next ch-3 sp, (ch 4, cl in next ch-3 sp) 2 times, ch 7, *tr in next 3 tr, ch 5, tr in next 3 tr, ch 7, cl in next ch-3 sp, (ch 4, cl in next ch-3 sp) 2 times, ch 7; repeat from * around, join.

Rnd 9: Ch 4, tr next 2 sts tog; for **picot, ch 3, sl st in top of last st made;** ch 5, sc in center ch of next ch-5 sp, ch 5, tr next 3 sts tog, picot, ch 8, cl in next ch-4 sp, ch 5, cl in top of next cl, ch 5, sl st in top of last st made *(corner picot made),* ch 5, cl in next ch-4 sp, ch 8, *tr next 3 sts tog, picot, ch 5, sc in center ch of next ch-5 sp, ch 5, tr next 3 sts tog, picot, ch 8, cl in next ch-4 sp, ch 5, cl in top of next cl, ch 5, sl st in top of last st made *(corner picot made),* ch 5, cl in next ch-4 sp, ch 8; repeat from * around, join. Fasten off.

Joining Motif

Rnds 1–8: Repeat rnds 1–8 of First Motif.

Rnd 9: Repeat rnd 9 of First Motif joining as needed *(see Special Stitches)*.

Make nine rows with nine Motifs in each row.

Border

Rnd 1: Working around entire outer edge, join with sl st in corner picot, *[ch 4, (2 tr, ch 3, 3 tr, ch 3, 3 tr) in same ch sp, ch 5, 3 tr in top of next cl, ch 7, 3 tr in next picot, ch 9, 3 tr in next picot, ch 7, 3 tr in top of next cl, (ch 5, 3 tr in joining between Motifs, ch 5, 3 tr in top of next cl, ch 7, 3 tr in next picot, ch 9, 3 tr in next picot, ch 7, 3 tr in top of next cl) across to next corner, ch 5], (3 tr, ch 3, 3 tr, ch 3, 3 tr) in corner picot; repeat from * 2 more times; repeat between [ ], join with sl st in top of ch-4.

Rnd 2: Ch 4, tr next 2 sts tog, picot; *work following steps to complete rnd:*

A: (Ch 7, tr next 3 sts tog, picot) 3 times;

B: (Ch 5, sc in fourth ch of next ch sp, ch 5, tr next 3 sts tog, picot) 3 times;

C: (Ch 7, tr next 3 sts tog, picot) 2 times;

D: Repeat steps B and C alternately across to next corner, ending with step B;

E: (Ch 7, tr next 3 sts tog, picot) 4 times;

F: Repeat steps B–E 2 more times;

G: Repeat steps B and C alternately across to next corner, ending with step B;

H: Ch 7, join. Fasten off.

Luncheon Decor

by Emma Willey

Edging

Finished Size: 1½" wide.

Materials:
- ❑ 350 yds. ecru size 10 crochet cotton thread
- ❑ 72" round tablecloth
- ❑ No. 9 steel hook or hook needed to obtain gauge

Gauge: 7 sc = 1".

Basic Stitches: Ch, sl st, sc, dc.

Special Stitch: For **treble crochet cluster (tr cl)**, yo 2 times, insert hook in ch sp or ring, yo, pull lp through, (yo, pull through 2 lps on hook) 2 times, *yo 2 times, insert hook in same ch sp or ring, yo, pull lp through, (yo, pull through 2 lps on hook) 2 times leaving last lps on hook; repeat from * number of times needed for number of tr in cluster, yo and pull through all lps on hook.

Edging

Rnd 1: Place slip knot on hook; working around outer edge of tablecloth, push hook through fabric, yo, pull lp through, yo, complete as sc; placing sts ⅛" apart, work 1,667 more sc around, join with sl st in first sc. *(1,668 sc made)*

Rnd 2: Ch 5, *(counts as first dc and ch-2)*, skip next 2 sts, (dc in next st, ch 2, skip next 2 sts) around, join with sl st in third ch of ch-5. *(556 ch sps)*

Rnd 3: (Sl st, ch 4, dc) in first ch sp, ch 3, sc in next ch sp, ch 3, *(dc, ch 1, dc) in next ch sp, ch 3, sc in next ch sp, ch 3; repeat from * around, join with sl st in third ch of ch-4. *(834 ch sps)*

Rnd 4: (Ch 1, sc) in first ch sp, ch 7, skip next 2 ch sps, (sc in next ch sp, ch 7, skip next 2 ch sps) around, join with sl st in first sc.

Rnd 5: (Sl st, ch 4, **2-tr cl**—*see Special Stitch*—ch 3, 3-tr cl, ch 3, 3-tr cl) in first ch sp, ch 5, sc in next ch sp, ch 5, *(3-tr cl, ch 3, 3-tr cl, ch 3, 3-tr cl) in next ch sp, ch 5, sc in next ch sp, ch 5; repeat from * around, join with sl st in top of ch-4. Fasten off. 🔑

Doily

Finished Size: 12" across.

Materials:
- ❑ 350 yds. ecru size 10 crochet cotton thread
- ❑ No. 9 steel hook or hook needed to obtain gauge

Gauge: Rnds 1–3 = 2".

Basic Stitches: Ch, sl st, sc, dc.

Doily

Rnd 1: Ch 6, sl st in first ch to form ring, ch 4, 2-tr cl *(see Edging Special Stitch)*, ch 3, (3-tr cl, ch 3) 5 times in ring, join with sl st in top of ch-4. *(6 tr cls, 6 ch-3 sps made)*

Rnd 2: (Sl st, ch 6, dc) in first ch sp, ch 3, (dc, ch 3) 2

continued on page 39

Motif Tablecloth

by Dot Drake

Finished Size: Each Motif is approximately 5" × 5".

Materials:
- 14,000 yds. white size 10 crochet cotton thread *(for 35" × 35" square table, add 35 yds. for each additional Motif for larger size)*
- Bobby pins *(use for markers)*
- No. 8 steel hook or hook needed to obtain gauge

Gauge: Rnds 1–5 = 1½" across.

Basic Stitches: Ch, sl st, sc, hdc, dc, tr.

Special Stitches: For **picot,** ch 3, sl st in **front lp and left bar** of last sc made *(see illustration).*
For **V st,** (dc, ch 5, dc) in Corner ch sp.
For **double crochet cluster (dc cl),** working in ch sp before and after corner edge, (yo, insert hook in next ch sp, yo, pull through ch sp, yo, pull through 2 lps on hook, yo, insert hook in same ch sp, yo, pull through ch sp, yo, pull through 2 lps on hook) 2 times, yo, pull through all 5 lps on hook.

Tablecloth

Using the following Motif and Panel instructions, make seven Panels each with nine Motifs long, make two End Panels each with seven Motifs long. For a larger square table, make amount of Panels with amount of Motifs needed for length and width of table plus one Motif at each end of Panel to hang over edge of table, make two End Panels two Motifs shorter than Panels.

For **First Panel,** make one Motif A, then make Motif B number of times needed for length of table, joining each Motif B on edge opposite last joined edge *(see assembly illustration).*

For **Second Panel,** make one Motif B joined to side of first Motif on last Panel, then make Motif C to same length as First Panel, joining each Motif C to side of next Motif B on last Panel and to side of last Motif made on this Panel *(see assembly illustration).*

Repeat Second Panel for number of Panels needed for width of table.

For **End Panel,** skip first Motif on First Panel, make one Motif B joined to side of second Motif on First Panel, then make Motif C number of times as same length of First Panel minus one Motif at end, joining each Motif C

to side of Motif B and to side of last Motif made on this Panel *(see assembly illustration).* Repeat End Panel on last Panel made on opposite edge.

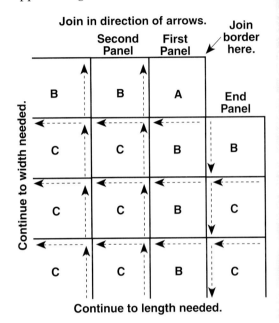

Motif A

Rnd 1: Ch 6, sl st in first ch to form ring, ch 1, 12 sc in ring, join with sl st in first sc. *(12 sc made)*

Rnd 2: Ch 3, skip next st, (sc in next st, ch 3, skip next st) around, join with sl st in first ch of first ch-3. *(6 ch sps)*

Rnd 3: For **Petals,** (sc, hdc, 3 dc, hdc, sc) in each ch sp around. *(6 Petals)*

Rnd 4: Working behind Petals, (ch 4, sc in bottom back 2 strands of sc on next Petal—*see illustration)* around.

Rnd 5: For **Petals,** (sc, hdc, 5 dc, hdc, sc) in each ch sp around, join with sl st in first sc.

Rnd 6: Working behind Petals, sl st in bottom back strands of next 4 sts on next Petal, sc in bottom back 2 strands of next dc, ch 9, (sc in bottom back 2 strands of third dc on next Petal, ch 9) 6 times, join.

Rnd 7: Working in ch sps, ch 1, (3 sc, **picot**—*see Special Stitches,* 5 sc, picot, 3 sc) in each ch sp around, join.

Rnd 8: Ch 8 *(first 3 chs of ch-8 counts as first dc),* *tr in third sc of next 5-sc group, ch 12, tr in sp
continued on page 38

Motif Tablecloth

continued from page 37

between next two 3-sc groups, ch 5, dc in third sc of next 5-sc group, ch 5, tr in sp between next two 3-sc groups, ch 12, tr in third sc of next 5-sc group, ch 5*, dc in sp between next two 3-sc groups, ch 5; repeat between first and second *, join with sl st in third ch of ch-8. *(4 ch-12 sps, 8 ch-5 sps, 12 sts)*

Rnd 9: Ch 1, sc in first st, work 5 sc in each ch-5 sp and sc in each st around with 18 sc in each ch-12 sp, join with sl st in first sc. *(124 sc)*

Rnd 10: (Ch 7, tr) in first st, *ch 3, skip next 10 sts, tr in next st, (ch 2, tr in next st) 9 times, ch 3, skip next 10 sts, (tr, ch 3, tr) in next st; repeat from * 2 more times, ch 3, skip next 10 sts, tr in next st, (ch 3, tr in next st) 9 times, ch 3, skip next 10 sts, join with sl st in fourth ch of ch-7. *(First four chs of ch-7 counts as first tr—48 tr, 47 ch sps.)*

Rnd 11: Ch 1, (sc, ch 5, sc, ch 5, sc, ch 5, sc) in first ch sp, *[3 sc in next ch sp, (sc in next st, 2 sc in next ch sp) 9 times, sc in next st, 3 sc in next ch sp], (sc, ch 5, sc, ch 5, sc, ch 5, sc) in next ch sp; repeat from * 2 more times; repeat between [ ], join with sl st in first sc. *(152 sts, 12 ch sps)*

Rnd 12: (Sl st, ch 1, sc) in first ch sp, (ch 5, sc in next ch sp) 2 times, *[ch 9, skip next 12 sts, sc in next st, (ch 5, skip next st, sc in next st) 5 times, ch 9, skip next 13 sts], sc in next ch sp, (ch 5, sc in next ch sp) 2 times; repeat from * 2 more times; repeat between [ ], join. *(36 ch sps)*

Rnd 13: (Sl st, ch 1, sc) in first ch-5 sp, ch 5, sc in next ch-5 sp, *[ch 9, skip next ch-9 sp, sc in next ch-5 sp, (ch 5, sc in next ch-5 sp) 2 times; for **Corner**, ch 9, sc in same ch sp as last sc; (ch 5, sc in next ch-5 sp) 2 times, ch 9, skip next ch-9 sp], sc in next ch-5 sp, ch 5, sc in next ch-5 sp; repeat from * 2 more times; repeat between [ ], join. Fasten off.

Motif B (joins on one side)

Note: *When joining Motifs, hold pieces wrong sides together matching corner ch-9 sps.*

Rnds 1–12: Repeat rnds 1–12 of Motif A.

Rnd 13: (Sl st, ch 1, sc) in first ch-5 sp, ch 5, sc in next ch-5 sp, ch 9, skip next ch-9 sp, sc in next ch-5 sp, (ch 5, sc in next ch-5 sp) 2 times: *work following steps to complete rnd:*

A: Ch 4, sc in corner ch-9 sp on previous Motif *(see assembly illustration),* ch 4, sc in same ch-5 sp where last sc was made on this Motif, (ch 2, sc in next ch-5 sp on previous Motif, ch 2, sc in next ch-5 sp on this Motif) 2 times, ch 9, skip next ch-9 sp, sc in next ch-5 sp, ch 2, sc in next ch-5 sp on previous Motif, ch 2, sc in next ch-5 sp on this Motif, ch 9, skip next ch-9 sp, sc in next ch-5 sp, (ch 2, sc in next ch-5 sp on previous Motif, ch 2, sc in next ch-5 sp on this Motif) 2 times, ch 4, sc in corner ch-9 sp on previous Motif, ch 4, sc in same ch-5 sp where last sc was made on this Motif;

B: Working on this Motif, (ch 5, sc in next ch-5 sp) 2 times, *ch 9, skip next ch-9 sp, sc in next ch-5 sp, ch 5, sc in next ch-5 sp, ch 9, skip

next ch-9 sp, sc in next ch-5 sp, (ch 5, sc in next ch-5 sp) 2 times; for **corner,** ch 9, sc in same ch sp as last sc, (ch 5, sc in next ch-5 sp) 2 times; repeat from *; ch 9, skip last ch-9 sp, join with sl st in first sc. Fasten off.

Motif C (joins on two sides)

Rnds 1–12: Repeat rnds 1–12 of Motif A.

Rnd 13: (Sl st, ch 1, sc) in first ch-5 sp, ch 5, sc in next ch-5 sp, ch 9, skip next ch-9 sp, sc in next ch-5 sp, (ch 5, sc in next ch-5 sp) 2 times; *work following steps to complete rnd:*

A: Ch 4, sc in corner ch-9 sp on previous Motif, ch 4, sc in same ch-5 sp where last sc was made on this Motif, (ch 2, sc in next ch-5 sp on previous Motif, ch 2, sc in next ch-5 sp on this Motif) 2 times, ch 9, skip next ch-9 sp, sc in next ch-5 sp, ch 2, sc in next ch-5 sp on previous Motif, ch 2, sc in next ch-5 sp on this Motif, ch 9, skip next ch-9 sp, sc in next ch-5 sp, (ch 2, sc in next ch-5 sp on previous Motif, ch 2, sc in next ch-5 sp on this Motif) 2 times, ch 4, sc in corner ch-9 sp on previous Motif of last Panel, ch 4, sc in same ch-5 sp where last sc was made on this Motif;

B: (Ch 2, sc in next ch-5 sp on previous Motif, ch 2, sc in next ch-5 sp on this Motif) 2 times, ch 9, skip next ch-9 sp, sc in next ch-5 sp, ch 2, sc in next ch-5 sp on previous Motif, ch 2, sc in next ch-5 sp on this Motif, ch 9, skip next ch-9 sp, sc in next ch-5 sp, (ch 2, sc in next ch-5 sp on previous Motif, ch 2, sc in next ch-5 sp on this Motif) 2 times, ch 4, sc in corner ch-9 sp on previous Motif, ch 4, sc in same ch-5 sp where last sc was made on this Motif;

C: (Ch 5, sc in next ch-5 sp) 2 times, ch 9, skip next ch-9 sp, sc in next ch-5 sp, ch 9, skip next ch-9 sp, sc in next ch-5 sp, (ch 5, sc in next ch-5 sp) 2 times; for **Corner,** ch 9, sc in same ch sp as last sc, (ch 5, sc in next ch-5 sp) 2 times, ch 9, skip last ch-9 sp, join with sl st in first sc. Fasten off.

Border

Rnd 1: With right side of work facing you, join with sl st in first ch sp at top outer Corner on first Motif of First Panel, (ch 8, dc) in same ch sp as last sl st, *(ch 4, dc in next ch-5 sp) 2 times, (ch 4, dc, ch 4, dc) in next ch-9 sp, ch 4, dc in next ch-5 sp, (ch 4, dc, ch 4, dc) in next ch-9 sp, (ch 4, dc in next ch-5 sp) 2 times, dc next 2 joined ch sps tog; repeat from * across to last Motif, working on last Motif, (ch 4, dc in next ch-5 sp) 2 times, (ch 4, dc, ch 4, dc) in next ch-9 sp, ch 4, dc in next ch-5 sp, (ch 4, dc, ch 4, dc) in next ch-9 sp, (ch 4, dc in next ch-5 sp) 2 times, ch 4; *work following steps to complete the rnd:*

A: V st *(see Special Stitches)* in next corner ch sp, (ch 4, dc in next ch-5 sp) 2 times, (ch 4, dc, ch 4, dc) in next ch-9 sp, ch 4, dc in next ch-5 sp, (ch 4, dc, ch 4, dc) in next ch-9 sp, (ch 4, dc in next ch-5 sp) 2 times, ch 4; for **corner**

edge, dc next 2 joined ch sps tog; (ch 4, dc in next ch-5 sp) 2 times, (ch 4, dc, ch 4, dc) in next ch-9 sp, ch 4, dc in next ch-5 sp, (ch 4, dc, ch 4, dc) in next ch-9 sp, (ch 4, dc in next ch-5 sp) 2 times, ch 4;

B: V st, *(ch 4, dc in next ch-5 sp) 2 times, (ch 4, dc, ch 4, dc) in next ch-9 sp, ch 4, dc in next ch-5 sp, (ch 4, dc, ch 4, dc) in next ch-9 sp, (ch 4, dc in next ch-5 sp) 2 times, dc next 2 joined ch sps tog; repeat from * across to last Motif, working on last Motif, (ch 4, dc in next ch-5 sp) 2 times, (ch 4, dc, ch 4, dc) in next ch-9 sp, ch 4, dc in next ch-5 sp, (ch 4, dc, ch 4, dc) in next ch-9 sp, (ch 4, dc in next ch-5 sp) 2 times, ch 4;

C: Repeat A-B two more times.

D: Repeat A at end, joining with sl st in third ch of ch-8.

Rnd 2: Ch 3, (4 dc, ch 2, 4 dc) in first Corner; *work following steps to complete the rnd:*

A: (Dc in next st, 4 dc in next ch-4 sp) across to st before next Corner;

B: Dc in next st, (4 dc, ch 2, 4 dc) in Corner;

C: (Dc in next st, 4 dc in next ch-4 sp) across to next st before next Corner Edge, dc in next st, dc cl *(see Special Stitches)* place marker here, (dc in next st, 4 dc in next ch sp) across to next st before next Corner;

D: Repeat B and C.

E: Repeat B and A.

F: Repeat B and C.

G: Repeat B and A.

H: Repeat B and C, join with sl st in fourth ch of ch-8.

Rnd 3: Ch 1, sc in first 5 sts, *(sc, picot) in corner ch sp, (sc in next 5 sts, picot) across to corner ch sp, (sc, picot) in corner ch sp, (sc in next 5 sts, picot) across to 5 sts before marker, sc in next 5 sts, skip marked st, remove marker, sc in next 6 sts, picot, sc in next 4 sts, (sc in next st, picot, sc in next 4 sts) across to corner ch sp; repeat from * around, ending with picot at last st, join with sl st in first sc. Fasten off. ⬤━⚷

Luncheon Decor

continued from page 35

times in each ch sp around, join with sl st in third ch of ch-6.

Rnd 3: (Sl st, ch 5, dc) in first ch sp, ch 3, sc in next ch sp, ch 3, *(dc, ch 1, dc) in next ch sp, ch 3, sc in next ch sp, ch 3; repeat from * around, join with sl st in third ch of ch-5.

Rnd 4: (Sl st, ch 1, sc) in first ch sp, ch 7, dc next 2 ch-3 sps tog, ch 7, (sc in next ch-1 sp, ch 7, dc next 2 ch-3 sps tog, ch 7) around, join with sl st in first sc.

Rnd 5: (Sl st, ch 4, 2-tr cl, ch 3, 3-tr cl, ch 3, 3-tr cl, ch 5) in first ch sp, sc in next ch sp, ch 5, *(3-tr cl, ch 3, 3-tr cl, ch 3, 3-tr cl, ch 5) in next ch sp, sc in next ch sp, ch 5; repeat from * around, join with sl st in top of ch-4.

Rnd 6: (Sl st, ch 7) in first ch sp, (dc in next ch sp, ch 4) around, join with sl st in third ch of ch-7.

Rnd 7: (Sl st, ch 4, dc) in first ch sp, ch 4, sc in next ch sp, ch 4, *(dc, ch 1, dc, ch 4) in next ch sp, sc in next ch sp, ch 4; repeat from * around, join with sl st in third ch of first ch-4.

Rnd 8: (Sl st, ch 1, sc) in first ch sp, ch 7, dc next 2 ch-4 sps tog, ch 7, (sc in next ch-1 sp, ch 7, dc next 2 ch-4 sps tog, ch 7) around, join with sl st in first sc.

Rnd 9: (Sl st, ch 4, 2-tr cl, ch 3, 3-tr cl, ch 3, 3-tr cl, ch 5) in first ch sp, sc in next ch sp, ch 5, *(3-tr cl, ch 3, 3-tr cl, ch 3, 3-tr cl, ch 5) in next ch sp, sc in next ch sp, ch 5; repeat from * around, join with sl st in top of ch-4.

Rnd 10: (Sl st, ch 7) in first ch sp, (dc in next ch sp, ch 4) around, join with sl st in third ch of ch-7.

Rnd 11: (Sl st, ch 4, dc) in first ch sp, ch 4, sc in next ch sp, ch 4, *(dc, ch 1, dc, ch 4) in next ch sp, sc in next ch sp, ch 4; repeat from * around, join with sl st in third ch of ch-4.

Rnd 12: (Sl st, ch 1, sc) in first ch sp, ch 7, dc next 2 ch-4 sps tog, ch 7, (sc in next ch-1 sp, ch 7, dc next 2 ch-4 sps tog, ch 7) around, join with sl st in first sc.

Rnd 13: (Sl st, ch 4, 2-tr cl, ch 3, 3-tr cl, ch 3, 3-tr cl, ch 3) in first ch sp, sc in next ch sp, ch 3, *(3-tr cl, ch 3, 3-tr cl, ch 3, 3-tr cl, ch 3) in next ch sp, sc in next ch sp, ch 3; repeat from * around, join with sl st in top of ch-4.

Rnd 14: (Sl st, ch 4, 2-tr cl, ch 3) in first ch sp, 3-tr cl in next ch sp, ch 5, dc next 2 ch sps tog, ch 5, *(3-tr cl in next ch sp, ch 3) 2 times, dc next 2 ch sps tog, ch 3; repeat from * around, join.

Rnd 15: (Sl st, ch 4, 2-tr cl, ch 7) in first ch sp, sc in next ch sp, sc in next st, sc in next ch sp, (ch 7, 3-tr cl in next ch sp, ch 7, sc in next ch sp, sc in next st, sc in next ch sp) around, ch 4, join with tr in top of ch-4 *(joining sp made).*

Rnd 16: (Ch 1, sc) in joining sp, (ch 7, sc in next ch sp) around, ch 4, join with tr in first sc.

Rnds 17-19: (Ch 1, sc, ch 3, sc) in joining sp, ch 7, (sc, ch 3, sc, ch 7) in each ch sp around, ch 4, join with tr in first sc.

Rnd 20: Ch 1, sc in joining ch sp, ch 5, (3-tr cl, ch 3, 3-tr cl, ch 3, 3-tr cl, ch 5) in next ch sp, *sc in next ch sp, ch 5, (3-tr cl, ch 3, 3-tr cl, ch 3, 3-tr cl, ch 5) in next ch sp; repeat from * around, join with sl st in first sc. Fasten off. ⬤━⚷

Spiderweb Set

by Ann Parnell

Finished Sizes: Place Mat is 12¼" × 16½". Napkin Envelope is 8¼" × 10" unfolded.

Materials:
- ❑ 6 oz. ecru woven acrylic sport yarn
- ❑ Tapestry needle
- ❑ B hook or hook needed to obtain gauge

Gauge: 7 dc = 1"; 3 dc rows = 1".

Basic Stitches: Ch, sl st, sc, dc.

Place Mat
Row 1: Ch 118, dc in sixth ch from hook, (ch 1, skip next ch, dc in next ch) 5 times, dc in next 2 chs; *repeat between ( ) 10 times, dc in next 2 chs; repeat from * 3 more times; repeat between ( ) across, turn. *(63 dc made)*

Row 2: Ch 4 *(counts as first dc and ch-1)*, (skip next ch, dc in next dc, ch 1) 5 times, *skip next ch, dc in next 3 dc, ch 1*; [repeat between ( ) 9 times; repeat between **]; repeat between [ ] 3 times; repeat between ( ) 5 times, skip next ch, dc in next ch, turn. *(63 dc)*

Row 3: Ch 4, (skip next ch, dc in next dc, ch 1) 4 times, [skip next ch, *dc in next dc, dc in next ch, dc in next dc*, ch 5, skip next dc; repeat between **, ch 1; repeat between ( ) 7 times]; repeat between [ ] 3 times, skip next ch; repeat between **, ch 5, skip next dc; repeat between **, ch 1; repeat between ( ) 4 times, skip next ch, dc in last dc, turn. *(68 dc)*

Row 4: Ch 4, (skip next ch, dc in next dc, ch 1) 3 times, [skip next ch, *dc in next dc, dc in next ch, dc in next dc*, ch 3, sc in next ch-5 lp, ch 3, skip next dc; repeat between **, ch 1; repeat between ( ) 5 times]; repeat between [ ] 3 times, skip next ch; repeat between **, ch 3, sc in next ch-5 lp, ch 3, skip next dc; repeat between **, ch 1; repeat between ( ) 3 times, skip next ch, dc in last dc, turn. *(58 dc)*

Row 5: Ch 4, (skip next ch, dc in next dc, ch 1) 2 times, [skip next ch, *dc in next dc, dc in next ch, dc in next dc*, ch 4, sc in next ch-3 lp, sc in next sc, sc in next ch-3 lp, ch 4, skip next 2 dc; repeat between **, ch 1; repeat between ( ) 3 times]; repeat between [ ] 3 times, skip next ch; repeat between **, ch 4, sc in next ch-3 lp, sc in next sc, sc in next ch-3 lp, ch 4, skip next 2 dc; repeat between **, ch 1; repeat between ( ) 2 times, skip next ch, dc in last dc, turn. *(48 dc)*

Row 6: Ch 3, dc in next 6 dc and chs, *(ch 4, sc in next ch-4 lp, sc in next 3 sc, sc in next ch-4 lp, ch 4, skip next 2 dc), dc in next 9 dc and chs; repeat from * 3 more times; repeat between ( ), dc in last 7 dc and chs, turn. *(50 dc)*

Row 7: Ch 4, (skip next dc, dc in next dc, ch 1) 2 times, *[skip next dc, dc in next dc, 2 dc in next ch-4 lp, ch 4, skip next sc, sc in next 3 sc, ch 4, skip next sc, 2 dc in next ch-4 lp, dc in next dc, ch 1]; repeat between ( ) 3 times*; repeat between ** 3 times; repeat between [ ]; repeat between ( ) 2 times, skip next dc, dc in last dc, turn. *(48 dc)*

Row 8: Ch 4, (skip next ch, dc in next dc, ch 1) 3 times, *[skip next dc, dc in next dc, 2 dc in next ch-4 lp, ch 3, skip next sc, sc in next sc, ch 3, skip next sc, 2 dc in next ch-4 lp, dc in next dc, ch 1]; repeat between ( ) 5 times*, repeat between ** 3 times; repeat between [ ]; repeat between ( ) 3 times, skip next dc, dc in last dc, turn. *(58 dc)*

Row 9: Ch 4, (skip next ch, dc in next dc, ch 1) 4 times, *[skip next dc, dc in next dc, 2 dc in next ch-3 lp, ch 1, 2 dc in next ch-3 lp, dc in next dc, ch 1]; repeat between ( ) 7 times*; repeat between ** 3 times; repeat between [ ]; repeat between ( ) 4 times, skip next dc, dc in last dc, turn. *(68 dc)*

Row 10: Ch 4, (skip next ch, dc in next dc, ch 1) 5 times, *[skip next dc, dc in next dc, dc in next ch, dc in next dc, ch 1]; repeat between ( ) 9 times*; repeat between ** 3 times; repeat between [ ]; repeat between ( ) 5 times, skip next dc, dc in last dc, turn. *(63 dc)*

Row 11: Repeat row 2.

Rows 12–41: Repeat rows 2–11 consecutively.

Rnd 42: For border, working 2 sc in end of each row and 2 sc in each corner; sc in each dc and in each ch around, join with sl st in first sc. **Do not turn.**

Rnd 43: Sl st in each st around. Fasten off.

Napkin Envelope
Row 1: Ch 74, dc in sixth ch from hook, (ch 1, skip next ch, dc in next ch) 5 times, dc in next 2 chs; *repeat between ( ) 10 times, dc in next 2 chs; repeat from * one more time; repeat between ( ) across, turn. *(39 dc made)*

Row 2: Ch 4 *(counts as first dc and ch-1)*, (skip next ch, dc in next dc, ch 1) 5 times, *skip next ch, dc in next 3 dc, ch 1*; [repeat between ( ) 9 times; repeat between **]; repeat between [ ] one more time; repeat between ( ) 5 times, skip next ch, dc in next ch, turn. *(39 dc)*

Row 3: Ch 4, (skip next ch, dc in next dc, ch 1) 4 times, [skip next ch, *dc in next dc, dc in next ch, dc in next dc*, ch 5, skip next dc; repeat between **; ch 1; repeat between ( ) 7 times];

continued on page 44

Sideboard Cover

by Dot Drake

Finished Size: 12½" × 36½".

Materials:
- ❏ 800 yds. ecru size 10 crochet cotton thread
- ❏ No. 7 steel hook or hook needed to obtain gauge

Gauge: Motif is 4" square.

Basic Stitches: Ch, sl st, sc, hdc, dc, tr.

Special Stitches: For **popcorn (pc)**, 4 dc in ring, drop lp from hook, insert hook in first dc of group, pull dropped lp through st.
For **corner shell**, (3 tr, ch 3, 3 tr) in next ch sp.
For **beginning corner shell (beg corner shell)**, sl st in next 2 sts, (sl st, ch 4, 2 tr, ch 3, 3 tr) in first ch sp.
For **picot**, ch 3, sl st in top of last st made.
For **beginning corner joining (beg corner joining)**, sl st in next 2 sts, (sl st, ch 4, 2 tr) in ch sp of corner shell, ch 1, sc in corresponding ch sp of corner shell on adjacent Motif, ch 1, 3 tr in same ch sp on this Motif.
For **side joining**, ch 2, sc in next corresponding ch sp on adjacent Motif, ch 2, sc in next ch sp on this Motif, picot, (ch 3, sc in corresponding ch sp on adjacent Motif, ch 3, sc in next ch sp on this Motif, picot) across to next corner shell, ch 2, sc in corresponding ch sp on adjacent Motif, ch 2.
For **corner joining**, 3 tr in ch sp of next corner shell on this Motif, ch 1, sc in corresponding ch sp of corner shell on adjacent Motif *(if there are two Motifs at this point, work one sc in each ch sp of each corner ch sp)*, ch 1, 3 tr in same ch sp on this Motif.

First Motif
Rnd 1: Ch 6, sl st in first ch to form ring, ch 3, 3 dc in ring, drop lp from hook, insert hook in top of ch-3, pull dropped lp through st *(beg pc made)*, ch 5, ***pc** (see Special Stitches)*, ch 5; repeat from * 4 more times, join with sl st in first pc. *(6 ch sps made)*
Rnd 2: For Petals, (sl st, sc, hdc, 3 dc, hdc, sc) in first ch sp, (sc, hdc, 3 dc, hdc, sc) in each ch sp around, join with sl st in first sc. *(6 Petals)*
Rnd 3: Sl st in each st around, **do not join.**
Rnd 4: Working behind Petals, *ch 5, sl st in bottom back 2 strands of first sc *(see illustration)* on next Petal; repeat from * around. *(6 ch sps)*
Rnd 5: For Petals, ch 1, (sc, ch 3, tr, ch 1, tr, ch 1, tr, ch 1, tr, ch 1, tr, ch 3, sc) in each ch sp around, join

with sl st in first sc. *(6 Petals)*
Rnd 6: Ch 1, 3 sc in first ch-3 sp, [*(sc in next st, sc in next ch-1 sp) 4 times, sc in next st, 3 sc in next ch-3 sp], sl st in space between next 2 sts, 3 sc in next ch-3 sp; repeat from * 4 more times; repeat between [ ], join with sl st in joining sl st of last rnd. *(90 sc)*
Rnd 7: Sl st in first 4 sc, ch 1, sc in next sc, ch 9, skip next 5 sc, sc in next sc, (ch 9, skip next 8 sc, sc in next sc, ch 9, skip next 5 sc, sc in next sc) 5 times, ch 9, join with sl st in first sc. *(12 ch sps)*
Rnd 8: (Sl st, ch 4, 2 tr, ch 3, 3 tr) in first ch sp *(corner shell made)*, [*ch 5, sc in next ch sp, **picot** (see Special Stitches), ch 7, sc in next ch sp, picot, ch 5], **corner shell**; repeat from * 2 more times; repeat between [ ], join with sl st in top of ch-4. *(4 corner shells, 12 ch sps)*
Rnds 9–11: Beg corner shell *(see Special Stitches)*, [*ch 5, sc in next ch sp, picot, (ch 7, sc in next ch sp, picot) across to next corner shell, ch 5], corner shell; repeat from * 2 more times; repeat between [ ], join. At end of last rnd, fasten off. *(4 corner shells, 24 ch sps)*

One-Side Joining Motif
Rnds 1–10: Repeat rnds 1–10 of First Motif.
Note: See Special Stitches for working joinings.
Rnd 11: Work beg corner joining, side joining, corner joining, [*ch 5, sc in next ch sp, picot, (ch 7, sc in next ch sp, picot) across to next corner shell, ch 5], corner shell; repeat from *; repeat between [ ], join. Fasten off. *(4 corner shells, 24 ch sps)*

Two-Side Joining Motif
Rnds 1–10: Repeat rnds 1–10 of First Motif.
Rnd 11: Work beg corner joining, (side joining, corner joining) 2 times, *ch 5, sc in next ch sp, picot, (ch 7, sc in next ch sp, picot) across to next corner shell, ch 5*, corner shell; repeat between first and second *, join. Fasten off. *(4 corner shells, 24 ch sps)*

Assembly
Work First Motif, work Motifs with one-side joining or two-side joining as indicated by

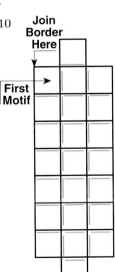

continued on page 44

Sideboard Cover

continued from page 43

blue lines on assembly illustration.

Border

With right side of work facing you, join with sc in corner shell according to arrow on assembly illustration, (sc, ch 5, 2 sc) in same ch sp as sc; *work following steps to complete rnd:*

A: Sc in next 3 sts, (3 sc, ch 3, sc, ch 3, 3 sc) in next ch-5 sp, (3 sc, ch 3, sc, ch 5, sc, ch 3, 3 sc) in each of next 4 ch-7 sps, (3 sc, ch 3, sc, ch 3, 3 sc) in next ch-5 sp, sc in next 3 sts, sc in next ch sp at corner joining;

B: [*Picot, sc in next joining ch-1, sc in next ch sp at corner joining, sc in next 3 sts, (3 sc, ch 3, sc, ch 3, 3 sc) in next ch-5 sp, (3 sc, ch 3, sc, ch 5, sc, ch 3, 3 sc) in each of next 4 ch-7 sps, (3 sc, ch 3, sc, ch 3, 3 sc) in next ch-5 sp, sc in next 3 sts], sc in next ch sp at corner joining; repeat from * 4 more times; repeat between [ ];

C: (2 sc, ch 5, 2 sc) in ch-3 sp of next corner shell, sc in next 3 sts, (3 sc, ch 3, sc, ch 3, 3 sc) in next ch-5 sp, (3 sc, ch 3, sc, ch 5, sc, ch 3, 3 sc) in each of next 4 ch-7 sps, (3 sc, ch 3, sc, ch 3, 3 sc) in next ch-5 sp, sc in each of next 3 sts;

D: Working across extended Motif, [*sc in next 3 sts, (3 sc, ch 3, sc, ch 3, 3 sc) in next ch-5 sp, (3 sc, ch 3, sc, ch 5, sc, ch 3, 3 sc) in each of next 4 ch-7 sps, (3 sc, ch 3, sc, ch 3, 3 sc) in next ch-5 sp, sc in next 3 sts], (2 sc, ch 5, 2 sc) in ch-3 sp of next corner shell; repeat from *; repeat between [ ];

E: Sc in next 3 sts, (3 sc, ch 3, sc, ch 3, 3 sc) in next ch-5 sp, (3 sc, ch 3, sc, ch 5, sc, ch 3, 3 sc) in each of next 4 ch-7 sps, (3 sc, ch 3, sc, ch 3, 3 sc) in next ch-5 sp, sc in next 3 sts;

F: (2 sc, ch 5, 2 sc) in ch-3 sp of next corner shell; repeat steps A–E, join with sl st in first sc. Fasten off. ⚷

Spiderweb Set

continued from page 40

repeat between [ ] one more time, skip next ch; repeat between **; ch 5, skip next dc; repeat between **, ch 1; repeat between ( ) 4 times, skip next ch, dc in last dc, turn. *(42 dc)*

Row 4: Ch 4, (skip next ch, dc in next dc, ch 1) 3 times, [skip next ch, *dc in next dc, dc in next ch, dc in next dc*, ch 3, sc in next ch-5 lp, ch 3, skip next dc; repeat between **, ch 1; repeat between ( ) 5 times]; repeat between [ ] one more time, skip next ch; repeat between **, ch 3, sc in next ch-5 lp, ch 3, skip next dc; repeat between **, ch 1; repeat between ( ) 3 times, skip next ch, dc in last dc, turn. *(36 dc)*

Row 5: Ch 4, (skip next ch, dc in next dc, ch 1) 2 times, [skip next ch, *dc in next dc, dc in next ch, dc in next dc*, ch 4, sc in next ch-3 lp, sc in next sc, sc in next ch-3 lp, ch 4, skip next 2 dc; repeat between **, ch 1; repeat between ( ) 3 times]; repeat between [ ] one more time, skip next ch; repeat between **, ch 4, sc in next ch-3 lp, sc in next sc, sc in next ch-3 lp, ch 4, skip next 2 dc; repeat between **, ch 1; repeat between ( ) 2 times, skip next ch, dc in last dc, turn. *(30 dc)*

Row 6: Ch 3, dc in next 6 dc and chs, *(ch 4, sc in next ch-4 lp, sc in next 3 sc, sc in next ch-4 lp, ch 4, skip next 2 dc), dc in next 9 dc; repeat from * one more time; repeat between ( ), dc in last 7 dc and chs, turn. *(32 dc)*

Row 7: Ch 4, (skip next dc, dc in next dc, ch 1) 2 times, *[skip next dc, dc in next dc, 2 dc in next ch-4 lp, ch 4, skip next sc, sc in next 3 sc, ch 4, skip next sc, 2 dc in next ch-4 lp, dc in next dc, ch 1]; repeat between ( ) 3 times*; repeat between ** one more time; repeat between [ ]; repeat between ( ) 2 times, skip next dc, dc in last dc, turn. *(30 dc)*

Row 8: Ch 4, (skip next ch, dc in next dc, ch 1) 3 times, *[skip next dc, dc in next dc, 2 dc in next ch-4 lp, ch 3, skip next sc, sc in next sc, ch 3, skip next sc, 2 dc in next ch-4 lp, dc in next dc, ch 1]; repeat between ( ) 5 times*; repeat between ** one more time; repeat between [ ]; repeat between ( ) 3 times, skip next dc, dc in last dc, turn. *(36 dc)*

Row 9: Ch 4, (skip next ch, dc in next dc, ch 1) 4 times, *[skip next dc, dc in next dc, 2 dc in next ch-3 lp, ch 1, 2 dc in next ch-3 lp, dc in next dc, ch 1]; repeat between ( ) 7 times*; repeat between ** one more time; repeat between [ ]; repeat between ( ) 4 times, skip next dc, dc in last dc, turn. *(42 dc)*

Row 10: Ch 4, (skip next ch, dc in next dc, ch 1) 5 times, *[skip next dc, dc in next dc, dc in next ch, dc in next dc, ch 1]; repeat between ( ) 9 times*; repeat between ** one more time; repeat between [ ]; repeat between ( ) 5 times, skip next dc, dc in last dc, turn. *(39 dc)*

Row 11: Repeat row 2.

Rows 12–37: Repeat rows 2-11 consecutively. At end of last row, fasten off. Fold bottom of row 1 up to top of row 21, spider webs will be on top of each other. With tapestry needle and yarn, sew side seams making pocket.

Border: Join with sl st in first dc of row 1, sl st in each dc and in each ch around opening of envelope with 2 sl sts in end of each row. Fasten off. ⚷

Kitchen Charm

The smell of hot-from-the-oven bread, fresh-brewed coffee and bacon sizzling in the pan—it's too bad we can't bottle them all to help us remember those wonderful days at Grandma's house! The next best thing is to recreate your own country-style kitchen with the baker's dozen designs in this chapter! We have pretty potholders to crochet from thread, hot pads and place mats to create from fabric strips. There's a rug to make with several strands of yarn and projects that help you use your scraps!

Round Rug

by Maggie Weldon

Finished Size: 33½" across.

Materials:
- ❑ 21 oz. each white and blue worsted yarn
- ❑ Q bulky hook or hook needed to obtain gauge

Gauge: 1 V st = 1½" across; 2 V st rows = 3".

Basic Stitches: Ch, sl st, dc.

Special Stitches: For **beginning V st (beg V st),** (ch 4, dc) in first st **or** ch sp.
For **V st,** (dc, ch 1, dc) in next st **or** ch sp.

Rug

Note: *Work with four strands of same color yarn held together throughout.*

Rnd 1: With white, ch 4, sl st in first ch to form ring, ch 3 *(counts as first dc),* 11 dc in ring, join with sl st in top of ch-3. *(12 dc made)*

Rnd 2: Beg V st *(see Special Stitches)* in first st, **V st** in each st around, join with sl st in third ch of ch-4. Fasten off. *(12 V sts)*

Rnd 3: Join blue with sl st in ch sp of any V st, (ch 3, 2 dc) in same ch sp, 3 dc in ch sp of each V st around, join with sl st in top of ch-3. *(36 dc)*

Rnd 4: Ch 3, 2 dc in next st, (dc in next 2 sts, 2 dc in next st) 11 times, dc in last st, join. Fasten off. *(48 dc)*

Rnd 5: Join white with sl st in any st, ch 3, 2 dc in next st, (dc in next 3 sts, 2 dc in next st) 11 times, dc in last 2 sts, join. *(60 dc)*

Rnd 6: Beg V st, skip next st, (V st in next st, skip next st) around, join with sl st in third ch of ch-4. Fasten off. *(30 V sts)*

Rnd 7: Join blue with sl st in ch sp of any V st, (ch 3, 2 dc) in same ch sp, 3 dc in ch sp of each V st around, join with sl st in top of ch-3. *(90 dc)*

Rnd 8: Ch 3, 2 dc in next st, (dc in next 14 sts, 2 dc in next st) 5 times, dc in last 13 sts, join. Fasten off. *(96 dc)*

Rnd 9: Join white with sl st in any st, ch 3, dc in next st, 2 dc in next st, (dc in next 7 sts, 2 dc in next st) 11 times, dc in last 5 sts, join. *(108 dc)*

Rnd 10: (Ch 5, dc) in first st *(counts as first dc and ch-2),* skip next 2 sts, *(dc, ch 2, dc) in next st, skip next 2 sts; repeat from * around, join with sl st in third ch of ch-5. Fasten off.

Rnd 11: Join blue with sl st in any ch sp, (ch 3, 2 dc) in same ch sp, 4 dc in each of next 2 ch sps, (3 dc in next ch sp, 4 dc in each of next 2 ch sps) around, join with sl st in top of ch-3. *(132 dc)*

Rnd 12: Ch 3, 2 dc in next st, (dc in next 10 sts, 2 dc in next st) 11 times, dc in last 9 sts, join. Fasten off. *(144 dc)*

Chicken Place Mat Set

by Leisa Hargrove

Finished Sizes: Place Mat is 16" × 18". Coaster is 3¾" × 4½". Napkin Ring is 7½" around.

Materials:
- ❑ 45" lightweight cotton fabric:
   ¾ yd. white print
   Small amount each red and yellow
- ❑ Small amount red size 10 crochet cotton thread
- ❑ No. 0 steel and P wooden hooks or hook needed to obtain gauge

Gauge: **P hook,** 6 sc = 3"; 7 sc rows = 3".

Basic Stitches: Ch, sl st, sc.

Notes: Wash fabric to preshrink and set colors before starting.
Cut fabric in ¾" strips. Sew end to end. Roll into a ball.
Use P hook unless otherwise stated.

Place Mat
Row 1: For **body,** with white, ch 17, sc in second ch from hook, sc in each ch across, turn. *(16 sc made)*

Rows 2–8: Ch 1, 2 sc in first st, sc in each st across to last st, 2 sc in last st, turn. At end of last row *(30).*

Rows 9–19: Ch 1, sc in each st across, turn.

Rows 20–23: Ch 1, skip first st, sc in each st across to last 2 sts, skip next st, sc in last st, turn. At end of last row *(22).*

Row 24: For **tail,** ch 1, sc in first 6 sts leaving last 16 sts unworked, turn. *(6)*

Rows 25–26: Ch 1, skip first st, sc in each st across to last 2 sts, skip next st, sc in last st, turn. *(4, 2)*

Row 27: Ch 1, skip first st, sc in last st. Fasten off.

Row 24: For **head,** skip next 6 unworked sts on row 23, join white with sc in next st, sc in each st across, turn. *(10)*

Rows 25–32: Repeat rows 20 and 9 alternately. At end of last row, **do not turn.** *(2)*

Rnd 33: Working around outer edge, ch 1, 2 sc in end of first row, sc in end of each row and in each st around with 3 sc in tip of tail and in end of last row on head, join with sl st in first sc. Fasten off.

continued on page 52

Countryside Curtain

by Elizabeth Ann White

Finished Size: 24"-wide × 26"-long.

Materials:
- ❏ 1,200 yds. cream size 10 crochet cotton thread
- ❏ Embroidery needle
- ❏ No. 8 steel hook or hook needed to obtain gauge

Gauge: 19 sts and ch = 2"; 9 dc rows = 2".

Basic Stitches: Ch, sl st, dc.

Special Stitches: For **beginning mesh (beg mesh),** ch 5, dc in next dc.
For **mesh,** ch 2, skip next 2 ch **or** 2 dc, dc in next dc.
For **end mesh,** ch 2, dc in top of ch-3.
For **block,** dc in next 3 dc **or** 2 dc in next ch sp, dc in next dc.

Curtain
Notes: *See Special Stitches for working pattern instructions.*

Even numbered rows are right side of work.

Row 1: Ch 230, dc in eighth ch from hook, *(counts as ch 3 and first mesh),* (ch 2, skip next 2 ch, dc in next ch) across, turn. *(75 mesh made)*

Row 2: Beg mesh, (block, mesh) 36 times, block, end mesh, turn.

Rows 3–116: Beg mesh, work across according to graph on page 54, turn. At end of row 116, fasten off.

For **casing,** fold rows 114–116 to wrong side; sew top edge of row 116 to top edge of row 109.

For **edging,** leaving casing open, starting at top right-hand corner, working across folded edge, skip end mesh, join with *sc in next mesh, (5 dc in next mesh, sc in next mesh) across to next end or beginning mesh at corner, 9 dc in end or beginning mesh at corner; repeat from * around, join with sl st in first sc. Fasten off. ⌐☞

graph on page 54

Chicken Place Mat Set

continued from page 51

Comb
Row 1: With right side facing you, working in center 3 sts on top of head, join red strip with sc in first st, sc in next 2 sts, turn. *(3 sc made)*

Row 2: (Ch 5, sl st) in first st, (sl st, ch 5, sl st) in each of next 2 sts. Fasten off.

Beak
Row 1: With right side facing you, skip next 2 sts on head below Comb, join yellow with sc in next st, sc in next 2 sts, turn. *(3 sc made)*

Row 2: Ch 1, sc in first st, skip next st, sc in last st, turn. *(2)*

Row 3: Ch 1, skip first st, sc in last st. Fasten off.

Wattle
Join red strip with sl st in same st as third st of Beak was worked in, ch 5, sl st in same st. Fasten off.

Egg Coaster
Notes: *Work in continuous rnds. Do not join or turn unless otherwise stated. Mark first st of each rnd.*

Rnd 1: With white, ch 2, 6 sc in second ch from hook. *(6 sc made)*

Rnd 2: 2 sc in each of first 3 sts, sc in next st, 3 sc in next st, sc in last st. *(11)*

Rnd 3: (Sc in next st, 2 sc in next st) 3 times, sc in next 2 sts, 3 sc in next st, sc in last 2 sts. *(16)*

Rnd 4: (2 sc in next st, sc in next 2 sts) 3 times, sc in next 3 sts, 3 sc in next st, sc in last 3 sts, join with sl st in first sc. Fasten off. *(21)*

Rnd 5: For **edge,** with 0 hook and red crochet cotton, join with sl st in any st, ch 4, (sl st in next st, ch 4) around, join with sl st in first sl st. Fasten off.

Napkin Ring
Rnd 1: With white, ch 15, sl st in first ch to form ring, ch 1, sc in each ch around, join with sl st in first sc. *(15 sc made)*

Rnds 2–3: Ch 1, sc in each st around, join. At end of last rnd, fasten off.

Rnd 4: For **edge,** with 0 hook and red crochet cotton, join with sl st in any st, ch 4, (sl st in next st, ch 4) around, join with sl st in first sl st. Fasten off.

Rnd 5: Working in **remaining lps** on opposite side of starting ch on rnd 1, with 0 hook and red crochet cotton, join with sl st in any ch, ch 4, (sl st in next ch, ch 4) around, join with sl st in first sl st. Fasten off. ⌐☞

Countryside Curtain

continued from page 52

■ = Block

☐ = Beg Mesh, Mesh or End Mesh

Rnd 37: Working in **back lps,** (ch 3, 2 dc) in next st, 3 dc in each st around, join with sl st in top of ch-3.

Rnd 38: Ch 3, skip next st, (sl st in next st, ch 3, skip next st) around, join with sl st in first ch of first ch-3. Fasten off.

Rnd 39: Working in **remaining lps** of rnd 36, join white with sc in first st, sc in next 3 sts changing to blue, sc in next 4 sts changing to white, (sc in next 4 sts changing to blue, sc in next 4 sts changing to white) around.

Rnd 40: (Sc in next 4 sts changing to blue, sc in next 4 sts changing to white) around.

Rnd 41: (Sc in next 4 sts changing to blue, sc in next 4 sts changing to white) around to last 8 sts, sc in next 4 sts changing to blue, sc in next 4 sts, **do not change colors.**

Rnds 42–43: (Sc in next 4 sts changing to white, sc in next 4 sts changing to blue) around.

Rnd 44: (Sc in next 4 sts changing to white, sc in next 4 sts changing to blue) around to last 8 sts, sc in next 4 sts changing to white, sc in next 4 sts, **do not change colors.**

Rnds 45–46: (Sc in next 4 sts changing to blue, sc in next 4 sts changing to white) around.

Rnd 47: (Sc in next 4 sts changing to blue, sc in next 4 sts changing to white) around to last 8 sts, sc in next 4 sts changing to blue, sc in next 4 sts, **do not change colors.**

Rnds 48–56: Repeat rnds 42–47 consecutively, ending with rnd 44. At end of last rnd, fasten off blue.

Rnd 57: With white, sc in each st around, join with sl st in first sc.

Rnd 58: Ch 1, sc in first st, ch 1, skip next st, (sc in next st, ch 1, skip next st) around, join.

Rnd 59: (Sl st, ch 3, 2 dc) in first ch sp, 3 dc in each ch sp around, join with sl st in top of ch-3.

Rnd 60: Ch 3, skip next st, (sl st in next st, ch 3, skip next st) around, join with sl st in first sl st. Fasten off.

Rnd 61: Working in starting ch on opposite side of row 1 on Dress, join white with sl st in first st, ch 2, 2 hdc in same st as sl st, 3 hdc in each st around.

Rnd 62: Ch 3, skip next st, (sl st in next st, ch 3, skip next st) around, join with sl st in first ch of first ch-3. Fasten off.

Weave cord through sts of rnd 58, tie ends in bow.

Apron

Rnd 1: Working in **remaining lps** of rnd 10, join white with sc in any st, sc in each st around.

Rnd 2: Sc in each st around, join with sl st in next st. Fasten off.

Straps (make 2)

Row 1: With white, ch 23, sc in second ch from hook, sc in each ch across, turn. *(22 sc made)*

Row 2: Sl st in each st across with 3 sc in last st, working in starting ch on opposite side of row 1, sl st in each ch across. Fasten off.

Sew one end of each Strap with 6 sts between to one top edge of Apron. Sew remaining ends together to center top edge in back of Apron.

Sew one button to end of each Strap in front.

Tie 8" piece of ⅛" ribbon in bow at center front of rnd 9 on Dress.

Sleeve (make 2)

Rnd 1: With white, ch 16, sl st in first ch to form ring, ch 1, sc in first 4 chs changing to blue, sc in next 4 chs changing to white, sc in next 4 chs changing to blue, sc in last 4 chs changing to white. *(16 sc made)*

Rnds 2–3: Repeat rnds 40 and 41 of Dress.

Rnds 4–14: Repeat rnds 42–47 of Dress consecutively, ending with rnd 46.

Rnd 15: (Sc in next 4 sts changing to blue, sc in next 4 sts changing to white) around. Fasten off blue.

Rnd 16: With white, sc in each st around, join with sl st in first st.

Rnd 17: Working in **back lps,** (ch 2, 2 hdc) in first st, 3 hdc in each st around.

Rnd 18: Ch 3, skip next st, (sl st in next st, ch 3, skip next st) around, join with sl st in first ch of first ch-3. Fasten off.

Rnd 19: Working in **remaining lps** of rnd 16, for **hand,** join off-white with sc in first st, sc in each st around. *(16)*

Rnds 20–23: Sc in each st around.

Rnds 24–26: (Sc next 2 sts tog) around. At end of last rnd, fasten off.

Gather and sew rnd 1 to side at top of Apron Strap. Glue or tack Head to inside opening of Dress.

Rolling Pin
Roller

Rnd 1: With tan, ch 18, sl st in first ch to form ring, ch 1, sc in each ch around. *(18 sc made)*

Rnds 2–18: Sc in each st around. At end of last rnd, join with sl st in next sc. Fasten off.

Knob (make 2)

Rnd 1: With tan, ch 2, 5 sc in second ch from hook. *(5 sc made)*

Rnd 2: (2 sc in next st, sc in next st) 2 times, 2 sc in last st. *(8)*

Rnd 3: Sc in each st around.

Rnd 4: 2 sc in first st, sc in each st around to last st, 2 sc in last st. *(10)*

Rnd 5: Sc in each st around.

Rnd 6: Sc in next 4 sts, sc next 2 sts tog, sc in next 4 sts. *(9)*

Rnd 7: Sc in each st around.

Rnd 8: 2 sc in each st around, join with sl st in next sc. Fasten off.

Sew Knobs to ends of Roller stuffing before closing.

Cut ribbon in half. For **bow (make 2),** holding one piece of ⅝" ribbon and one piece of ⅛" ribbon together as one, tie in bow around end of Pin as shown in photo.

Glue remaining flowers to bows.

Tack Rolling Pin to hands as shown. ✐

Country Apples Set

by Dorothy Moder Frantz

Finished Sizes: Rug is 27" × 28" including stem; Hot Pad is 10" × 11" including stem; Wall Hanging is 10" × 11" including stem; Napkin Holder is 5½" × 9".

Materials:
- ❏ 1½"-wide fabric strips:
  - 200 yds. bright green for Rug
  - 30 yds. white for Napkin Holder
  - 8 yds. dk. red for Napkin Holder
  - 50 yds. red or bright green for Hot Pad/Wall Hanging
  - 5 yds. green print for Leaves
  - 3 yds. brown for each Stem
- ❏ 3 yds. black yarn
- ❏ Black buttonhole thread
- ❏ Sewing and tapestry needles
- ❏ P wooden hook or hook needed to obtain gauge

Gauge: 3 sc = 2"; sc rnd = 1"; 3 hdc = 2"; hdc

continued on page 64

Collectable Thread Potholders

Rickrack Potholder

Finished Size: 6" across.

Materials:
- ❑ Size 8 crochet cotton thread:
  - 70 yds. green
  - 18 yds. white
- ❑ 2 yds. white ¼" rickrack
- ❑ White sewing thread and needle
- ❑ No. 7 steel hook or hook needed to obtain gauge

Gauge: Rnds 1–4 = 2" across; 8 dc = 1", 4 dc rows = 1".

Basic Stitches: Ch, sl st, sc, dc, tr.

Side (make 2)

Rnd 1: With green, ch 3, sl st in first ch to form ring, ch 4, (dc in ring, ch 1) 9 times, join with sl st in top of ch-3. *(10 ch sps made)*

Rnd 2: Sl st in first ch sp, ch 4; for **V st, (dc, ch 1, dc)** in next ch sp, ch 1, (dc in next ch sp, ch 1, V st in next ch sp, ch 1) around, join with sl st in third ch of ch-4. *(15 ch sps)*

Rnd 3: Sl st in first ch sp, ch 4, dc in next ch sp, ch 1, V st in next ch sp, ch 1, *(dc in next ch sp, ch 1) 2 times, V st in next ch sp, ch 1; repeat from * around, join. *(20 ch sps)*

Rnd 4: Repeat rnd 2. *(30 ch sps)*

Rnd 5: Sl st in first ch sp, ch 4, (dc in next ch sp, ch 1) around, join.

Rnd 6: Repeat rnd 2. *(45 ch sps)*

Rnd 7: (Sl st, ch 4, dc) in first ch sp, ch 1, (dc in next ch sp, ch 1) around, join. *(46 ch sps)*

Rnds 8-10: Repeat rnds 2 and 7 alternately, ending with rnd 2. At end of last rnd, fasten off. *(105 ch sps)*

With right side facing you, weave rickrack on rnds 2, 4, 6, 8 and 10, weaving under one st and over V st of each rnd *(see photo).*

Tack rickrack ends together on wrong side.

Trim

Rnd 1: With wrong sides together, working through both thicknesses, join white with sc in any dc on rnd 10; skipping V sts, ch 3, (sc in next dc, ch 3) around, join with sl st in first sc.

Rnd 2: Ch 1, sc in first st, (4 dc, tr, 4 dc) in next ch sp, *sc in next ch sp, (4 dc, tr, 4 dc) in next ch sp; repeat from * around, join with sl st in first sc. Fasten off.

For **hanging loop,** with wrong side facing you, join white with sl st in any unworked sc on rnd 1 of Trim, ch 10, sl st in next unworked sc, **turn;** 10 sc in ch lp, sl st in same st as first sl st. Fasten off. ❑❑

Posy Petals

Finished Size: 6" across.

Materials:
- ❑ Size 10 crochet cotton thread:
  - 100 yds. raspberry
  - 50 yds. white
  - 15 yds. green
- ❑ White and green sewing thread
- ❑ Sewing needle
- ❑ No. 9 steel hook or hook needed to obtain gauge

Gauge: 9 dc = 1"; 8 dc **back lp rows** = 2".

Basic Stitches: Ch, sl st, dc, tr.

Back

Rnd 1: With raspberry, ch 4, sl st in first ch to form ring, ch 3, 14 dc in ring, join with sl st in top of ch-3. *(15 dc made)*

Note: *Work in* **back lps** *(see Stitch Guide) unless otherwise stated.*

Rnd 2: (Ch 3, dc) in first st, 2 dc in each st around, join. *(30)*

Rnd 3: (Ch 3, dc) in first st, dc in next st, (2 dc in next st, dc in next st) around, join. *(45)*

Rnd 4: Ch 3, dc in next st, 2 dc in next st, (dc in next 2 sts, 2 dc in next st) around, join. *(60)*

Rnd 5: (Ch 3, dc) in first st, dc in next 3 sts, (2 dc in next st, dc in next 3 sts) around, join. *(75)*

Rnd 6: (Ch 3, dc) in first st, dc in next 4 sts, (2 dc in next st, dc in next 4 sts) around, join. *(90)*

Rnd 7: (Ch 3, dc) in first st, dc in next 5 sts, (2 dc in next st, dc in next 5 sts) around, join. *(105)*

Rnd 8: (Ch 3, dc) in first st, dc in next 6 sts, (2 dc in next st, dc in next 6 sts) around, join. *(120)*

Rnd 9: Ch 3, dc in next 6 sts, 2 dc in next st, (dc in next 6 sts, 2 dc in next st) around, join. *(137)*

Rnd 10: Ch 3, dc in next 8 sts, (2 dc in next st, dc in next 8 sts) around to last 2 sts, dc in last 2 sts, join. Fasten off. *(151)*

Front

Rnds 1-6: Repeat rnds 1-6 of Back. At end of last rnd, fasten off.

Rnd 7: Working this rnd in **both lps,** join white with sl st in first st; for **beginning popcorn, ch 3, 4 dc in same st, drop lp from hook, insert hook in third ch of ch-3, pull dropped lp**

continued on page 63

Heart & Home Set

by Donna Lee-Piglowski

Towel Holder

Finished Size: 5½" long without towel.

Materials:
- ❑ Cotton worsted yarn:
    1 oz. eggshell
    Small amount each blue, yellow and pink
- ❑ Kitchen towel
- ❑ White sewing thread
- ❑ Sewing and tapestry needles
- ❑ G hook or hook needed to obtain gauge

Gauge: 4 sc = 1"; 4 sc rows = 1".

Basic Stitches: Ch, sl st, sc, hdc, dc.

Towel Holder

Row 1: With eggshell, ch 62, sc in second ch from hook, sc in each ch across, turn. *(61 sc made)*

Row 2: Ch 1, sc first 2 sts tog, (sc next 2 sts tog) 14 times, sc in next st, (sc next 2 sts tog) 15 times, turn. *(31)*

Row 3: Ch 1, sc first 2 sts tog, (sc next 2 sts tog) 6 times, sc in next 3 sts, (sc next 2 sts tog) 7 times, turn. *(17)*

Rows 4–12: Ch 1, sc in each st across, turn.

Rows 13–18: Ch 1, sc first 2 sts tog, sc in each st across to last 2 sts, sc last 2 sts tog, turn. At end of last row, fasten off. *(5 sc)*

Row 19: For **trim**, working in ends of rows and in sts, join blue with sc in row 1, sc in next 17 rows; working in **front lps** *(see Stitch Guide)* of row 18, 2 sc in first st, sc in next 3 sts, 2 sc in last st, sc in next 18 rows, **do not turn.** Fasten off. *(43)*

Row 20: Join yellow with sc in first st, *skip next st, (sc, hdc, dc) in next st; repeat from * across to last 2 sts, skip next st, sc in last st, **do not turn.** Fasten off. *(62 sts)*

Row 21: Join blue with sl st in last st, ch 1; for **reverse sc** *(see Stitch Guide),* working from left to right, insert hook in next st to the right, complete as sc; reverse sc in next st, skip next st, (reverse sc in next 2 sts, skip next st) across to last st, sl st in last st. Fasten off.

Finishing

Using cross-stitch *(see Stitch Guide),* embroider according to graph on page 62.

For **first tie,** working in **back lps** of row 18, join eggshell with sl st in first st, ch 50. Fasten off.

For **second tie,** skip next 3 sts, join with sl st in next st, ch 50. Fasten off.

Cut towel in half. Machine or hand zig-zag raw edge. Sew to row 1 of Towel Holder. ○─⌐

Utensil Holder

Finished Size: Fits 46 oz. juice can.

Materials:
- ❑ Cotton worsted yarn:
    2 oz. eggshell
    1 oz. blue
    Small amount each yellow and pink
- ❑ Tapestry needle
- ❑ G hook or hook needed to obtain gauge

Gauge: 4 sc = 1" 4 sc rows = 1".

Basic Stitches: Ch, sl st, sc.

Cover

Bottom

Note: Work in continuous rnds. Do not join or turn unless otherwise stated. Mark first st of each rnd.

Rnd 1: With blue, ch 2, 6 sc in second ch from hook. *(6 sc made)*

Rnd 2: 2 sc in each st around. *(12)*

Rnd 3: (Sc in next st, 2 sc in next st) around. *(18)*

Rnd 4: (Sc in next 2 sts, 2 sc in next st) around. *(24)*

Rnd 5: (Sc in next 3 sts, 2 sc in next st) around. *(30)*

Rnd 6: (Sc in next 4 sts, 2 sc in next st) around. *(36)*

Rnd 7: (Sc in next 5 sts, 2 sc in next st) around. *(42)*

Rnd 8: (Sc in next 6 sts, 2 sc in next st) around, join with sl st in first sc. *(48)*

Rnds 9–10: Working these rnds in **back lps** *(see Stitch Guide),* ch 1, sc in each st around, join. At end of last rnd, fasten off.

Rnds 11–12: Ch 1, sc in each st around, join. At end of last rnd, fasten off.

Side

Row 1: With eggshell, ch 49, sc in second ch from hook, sc in each ch across, turn. *(48 sc made)*

Rows 2–26: Ch 1, sc in each st across, turn. At end of last row, fasten off.

Using cross-stitch *(see Stitch Guide),* embroider Side according to graph on page 62.

Sew ends of rows together.

Edging

Rnd 1: With right side facing you, working this rnd in **back lps** of row 26 on Side, join blue with sc in first st, sc in next 9 sts, sc next 2 sts tog, (sc in next 10 sts, sc next 2 sts tog) around,

continued on page 62

join with sl st in first sc. Fasten off. *(44 sc made)*

Rnd 2: With wrong side facing you, working this rnd in **front lps**, join yellow with sc in first st, sc in each st around, join with sl st in first sc, **turn.**

Rnd 3: Sl st in each st around, join with sl st in first sl st. Fasten off.

Rnd 4: Working in **front lps** of row 26, join pink with sc in first st; for **reverse sc** *(see Stitch Guide),* working from left to right, insert hook in next st to the right, complete as sc; reverse sc in each st around, join with sl st in first sc. Fasten off.

Finishing

Matching sts of row 1 on Side to sts of rnd 12 on Bottom, working through both thicknesses, join pink with sc in any st, sc in each st around, join with sl st in first sc. Fasten off.

Working in **front lps** of rnd 9 on Bottom, join yellow with sc in any st, ch 1, reverse sc in each st around, join with sl st in first sc. Fasten off.

Insert can, pull Edging over top of can.

Place Mat

Finished Size: 11¾" x 18¼".

Materials:
- ❑ Cotton worsted yarn:
  - 5 oz. eggshell
  - Small amount each blue, yellow and pink
- ❑ Tapestry needle
- ❑ G hook or hook needed to obtain gauge

Gauge: 4 sc = 1"; 9 sc rows = 2".

Basic Stitches: Ch, sl st, sc.

Place Mat

Row 1: With eggshell, ch 70, sc in second ch from hook, sc in each ch across, turn. *(69 sc made)*

Rows 2–49: Ch 1, sc in each st across, turn.

Rnd 50: Working around outer edge, sc in each st and in end of each row around with 3 sc in each corner st, join with sl st in first sc. Fasten off.

Rnd 51: Join pink with sc in any st; for **reverse sc** *(see Stitch Guide),* working left to right, insert hook in next st to the right, complete as sc; reverse sc in each st around, join with sl st in first sc. Fasten off.

Using cross-stitch *(see Stitch Guide),* embroider according to graph on next page.

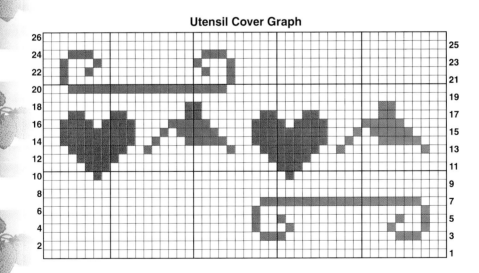

Utensil Cover Graph

X	Colors
▨	= Pink
☐	= Yellow
▨	= Blue

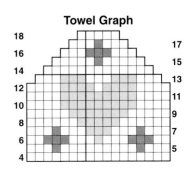

Towel Graph

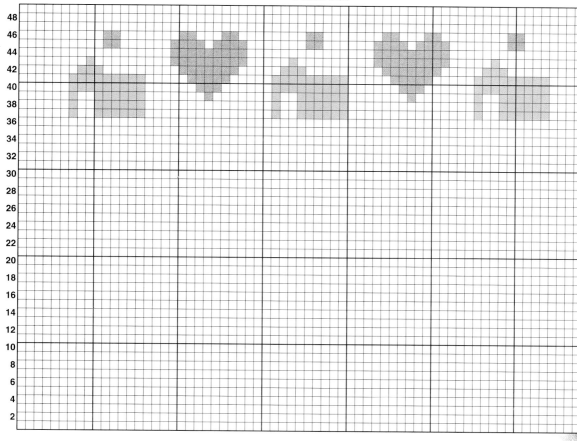

Collectable Thread Potholders

continued from page 59

through ch; ch 1, skip next st; *for **popcorn (pc), 5 dc in next st, drop lp from hook, insert hook in top of first dc of group, pull dropped lp through st;** ch 1, skip next st; repeat from * around, join. Fasten off. *(45 pc)*

Rnd 8: Join raspberry with sl st in first pc, ch 3, dc in next ch-1 sp, (dc in next pc, 2 dc in next ch-1 sp, dc in next pc, dc in next ch-1 sp) 2 times, *(dc in next pc, 2 dc in next ch-1 sp) 3 times, dc in next pc, dc in next ch-1 sp; repeat from * 7 more times, (dc in next pc, 2 dc in next ch-1 sp, dc in next pc, dc in next ch-1 sp) 4 times, join. *(120 dc)*

Rnds 9-10: Repeat rnds 9-10 of Back.

Flower (make 5)

With white, ch 3, sl st in first ch to form ring; for **petal,** (ch 4, 2 tr in ring, ch 4, sl st in ring) 5 times Fasten off. *(5 petals made)*

Leaves (make 5)

Row 1: With green, ch 4; for **first leaf,** 4 dc in fourth ch from hook, turn. *(5 dc made)*

Row 2: Ch 3, dc next 2 sts tog, dc in next st leaving last st unworked, turn. *(3)*

Row 3: For **tip,** ch 3, sl st in third ch from hook, sc in next st leaving last st unworked, **do not turn;** working in ends of rows, ch 3, sl st in bottom of row 2, ch 3, sl st in same ch as first 4 dc. **Do not fasten off.**

Rows 4-6: For **second leaf,** repeat rows 1-3 of first leaf. At end of last row, fasten off.

Sew center of Leaves evenly spaced around rnd 4 of front. Sew center of each Flower to center of each Leaf piece.

Trim

Rnd 1: With Front facing you, holding Front and Back wrong sides together, matching sts; working through both thicknesses in **both lps,** join white with sc in first st, sc in each st around, join with sl st in first sc. *(151 sc made)*

Rnd 2: Ch 1, sc in first st; for **hanging loop,** ch 12; sc in next st, skip next 2 sts; for **shell, (dc, ch 1) 4 times in next st, dc in same st;** skip next 2 sts, (sc in next st, skip next 2 sts, shell in next st, skip next 2 sts) around, sl st in first sc, ch 1, 15 sc in hanging loop, join with sl st in first sc. Fasten off. *(25 shells)*

Country Apples Set

continued from page 57

rnd = 1½"; 3 dc = 2"; 1 dc rnd = 2".

Basic Stitches: Ch, sl st, sc, hdc, dc.

Hot Pad/Wall Hanging
Rnd 1: Make a slip ring *(see Stitch Guide)* ch 3, 12 dc in ring pull ring closed, join with sl st in top of ch-3.

Rnd 2: (Ch 2, hdc) in first st, 3 hdc in next st, 2 hdc in next 11 sts, join with sl st in top of ch-2.

Rnd 3: (Ch 2, hdc) in first st, 2 hdc in next sts, (hdc in next st, 2 hdc in next st) 12 times, sc in next st, join.

Rnd 4: Ch 1, sl st in next st, sc in next 2 sts, 2 hdc in next 2 sts, hdc in next st, sc in next 6 sts, sl st in next 2 sts, sc in next st, hdc in next st, 2 hdc in next st, sc in next st, sl st in next 2 sts, sc in next st, 2 hdc in next st, hdc in next st, sc in next st, sl st in next 2 sts, sc in next 6 sts, hdc in next st, 2 hdc in next 2 sts, hdc in next st, sc in next 2 sts, sl st in last 3 sts, join with sl st in first sl st. Fasten off.

Hanging Stem
With brown, join with sl st in second sl st at end of rnd 4, ch 9, sl st in last sl st of rnd 4. Fasten off.

Stem
Row 1: With brown, join with sc in last st of rnd 4, turn.

Row 2: Ch 1, 2 sc in first st, turn.

Row 3: Ch 1, 2 sc in first st. Fasten off.

Leaf
With green print, ch 5, 2 sc in second ch from hook, hdc in next ch, sc in next ch, (sc, sl st, sc) in next ch; working on opposite side of starting ch, sc in next ch, hdc in next ch, 2 sc in next ch, join with sl st in first sc. Fasten off.

With black thread and needle, sew Leaf to Hot Pad or Wall Hanging according to photo.

Napkin Holder
First Side Bottom
Row 1: With white, make a slip ring *(see Stitch Guide)* ch 3, 5 dc in ring, pull ring closed, turn.

Row 2: (Ch 2, hdc) in first st, 3 hdc in next st, (hdc in next st, 2 hdc in next) 2 times, **do not turn.**

Row 3: Working in ends of rows, evenly space 10 sl sts across, turn.

Rows 4–6: Ch 1, sc in each st across, turn. At end of row 6, fasten off.

Second Side Bottom
Repeat rows 1–3 of First Side Bottom. At end of row 3, fasten off.

With white, whipstitch rows 3 and 6 together.

Trim
With dk. red, join with sc in first st on row 3 of First Side, sc in next 4 sts, 2 sc in next st, sc in last 5 sts. Fasten off. Repeat for Second Side

With tapestry needle and double strands of black yarn secure to back side of Holder making straight stitches according to photo.

Rug
Rnd 1: Make a slip ring *(see Stitch Guide)* ch 3, 16 dc in ring, pull ring closed, join with sl st in top of ch-3.

Rnd 2: (Ch 3, dc) in first st, 2 dc in each st around, join.

Rnd 3: (Ch 3, dc) in first st, (dc in next st, 2 dc in next st) 16 times, dc in last st, join.

Rnd 4: (Ch 3, dc) in first st, (dc in next 3 sts, 2 dc in next st) 12 times, dc in last 2 sts, join.

Rnd 5: (Ch 3, dc) in first st, (dc in next 5 sts, 2 dc in next st) 10 times, dc in last 3 sts, join.

Rnd 6: (Ch 3, dc) in first st, (dc in next 7 sts, 2 dc in next st) 9 times, dc in last 2 sts, join.

Rnd 7: (Ch 3, dc) in first st, (dc in next 9 sts, 2 dc in next st) 8 times, dc in last 4 sts, join.

Rnd 8: Ch 1, sl st in first 3 sts, sc in next 2 sts, hdc in next 3 sts, dc in next 3 sts, 2 dc in next 6 sts, dc in next 3 sts, hdc in next 8 sts, sc in next 8 sts, hdc in next 3 sts, 2 dc in next 4 sts, sc in next 3 sts, sl st in next 5 sts, sc in next 3 sts, 2 dc in next 4 sts, hdc in next 3 sts, sc in next 8 sts, hdc in next 8 sts, dc in next 3 sts, 2 dc in next 6 sts, dc in next 2 sts, hdc in next 3 sts, sc in next 2 sts, sl st in last 2 sts. Fasten off.

Stem
Row 1: With brown, join with sc in last st of rnd 8, turn.

Row 2: Ch 1, 2 sc in first st, turn.

Row 3: Ch 1, 2 sc in first st, sc in next st, turn.

Row 4: Ch 1, 2 sc in first st, sc in each st across, turn.

Row 5: 2 sc in first st, sc in each st across. Fasten off.

Leaf
With green print, ch 9, 2 sc in second ch from hook, hdc in next 4 chs, sc in next 2 chs, (sc, sl st, sc) in next ch; working on opposite side of starting ch, sc in next 2 chs, hdc in next 4 chs, 2 sc in next ch, join with sl st in first sc. Fasten off.

With black thread and needle, sew Leaf to Rug according to photo. ⌁

Boudoir Basics

What could be more appealing than to lounge around and be served breakfast in bed? All of this, while surrounded by luxurious crochet pieces that we've created ourselves! Looking for a bedspread in fine thread or fluffy yarn? It's here! Pillows and places for pictures? We have them, too! Turn the page to surround yourself with the very epitome of elegance—crochet!

Delicate Lampshade

by Wilma Bonner

Finished Size: Fits 3" × 4" × 4" lamp shade.

Materials:
- ❏ Size 10 crochet cotton thread:
    - 350 yds. moss green
    - 150 yds. med. rose
- ❏ 1 yd. moss green ³⁄₁₆" ribbon
- ❏ Dark green 3" × 4" × 4" lamp shade
- ❏ Fabric glue
- ❏ No. 8 steel hook or hook needed to obtain gauge

Gauge: 9 dc = 1".

Basic Stitches: Ch, sl st, sc, dc.

Lamp Shade Cover

Rnd 1: With green, ch 96 to fit around top of lamp shade, being careful not to twist ch, sl st in first ch to form ring, ch 4 *(counts as dc and ch-1),* skip next ch, (dc in next ch, ch 1, skip next ch) around, join with sl st in third ch of ch-4. *(48 dc made)*

Rnd 2: Ch 9, skip next 2 dc, (sc in next dc, ch 9, skip next 2 dc) around, join with sl st in first ch of first ch-9. *(16 ch sps)*

Rnd 3: Sl st in next 3 chs of first ch sp, ch 3, 4 dc in same ch sp as ch-3, ch 5, (5 dc in next ch sp, ch 5) around, join with sl st in top of ch-3.

Rnd 4: Ch 1, sc in first st, sc in next 2 dc; for **triple-picot, (ch 3, sl st in third ch from hook) 3 times;** sc in same dc as last sc made, sc in next 2 dc, ch 3, dc in third ch of next ch-5 sp, ch 3, *sc in next 2 dc, (sc, triple-picot, sc) in next dc, sc in next 2 dc, ch 3, dc in third ch of next ch-5 sp; repeat from * around, join with sl st in first sc.

Rnd 5: Ch 12, skip next 4 sc, sc in next sc, ch 3, dc in next dc, ch 3, (sc in next sc, ch 12, skip next 4 sc, sc in next sc, ch 3, dc in next dc, ch 3) around, join with sl st in first ch of ch-12. *(16 ch-12 ch sps, 16 dc)*

Rnd 6: (Sl st, ch 1, sc, ch 3, 12 dc) in first ch-12 sp, sc in next dc, (13 dc in next ch-12 sp, sc in next dc) around, join with sl st in top of ch-3.

Rnd 7: Ch 1, sc in first st, ch 7, skip next 5 dc, dc in next dc, ch 7, skip next 5 dc, sc in next dc, sc in next sc, (sc in next dc, ch 7, skip next 5 dc, dc in next dc, ch 7, skip next 5 dc, sc in next dc, sc in next sc) around, join with sl st in first sc.

Rnd 8: Ch 1, sc in first sc, 7 sc in next ch sp; for **V st, (dc, ch 2, dc)** in next dc; 7 sc in next ch sp, (sc in next 3 sc, 7 sc in next ch sp, V st in next dc, 7 sc in next ch sp) 15 times, sc in last 2 sc, join. Fasten off.

Note: *For* **sc back post (sc bp**—*see Stitch Guide), insert hook from right to left around post of st, complete as sc.*

Rnd 9: Working behind rnd 8, join green with **sc bp** *(see Note)* around first dc on rnd 7, ch 5, (sc bp around next dc on rnd 7, ch 5) around, join with sl st in first sc.

Rnd 10: (Ch 5, dc) in first st *(V st made),* ch 3, (V st in next dc, ch 3) around, join with sl st in third ch of ch-5. *(16 V sts, 16 ch-3 sps)*

Rnd 11: (Sl st, ch 3, dc, ch 2, 2 dc) in ch sp of first V st, ch 1, dc in next ch-3 sp, ch 1; *for **shell, (2 dc, ch 2, 2 dc)** in ch sp of next V st, ch 1, dc in next ch-3 sp, ch 1; repeat from * around, join with sl st in top of ch-3.

Rnd 12: Ch 3, dc in next dc, shell in first ch-2 sp, dc in next 2 dc, sc in next ch-1 sp, sc in next dc, sc in next ch-1 sp, (sl st in next dc, ch 3, dc in next dc, shell in next ch-2 sp, dc in next 2 dc, sc in next ch-1 sp, sc in next dc, sc in next ch-1 sp) around, join with sl st in joining sl st.

Rnd 13: Sl st across to first ch-2 sp, ch 1, sc in first ch-2 sp, ch 5, (sc in next ch-2 sp, ch 5) around, join with sl st in first sc.

Rnd 14: Ch 1, sc in first sc, (7 sc, triple-picot, 7 sc) in each ch-5 sp around with sc in each sc, join.

Rnd 15: Ch 1, sc in first sc, ch 11, skip next 14 sc, (sc in next sc, ch 11, skip next 14 sc) around, join.

Rnd 16: Ch 1, (sc, triple-picot, sc) in first sc, (7 sc, triple-picot, 7 sc) in next ch-11 sp, *(sc, triple-picot, sc) in next sc, (7 sc, triple-picot, 7 sc) in next ch-11 sp; repeat from * around, join. Fasten off.

For **Flowers,** with rose, working in front of rnd 7, join with sl st in first Vst, *ch 3; for **cluster, yo, insert hook in third ch from hook, yo, pull through ch, yo, pull through 2 lps on hook, yo, insert hook in same ch, yo, pull through ch, yo, pull through 2 lps on hook, yo, pull through all lps on hook;** ch 2, sl st in same ch as last st made, (ch 3, cluster, ch 2, sl st in same ch as last st made) 4 times, join with sl st in first ch of first ch-3, sl st in ch sp of first V st on rnd 8, fasten off; repeat from * in ch sp of each V st around.

Weave ribbon through sts on rnd 1. Attach Lamp Shade Cover over lamp shade with fabric glue. Let dry completely. Tie ribbon in bow.

Picture Mat

by Rose Beckett

Finished Size: 6" × 8".

Materials:
- ❏ 120 yds. size 50 crochet cotton thread
- ❏ Fabric stiffener
- ❏ No. 13 steel hook or hook needed to obtain gauge

Gauge: 33 dc = 2"; 8 dc rows = 1".

Basic Stitches: Ch, sl st, sc, dc.

Special Stitches: For **mesh,** ch 1, skip next st or ch, dc in next st.

For **beginning block (beg block),** ch 3, dc in next 2 sts.

For **block,** dc in next ch, dc in next st, **or,** dc in next 2 sts.

For **decrease (dec),** sl st in first 3 sts, **or,** leave last 2 sts unworked.

Work in **back lps** *(see Stitch Guide)* unless otherwise stated.

Mat Side (make 2)

Row 1: Ch 101, dc in fourth ch from hook, dc in each ch across, turn. *(99 dc made)*

Row 2: Beg block *(see Special Stitches),* mesh 21 times, block 5 times, mesh 21 times, block, turn.

Rows 3–10: Work according to graph across, turn.

Row 11: For **first side,** beg block, mesh 2 times, block 3 times, mesh, block, mesh 2 times, block, mesh 7 times, block 4 times leaving remaining sts unworked, turn.

Row 12: Sl st in first 5 sts, beg block, block 2 times, mesh 5 times, block, mesh 3 times, block 2 times, mesh, block 2 times, mesh 2 times, block, turn.

Rows 13–32: Work according to graph across, turn. At end of last row, fasten off.

Row 11: For **second side,** skip next 9 unworked sts on row 10, join with sl st in next st, beg block, block 3 times, mesh 7 times, block, mesh 2 times, block, mesh, block 3 times, mesh 2 times, block, turn.

Row 12: Beg block, mesh 2 times, block 2 times, mesh, block 2 times, mesh 3 times, block, mesh 5 times, block 3 times leaving last 4 sts unworked, turn.

Row 13: Sl st in first 5 sts, beg block, block, mesh 3 times, block, mesh 4 times, block 3 times, mesh, block, mesh 2 times, block, turn.

Rows 14–32: Work according to graph across, turn. At end of last row, fasten off.

Sew last rows on each side of Mat Side together.

Apply fabric stiffener. Shape. Let dry. ☞

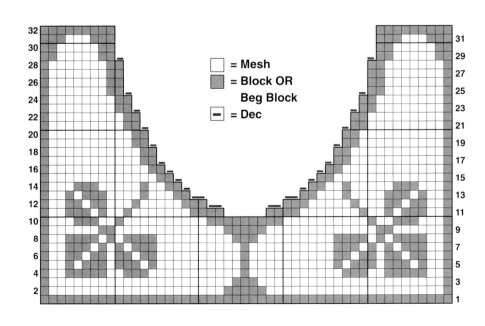

= Mesh
= Block OR Beg Block
─ = Dec

Vanity Set

by Isabelle Wolters

Puffed Hearts

Finished Size: 20" long.

Materials:
- ❑ Size 10 crochet cotton thread:
    - 200 yds. red
    - 150 yds. white
- ❑ Polyester fiberfill
- ❑ Satin ribbon:
    - ½ yd. of ⅝"-wide red picot-edge
    - 1¼ yds. of 2¼"-wide red
    - ¼ yd. of ⅛"-wide green
- ❑ 39 white 4mm pearl beads
- ❑ 2 yds. white 4mm strung beads
- ❑ 3 small red ribbon roses
- ❑ Bobby pins *(use for markers)*
- ❑ Sewing needle
- ❑ White, green and red sewing thread
- ❑ Craft glue
- ❑ ½" plastic ring
- ❑ No. 5 steel hook or hook needed to obtain gauge

Gauge: 7 sc = 1"; 7 sc **back lp** rows = 1".

Basic Stitches: Ch, sl st, sc, hdc.

Notes: Work in **back lps** *(see Stitch Guide)* throughout unless otherwise stated.
On each row, mark center st of each 3-sc group for bottom point of Heart; move marker up as you work.

Large Heart Side (make 2)
Row 1: With red, ch 2, 3 sc in second ch from hook, turn. *(3 sc made)*
Row 2: Ch 1, sc in first sc, 3 sc in **both lps** of next sc, sc in last sc, turn. *(5)*
Row 3: Ch 1, sc in first 2 sc, 3 sc in **both lps** of marked sc, sc in last 2 sc, turn. *(7)*
Rows 4–13: Ch 1, sc in each sc across to marked sc, 3 sc in **both lps** of marked sc, sc in each sc across to end of row, turn. At end of last row, **do not turn. Do not fasten off.** *(27)*

Lobes
Row 1: Working in ends of rows, ch 1; starting with same row, work 12 sc evenly spaced across first side, 1 sc in corner ch at base of row 1, 12 sc evenly spaced across second side to next corner, turn. *(25)*
Row 2: Ch 1, sc in first 4 sc, hdc in next sc, 2 hdc in each of next 3 sc, hdc in next sc, sc in next 2 sc, sl st in next 3 sc *(for break between Lobes of Heart)*, sc in next 2 sc, hdc in next sc, 2 hdc in each of next 3 sc, hdc in next sc, sc in last 4 sc, turn. *(31 sts and sl sts)*

Row 3: Ch 1, sc in first 4 sc, hdc in next 8 hdc, sc in next 2 sc, sl st in next 3 sl sts, sc in next 2 sc, hdc in next 8 hdc, sc in last 4 sc, turn.
Row 4: Ch 1, sc in first 4 sc, hdc in next 2 hdc, 2 hdc in each of next 4 hdc, hdc in next 2 hdc, sc in next 2 sc, sl st in next 3 sl sts, sc in next 2 sc, hdc in next 2 hdc, 2 hdc in each of next 4 hdc, hdc in next 2 hdc, sc in last 4 sc, turn. *(39)*
Rnd 5: For edging, ch 1, sc in first 18 sts, sl st in next 3 sl sts, sc in next 18 sts; working toward bottom point of Heart, sc in end of next 4 rows, sc in next 13 sts, 3 sc in **both lps** of marked st at bottom point of Heart, sc in next 13 sts, sc in end of next 4 rows, join with sl st in first sc. Fasten off. *(76 sts)*
Joining Rnd: Holding Heart Sides together with front of rnd 5 out, matching edges and working through both thicknesses in **both lps** of corresponding sts, join red with sc in first sl st between Lobes of Heart, sc in next 2 sl sts, work sc in each st to bottom point of Heart, work 3 sc in center st at bottom of Heart, work sc in each st around, stuffing before closing, join. Fasten off.

Ruffle
Rnd 1: Working in **back lps** of sts for this rnd, join white with sc in first sc of last rnd, sc in next 2 sc, ch 5, (sc in next st, ch 5) around, join with sl st in **both lps** of first sc.
Rnd 2: Working in **both lps** of sts for this rnd, ch 1, sc in same st as joining and in next 2 sc, (ch 3, sc in next ch-5 lp) around, ch 5, join with a sl st in first sc. Leaving a 6" end for sewing, fasten off.

Medium Heart Side (make 2)
Follow directions for rows 1–4 of Large Heart, then repeat row 4 until 9 rows have been completed. At end of row 9, **do not turn or fasten off.** *(19 sc)*

Lobes
Row 1: Follow directions for row 1 for Lobes of Large Heart, working 8 sc evenly along first side, 1 sc in corner, 8 sc along second side, turn. *(17 sc)*
Row 2: Ch 1, sc in first 2 sc, hdc in next sc, 2 hdc in each of next 3 sc, sc in next sc, sl st in next 3 sc *(for break between Lobes of Heart)*, sc in next sc, 2 hdc in each of next 3 sc, hdc in next sc, sc in last 2 sc, turn. *(23 sts)*
Row 3: Ch 1, sc in first 2 sc, hdc in next 7 hdc, sc in next sc, sl st in next 3 sl sts, sc in next sc, hdc in next 7 hdc, sc in last 2 sc, turn.

continued on page 72

continued from page 71

Row 4: Ch 1, sc in first 2 sc, hdc in next hdc, 2 hdc in each of next 4 hdc, hdc in next 2 hdc, sc in next sc, sl st in next 3 sl sts, sc in next sc, hdc in next 2 hdc, 2 hdc in each of next 4 hdc, hdc in next hdc, sc in last 2 sc, turn. *(31)*

Rnd 5: For **edging**, ch 1, sc in first 14 sts, sl st in next 3 sl sts, sc in next 14 sts; working toward bottom point of Heart, sc in ends of next 4 rows, sc in next 9 sts, 3 sc in **both lps** of marked st at bottom point of Heart, sc in next 9 sts, sc in end of next 4 rows, join with sl st in first sc. Fasten off. *(60)*

Follow directions for joining, stuffing and working Ruffle as for Large Heart.

Small Heart Side (make 2)

Follow directions for rows 1–4 of Large Heart, then repeat row 4 until 7 rows have been completed. At end of row 7, **do not turn or fasten off.** *(15 sc)*

Lobes

Row 1: Follow directions for row 1 of Lobes on Large Heart, working 6 sc evenly along first side, 1 sc in corner, and 6 sc along second side, turn. *(13 sc)*

Row 2: Ch 1, sc in first sc, hdc in next sc, 2 hdc in each of next 2 sc, sc in next sc, sl st in next 3 sc *(for break between Lobes of Heart),* sc in next sc, 2 hdc in each of next 2 sc, hdc in next sc, sc in last sc, turn. *(17 sts)*

Row 3: Ch 1, sc in first sc, hdc in next 5 hdc, sc in next sc, sl st in next 3 sl sts, sc in next sc, hdc in next 5 hdc, sc in last sc, turn.

Row 4: Ch 1, sc in first sc, hdc in next 2 hdc, 2 hdc in each of next 2 hdc, hdc in next hdc, sc in next sc, sl st in next 3 sl sts, sc in next sc, hdc in next hdc, 2 hdc in each of next 2 hdc, hdc in next 2 hdc, sc in last sc, turn. *(21)*

Rnd 5: For **edging**, ch 1, sc in first 9 sts, sl st in next 3 sl sts, sc in next 9 sts; working toward bottom point of Heart, sc in ends of next 4 rows, sc in next 7 sts, 3 sc in **both lps** of marked st at bottom point of Heart, sc in next 7 sts, sc in end of next 4 rows, join with sl st in first sc. Fasten off. *(46)*

Follow directions for joining, stuffing and working Ruffle as for Large Heart.

Finishing

1: On each Heart, fold Ruffle down between Lobes and tack in place with thread left at end of work.

2: Cut green ribbon into three equal lengths. For each Heart, make a ¾" bow by crossing ends at center and tacking together with green thread. Tack or glue bow between Lobes of Heart.

3: Glue a ribbon rose at center of each bow.

4: For each Heart, string 13 pearl beads onto length of white thread and knot thread ends together to form loop. Stitch loop below rose on Heart.

5: Turn under raw edge of picot ribbon and sew between Lobes at back of Large Heart.

6: Place Medium Heart on picot ribbon 2" above Large Heart and sew ribbon along back of Heart. Attach Small Heart above Medium Heart in same way.

7: For bow, with wide red ribbon, make a 7"-wide bow *(2 loops on each side)* and tie at center with strand of red crochet thread. Cut ribbon ends in a V. Tack or glue bow to top of picot ribbon.

8: For hanger, stitch plastic ring to back of picot ribbon.

9: With strung pearls, make two 6" loops at center of strand, tie loops together for bow; leaving ends loose, tie the loops twice more. Tack or glue knots to center of red bow.

10: Tack loose pearl strands behind Small Heart on each side of ribbon, then holding strands together, tie knot at front of ribbon between Small and Medium Hearts. Tack strands behind Medium Heart, then knot at front between Medium and Large Hearts. Tack ends behind Large Heart and trim away any excess pearls. ⚷

Vanity Box

Finished Size: 6½" diameter × 4" high without Handle.

Materials:

- ❏ 400 yds. size 20 crochet cotton thread
- ❏ Pencil
- ❏ Fabric stiffener
- ❏ No. 10 steel hook or hook needed to obtain gauge

Gauge: Rnds 1–5 = 2" across.

Basic Stitches: Ch, sl st, sc, dc, tr.

Top

To form center ring, wind thread around end of pencil 8 times; slip ring from pencil.

Rnd 1: Ch 1, 16 sc in ring, join with sl st in first sc. *(16 sc made)*

Rnd 2: Ch 1, 2 sc in each st around, join. *(32)*

Rnd 3: Ch 3, dc in next st, (ch 3, skip next st, dc in next 3 sts) around to last st, dc in last st, ch 3, join with sl st in top of ch-3.

Rnd 4: Ch 3, dc in next st, dc in next ch, ch 3, skip next ch, dc in next ch (dc in next 3 sts, dc in next ch, ch 3, skip next ch, dc in next ch) around to last st, dc in last st, join.

Rnd 5: Ch 3, dc in next 2 sts, dc in next ch, ch 3, skip next ch, dc in next ch (dc in next 5 sts, dc in next ch, ch 3, skip next ch, dc in next ch) around to last 2 sts, dc in last 2 sts, join.

Rnd 6: Ch 3, dc in next 3 sts, dc in next ch, ch 3, skip next ch, dc in next ch (dc in next 7 sts, dc in next ch, ch 3, skip next ch, dc in next ch) around to last 3 sts, dc in last 3 sts, join.

Rnd 7: Ch 3, dc in next 3 sts, skip next st, ch 3, dc in next ch sp, ch 3, skip next st, (dc in next 7 sts, skip next st, ch 3, dc in next ch sp, ch 3, skip next st) around to last 3 sts, dc in last 3 sts, join.

Rnd 8: Ch 3, dc in next 2 sts, skip next st, ch 3, (dc in next ch sp, ch 3) 2 times, skip next st, *dc in next 5 sts, ch 3, skip next st, (dc in next ch sp, ch 3) 2 times, skip next st; repeat from * around to last 2 sts, dc in last 2 sts, join.

Rnd 9: Ch 3, dc in next st, skip next st, ch 3, (dc in next ch sp, ch 3) 3 times, skip next st, *dc in next 3 sts, ch 3, skip next st, (dc in next ch sp, ch 3) 3 times, skip next st; repeat from * around to last st, dc in last st, join.

Rnd 10: (Sl st, ch 5) in next st, *(dc in next ch sp, ch 2) 4 times, dc in next st, ch 2, skip next st, dc in next st; repeat from * 6 more times, (dc in next ch sp, ch 2) 4 times, dc in next st, ch 2, join with sl st in third ch of beginning ch-5. *(48 ch sps)*

Rnd 11: (Sl st, ch 5) in first ch sp, dc in next ch sp, ch 2, 4 dc in next ch sp, ch 2, *(dc in next ch sp, ch 2) 5 times, 4 dc in next ch sp, ch 2; repeat from * 5 more times, (dc in next ch sp, ch 2) 3 times, join with sl st in third ch of beginning ch-5.

Rnd 12: (Sl st, ch 5) in first ch sp, ch 2, 4 dc in next ch sp, ch 2, skip next 4 sts, 4 dc in next ch sp, ch 2, *(dc in next ch sp, ch 2) 4 times, 4 dc in next ch sp, ch 2, skip next 4 sts, 4 dc in next ch sp, ch 2; repeat from * 5 more times, (dc in next ch sp, ch 2) 3 times, join.

Rnd 13: (Sl st, ch 5) in first ch sp, dc in next st, ch 2, skip next 3 sts, 4 dc in next ch sp, ch 2, skip next 3 sts, dc in next st, ch 2, *(dc in next ch sp, ch 2) 5 times, dc in next st, ch 2, skip next 3 sts, 4 dc in next ch sp, ch 2, skip next 3 sts, dc in next st, ch 2; repeat from * 5 more times, (dc in next ch sp, ch 2) 4 times, join.

Rnd 14: (Sl st, ch 5) in first ch sp, dc in next ch sp, ch 2, dc in next st, ch 2, skip next 2 sts, dc in next st, ch 2, *(dc in next ch sp, ch 2) 8 times, dc in next st, ch 2, skip next 2 sts, dc in next st, ch 2; repeat from * 5 more times, (dc in next ch sp, ch 2) 6 times, join. *(80 ch sps)*

Rnd 15: (Sl st, ch 4) in first ch sp, (dc in next ch sp, ch 1) around, join with sl st in third ch of ch-4.

Rnd 16: (Sl st, ch 5) in first ch sp, 2 dc in next ch sp, ch 3, skip next 2 ch sps, (2 dc in next ch sp, ch 2, 2 dc in next ch sp, ch 3, skip next 2 ch sps) around, dc in same ch sp as sl st, join with sl st in third ch of beginning ch-5.

Rnd 17: (Sl st, ch 5, 2 dc) in first ch-2 sp, sc in next ch-3 sp, *(2 dc, ch 2, 2 dc) in next ch-2 sp, sc in next ch-3 sp; repeat from * around, dc in same ch sp as sl st, join with sl st in third ch of ch-5.

Rnd 18: (Sl st, ch 3, 4 dc) in first ch sp, ch 2, sc in next sc, ch 2, (9 dc in next ch-2 sp, ch 2, sc in next sc, ch 2) around, 4 dc in same ch sp as sl st, join with sl st in top of ch-3. Fasten off.

Bottom

Rnds 1–18: Repeat rnds 1–18 of Top. **Do not fasten off.**

Rnd 19: Ch 1, sc in first st, ch 7, (sc in center st of next 9-dc group, ch 7) around, join with sl st in first sc. *(20 ch sps)*

Rnd 20: (Sl st, ch 3, 8 dc) in first ch sp, 9 dc in each ch sp around, join with sl st in top of ch-3. *(180 dc)*

Rnd 21: Ch 6, skip next 3 sts, (tr in next st, ch 3, skip next 3 sts) around, join with sl st in third ch of beginning ch-6. *(45 ch sps)*

Rnd 22: Sc in first ch sp, (ch 5, sc in next ch sp) around, ch 2, join with dc in first sc *(joining ch sp made).*

Rnds 23–25: Ch 1, sc in joining ch sp, (ch 5, sc in next ch sp) around, ch 2, join with dc in first sc.

Rnd 26: Ch 1, sc in joining ch sp, ch 3, (sc in next ch sp, ch 3) around, join with sl st in first sc.

Rnd 27: (Sl st, ch 3, 2 dc) in first ch sp, ch 5, skip next ch sp, 2 sc in next ch sp, sc in next st, 2 sc in next ch sp, ch 5, skip next ch sp, (3 dc in next ch sp, ch 5, skip next ch sp, 2 sc in next ch sp, sc in next st, 2 sc in next ch sp, ch 5, skip next ch sp) around, join with sl st in top of ch-3.

Rnd 28: Ch 5, skip next st, 3 dc in next st, ch 4, sc in center 3 sts of next 5-sc group, ch 4, (3 dc in first st of next 3-dc group, ch 2, skip next st, 3 dc in next st, ch 4, sc in center 3 sts of next 5-sc group, ch 4) around, 2 dc in same st as beginning ch-5, join with sl st in third ch of ch-5.

Rnd 29: Ch 4, dc in first ch-2 sp, (ch 1, dc in next st) 3 times, ch 4, sc in center st of next 3-sc group, ch 4, *dc in first st of next 3-dc group, (ch 1, dc in next st) 2 times, ch 1, dc in next ch-2 sp, (ch 1, dc in next st) 3 times, ch 4, sc in center st of next 3-sc group, ch 4; repeat from * around to last 2 sts, (dc in next st, ch 1) 2 times, join with sl st in third ch of beginning ch-4.

Rnd 30: Sc in first ch sp, ch 3, (sc, ch 3) in each ch-1 sp and in each sc around, join with sl st in first sc. Fasten off.

For **Handle,** wrap thread around tip of forefinger 20 times and slip from finger; cover this ring closely with sc, join with sl st in first sc. Fasten off. Sew Handle to center of Top as shown in photo.

Stiffen and shape over glass jar or anything of the desired shape.

Decorate as desire. ⌘

Rose Trellis Bedspread

by Dot Drake

Finished Size: 77" × 93½".

Materials:
- ❏ 6,975 yds. size 10 crochet cotton thread
- ❏ No. 8 steel hook or hook needed to obtain gauge

Gauge: 10 dc = 1"; 4 dc rows = 1".

Basic Stitches: Ch, sl st, sc, dc.

Special Stitches: For **beginning block (beg block),** ch 3, dc in next 3 sts.

For **block,** dc in next 3 sts, **or,** 2 dc in next ch sp, dc in next st.

For **mesh,** ch 2, skip next 2 chs or sts, dc in next st.

For **beginning cluster (beg cl),** ch 3, (yo, insert hook in same st as ch-3, yo, pull through st, yo, pull through 2 lps on hook) 2 times, yo, pull through all 3 lps on hook.

For **cluster (cl),** yo, insert hook in next st, yo, pull through st, yo, pull through 2 lps on hook, (yo, insert hook in same st, yo, pull through st, yo, pull through 2 lps on hook) 2 times, yo, pull through all 4 lps on hook.

First Row

First Motif

Row 1: Ch 102, dc in fourth ch from hook, dc in each ch across, turn. *(100 dc made)*

Row 2: Beg block *(see Special Stitches),* (mesh, block) across, turn.

Rows 3–37: Work according to graph on page 81 across, turn.

Rnd 38: Working in rnds, **beg cl** *(see Special Stitches)* in first st, ch 5, **cl** in same st as last cl, mesh 32 times, ch 2, skip next 2 sts, (cl, ch 5, cl) in last st, ch 2, skip row 37, dc in top of next row, (ch 2, dc in top of next row) 35 times; working in remaining lps on opposite side of starting ch on row 1, (cl, ch 5, cl) in first ch, (ch 2, skip next 2 chs, dc in next ch) 32 times, ch 2, skip next 2 chs, (cl, ch 5, cl) in last ch, ch 2, skip row 1, dc in bottom of next row, (ch 2, dc in bottom of next row) 35 times, ch 2, join with sl st in first cl, **turn.**

Rnd 39: Ch 1, sc in each cl, 2 sc in each ch-2 sp, sc in each dc and 5 sc in each ch-5 sp around, join with sl st in first sc. Fasten off.

Second Motif

Rows 1–37: Work rows 1–37 of First Motif.

Rnd 38: Work rnd 38 of First Motif. Fasten off.

Rnd 39: Hold last Motif and this Motif together according to joining illustration, join with sc in first cl on corner, 5 sc in next ch-5 sp, sc in next cl, sc in st above corresponding cl on last Motif, (2 sc in next ch-2 sp on this Motif, sc in next st on this Motif, skip next 2 sts on last Motif, sc in next st on last Motif) 36 times, 2 sc in next ch-2 sp on this Motif, sc in next cl, sc in st above next cl on last Motif; working on remainder of Motif, 5 sc in each ch-5 sp, sc in each cl, 2 sc in each ch-2 sp and sc in each dc around, join with sl st in first sc. Fasten off.

Repeat Second Motif 4 more times according to illustration for width.

First Motif	Second Motif				
First Row Rose	Rose	Rose	Rose	Rose	Rose
Second Row Rose	Rose	Rose	Rose	Rose	Rose
First Motif	**Second Motif**				

Second Row

First Motif

Joining to Motif on row above, work same as First Row Second Motif.

Second Motif

Rows 1–37: Work rows 1–37 of First Row First Motif.

Rnd 38: Work rnd 38 of First Row First Motif. Fasten off.

Rnd 39: Holding Motifs according to joining illustration, join with sc in first cl on corner, 5 sc in next ch-5 sp, sc in next cl, sc in st above corresponding cl of Motif on row above, (2 sc in next ch-2 sp on this Motif, sc in next st on this Motif, skip next 2 sts of Motif on row above, sc in next st of Motif on row above) 32 times, 2 sc in next ch-2 sp on this Motif, sc in next cl, sc in st above next cl of Motif on row above, 5 sc in next ch-5 sp, sc in next cl, sc in st above corresponding cl on last Motif, (2 sc in next ch-2 sp on this Motif, sc in next st on this Motif, skip next 2 sts on last Motif, sc in next st on last Motif) 36 times, 2 sc in next ch-2 sp on this Motif, sc in next cl, sc in st above next cl on last Motif; working on remainder of Motif, 5 sc in each ch-5 sp, sc in each cl, 2 sc in each ch-2 sp and sc in each dc around, join with sl st in first sc. Fasten off.

Repeat Second Motif 4 more times according to joining illustration.

continued on page 81

Boudoir Pillows

by Ann Kirtley

Hydrangea Pillow

Finished Size: 18" square without Fringe.

Materials:
- ❑ 10 oz. lt. blue worsted yarn
- ❑ ½ yd. matching satin fabric
- ❑ 3 yds. blue ⅜" ribbon
- ❑ 85 pearl 6mm beads
- ❑ Four 6 × 13mm pearl drop beads
- ❑ 14" square pillow form
- ❑ 4 bobby pins for markers
- ❑ Blue and white sewing thread and needle
- ❑ Tapestry needle
- ❑ G hook or hook needed to obtain gauge

Gauge: Rnds 1–3 = 3" across.

Basic Stitches: Ch, sl st, sc, dc, tr.

Pillow Form Cover
Cut two pieces each 15" square from satin. With right sides together, allowing ½" seams, sew three sides together. Clip corners and turn right side out. Insert pillow form. Sew last side closed.

Pillow Side (make 2)
Rnd 1: Ch 4, sl st in first ch to form ring, ch 4, (dc, ch 1) 7 times in ring, join with sl st in third ch of ch-4. *(8 ch sps made) Front of rnd 1 is right side of work.*

Rnd 2: (Sl st, ch 3, 2 dc, ch 1) in first ch sp, 3 dc in next ch sp, ch 2, (3 dc in next ch sp, ch 1, 3 dc in next ch sp, ch 2) around ending last repeat with ch 1, join with dc in top of ch-3.

Rnd 3: (Ch 5, 3 dc) in first ch-1 sp, ch 1, sc in next ch-1 sp, ch 1; *for **large shell (lg shell)**, **(3 dc, ch 2, 3 dc)** in next ch-2 sp; ch 1, sc in next ch-1 sp, ch 1; repeat from * 3 more times, 2 dc in same sp as first dc, join with sl st in third ch of ch-5. *(4 shells)*

Rnd 4: (Sl st, ch 5, 3 dc, ch 3) in next ch-2 sp, (dc, ch 3, dc) in next sc, ch 3, *shell in ch sp of next shell, ch 3, (dc, ch 3, dc) in next sc, ch 3; repeat from * 2 more times, 2 dc in same sp as first dc, join.

Rnd 5: (Sl st, ch 5, 3 dc, ch 3) in next ch-2 sp, skip next ch-3 sp, 10 dc in next ch-3 sp, ch 3, (skip next ch-3 sp, shell in ch sp of next shell, ch 3, skip next ch-3 sp, 10 dc in next ch-3 sp, ch 3) 3 times, 2 dc in same sp as first dc, join.

Rnd 6: (Sl st, ch 6, 3 dc, ch 3) in next ch-2 sp, skip next ch-3 sp, dc in next dc, (ch 1, dc in next dc) 9 times, ch 3, *skip next ch-3 sp, (3 dc, ch 3, 3 dc) in ch sp of next shell, ch 3, skip

next ch-3 sp, dc in next dc, (ch 1, dc in next dc) 9 times, ch 3; repeat from * 2 more times, 2 dc in same sp as first dc, join with sl st in third ch of ch-6.

Rnd 7: (Sl st, ch 3, 9 dc, ch 3) in next ch-3 sp, skip next ch-3 sp, sc in next dc, (ch 3, sc in next dc) 9 times, skip next ch-3 sp, skip next 3 dc, *ch 3, 10 dc in next ch-3 sp, ch 3, skip next ch-3 sp, sc in next dc, (ch 3, sc in next dc) 9 times, skip next ch-3 sp, skip next 3 dc; repeat from * 2 more times, ch 3, join with sl st in top of ch-3.

Rnd 8: Ch 4, dc in next dc, (ch 1, dc in next dc) 8 times, skip next ch-3 sp, sc in next ch-3 sp, (ch 3, sc in next ch-3 sp) 8 times, *dc in next dc, (ch 1, dc in next dc) 9 times, skip next ch-3 sp, sc in next ch-3 sp, (ch 3, sc in next ch-3 sp) 8 times; repeat from * 2 more times, join.

Rnd 9: Ch 1, sc in first st, (ch 3, sc in next dc) 8 times; for **small shell (sm shell)**, **(2 dc, ch 2, 2 dc)** in sp between last st and next sc; sc in next ch-3 sp, (ch 3, sc in next ch-3 sp) 7 times, sm shell in sp between next sc and next dc, *sc in next dc, (ch 3, sc in next dc) 9 times, sm shell in sp between last st and next sc, sc in next ch-3 sp, (ch 3, sc in next ch-3 sp) 7 times, sm shell in sp between next sc and next dc; repeat from * 2 more times, join with sl st in first sc.

Rnd 10: (Sl st, ch 1, sc) in next ch-3 sp, (ch 3, sc in next ch-3 sp) 8 times, sm shell in ch sp of next shell, sc in next ch-3 sp, (ch 3, sc in next ch-3 sp) 6 times, sm shell in ch sp of next shell, *sc in next ch-3 sp, (ch 3, sc in next ch-3 sp) 8 times, sm shell in ch sp of next shell, sc in next ch-3 sp, (ch 3, sc in next ch-3 sp) 6 times, sm shell in ch sp of next shell; repeat from * 2 more times, join.

Rnd 11: (Sl st, ch 1, sc) in next ch-3 sp, (ch 3, sc in next ch-3 sp) 7 times, sm shell in ch sp of next shell, sc in next ch-3 sp, (ch 3, sc in next ch-3 sp) 5 times, sm shell in ch sp of next shell, *sc in next ch-3 sp, (ch 3, sc in next ch-3 sp) 7 times, sm shell in ch sp of next shell, sc in next ch-3 sp, (ch 3, sc in next ch-3 sp) 5 times, sm shell in ch sp of next shell; repeat from * 2 more times, join.

Rnd 12: (Sl st, ch 1, sc) in next ch-3 sp, (ch 3, sc in next ch-3 sp) 6 times, sm shell in ch sp of next shell, sc in next ch-3 sp, (ch 3, sc in next ch-3 sp) 4 times, sm shell in ch sp of next shell, *sc in next ch-3 sp, (ch 3, sc in next ch-3 sp) 6 times, sm shell in ch sp of next shell, sc in next ch-3 sp, (ch 3, sc in next ch-3 sp) 4 times, sm shell in ch sp of next shell; repeat from * 2 more times, join.

Rnd 13: (Sl st, ch 1, sc) in next ch-3 sp, (ch 3, sc in next ch-3 sp) 5 times, sm shell in ch sp of next shell, sc in next ch-3 sp, (ch 3, sc in next ch-3 sp) 3 times, sm shell in ch sp of next shell, *sc in next ch-3 sp, (ch 3, sc in next ch-3 sp) 5 times, sm shell in ch sp of next shell, sc in next ch-3 sp, (ch 3, sc in next ch-3 sp) 3 times, sm shell in ch sp of next shell; repeat from * 2 more times, join.

Rnd 14: (Sl st, ch 1, sc) in next ch-3 sp, (ch 3, sc in next ch-3 sp) 4 times, dc in sp between next sc and next dc, ch 2, sm shell in ch sp of next shell, ch 2, dc in sp between last shell worked into and next sc, sc in next ch-3 sp, (ch 3, sc in next ch-3 sp) 2 times, dc in sp between next sc and next dc, ch 2, sm shell in ch sp of next shell, ch 2, dc in sp between last shell worked into and next sc, *sc in next ch-3 sp, (ch 3, sc in next ch-3 sp) 4 times, dc in

continued on page 78

sp between next sc and next dc, ch 2, sm shell in ch sp of next shell, ch 2, dc in sp between last shell worked into and next sc, sc in next ch-3 sp, (ch 3, sc in next ch-3 sp) 2 times, dc in sp between next sc and next dc, ch 2, sm shell in ch sp of next shell, ch 2, dc in sp between last shell worked and next sc; repeat from * 2 more times, join.

Rnd 15: (Sl st, ch 1, sc) in next ch-3 sp, (ch 3, sc in next ch-3 sp) 3 times, ch 2, (dc, ch 2) 2 times in next dc, sm shell in ch sp of next shell, ch 2, (dc, ch 2) 2 times in next dc, sc in next ch-3 sp, ch 3, sc in next ch-3 sp, ch 2, (dc, ch 2) 2 times in next dc, sm shell in ch sp of next shell, ch 2, (dc, ch 2) 2 times in next dc, *sc in next ch-3 sp, (ch 3, sc in next ch-3 sp) 3 times, ch 2, (dc, ch 2) 2 times in next dc, sm shell in ch sp of next shell, ch 2, (dc, ch 2) 2 times in next dc, sc in next ch-3 sp, ch 3, sc in next ch-3 sp, ch 2, (dc, ch 2) 2 times in next dc, sm shell in ch sp of next shell, ch 2, (dc, ch 2) 2 times in next dc; repeat from * 2 more times, join.

Rnd 16: (Sl st, ch 1, sc) in next ch-3 sp, (ch 3, sc in next ch-3 sp) 2 times, ch 3, skip next ch-2 sp, sm shell in next ch-2 sp, ch 2, sm shell in ch sp of next shell, ch 2, skip next ch-2 sp, sm shell in next ch-2 sp, ch 3, skip next ch-2 sp, dc in next ch-3 sp *(mark last st for corner),* ch 3, skip next ch-2 sp, sm shell in next ch-2 sp, ch 2, sm shell in ch sp of next shell, ch 2, skip next ch-2 sp, sm shell in next ch-2 sp, ch 3, *sc in next ch-3 sp, (ch 3, sc in next ch-3 sp) 2 times, ch 3, skip next ch-2 sp, sm shell in next ch-2 sp, ch 2, sm shell in ch sp of next shell, ch 2, skip next ch-2 sp, sm shell in next ch-2 sp, ch 3, skip next ch-2 sp, dc in next ch-3 sp *(mark last st for corner),* ch 3, skip next ch-2 sp, sm shell in next ch-2 sp, ch 2, sm shell in ch sp of next shell, ch 2, skip next ch-2 sp, sm shell in next ch-2 sp, ch 3; repeat from * 2 more times, join.

Rnd 17: (Sl st, ch 1, sc) in first ch-3 sp, ch 3, sc in next ch-3 sp, ch 3, (sm shell in ch sp of next shell, ch 3) 6 times, *skip next ch-3 sp, sc in next ch-3 sp, ch 3, sc in next ch-3 sp, ch 3, (sm shell in ch sp of next shell, ch 3) 6 times; repeat from * around, join.

Rnd 18: (Sl st, ch 6) in first ch-3 sp, (lg shell in ch sp of next shell, ch 3) 6 times, *skip next ch-3 sp, dc in next ch-3 sp, ch 3, (lg shell in ch sp of next shell, ch 3) 6 times; repeat from * around, join with sl st in third ch of ch-6.

Rnd 19: Ch 1, sc in first st, ch 7, sl st in top of sc just made, sc in next dc, 9 tr in ch sp of next shell, sc in next dc, sc in next ch-3 sp, *(5 tr; for **triple picot, ch 6, sl st in sixth ch from hook, ch 9, sl st in ninth ch from hook, ch 6, sl st in sixth ch from hook, sl st in top of last tr made;** 6 tr) in ch sp of next shell, skip next 2 dc, sc in next dc, sc in next ch-3 sp, sc in next dc, 9 tr in ch sp of next shell, skip next 2 dc, sc in next dc, sc in next ch-3

sp, ch 7, sl st in top of sc just made, sc in next dc, 9 tr in next ch sp, sc in next ch-3 sp; repeat from * around, join. Fasten off.

Assembly

With wrong sides together and Pillow Form between, matching each marked stitch of rnd 16 to corner of pillow form, using matching thread and sewing needle, sew last rnd of Pillow Sides together in **back lps** *(see Stitch Guide).*

Finishing

1: With white sewing thread and needle, on one Pillow Side, sew one bead to center of rnd 1. Sew one bead to top of each st on rnd 1. Sew one bead over each sc of rnd 3.

2: Cut ribbon into eight equal lengths, tie each piece in bow around each small shell on rnd 8 of Pillow.

3: Sew one bead below each bow. Sew one bead at top of each corner dc on rnd 16. Sew one bead to center of each tr group, center of each triple picot and at bottom of each ch-7 sp on last rnd.

4: With needle and thread, string four groups of five beads. Sew one group to each ch-7 sp of last rnd at corners. Sew one drop bead to each ch-7 sp on sides.

5: For **Fringe** *(see Stitch Guide),* cut 12 strands yarn each 11" long; with all strands held together, fold in half, insert hook through st, pull fold through st, pull ends through fold, tighten. Work Fringe in top of each triple picot on last rnd of Pillow. 🔑

Camellia Pillow

Finished Size: 20" square without Tassels.

Materials:
- ❏ 14 oz. off-white worsted yarn
- ❏ ½ yd. matching satin fabric
- ❏ 1½ yds. off-white ¼" ribbon
- ❏ 61 pearl 6mm beads
- ❏ 14" square pillow form
- ❏ Off-white sewing thread
- ❏ Sewing and tapestry needles
- ❏ G hook or hook needed to obtain gauge

Gauge: Rnds 1–3 = 2" across.

Basic Stitches: Ch, sl st, sc, hdc, dc, tr.

Special Stitch: For **triple treble (ttr),** yo 4 times, insert hook in st, yo, pull loop through, (yo, pull through 2 loops on hook) 5 times.

Pillow Form Cover

Cut two pieces each 15" square from satin. With right sides together, allowing ½" seams, sew three sides together. Clip corners and turn right side out. Insert pillow form. Sew last side closed.

Pillow

Front

Rnd 1: Ch 4, sl st in first ch to form ring, ch 1, 16 sc in ring, join with sl st in first sc. *(16 sc made)*

Rnd 2: Ch 1, sc in first st, ch 2, skip next st, (sc in next st, ch 2, skip next st) around, join. *(8 ch sps)*

Rnd 3: For **petals,** (sc, 3 dc, sc) in each ch sp around, join. *(8 petals)*

Rnd 4: Working behind petals, ch 1, **sc around post of first sc** *(see illustration),* ch 3, (sc around post of first sc on next petal, ch 3) around, join.

Post of sc

Rnd 5: For **petals,** (sc, 5 dc, sc) in each ch sp around, join.

Rnd 6: Working behind petals, ch 1, sc around post of first sc, ch 4, (sc around post of first sc on next petal, ch 4) around, join.

Rnd 7: For **petals,** (sc, 7 dc, sc) in each ch sp around, join.

Rnd 8: Working behind petals, ch 1, sc around post of first sc, ch 5, (sc around post of first sc on next petal, ch 5) around, join.

Rnd 9: For **petals,** (sc, 9 dc, sc) in each ch sp around, join.

Rnd 10: Working behind petals, ch 1, sc around post of first sc, ch 6, (sc around post of first sc on next petal, ch 6) around, join.

Rnd 11: For **petals,** (sc, 11 dc, sc) in each ch sp around, join.

Rnd 12: Working behind petals, ch 1, sc around post of first sc, ch 8, (sc around post of first sc on next petal, ch 8) around, join.

Rnd 13: For **petals,** (sc, 13 dc, sc) in each ch sp around, join.

Rnd 14: Working behind petals, ch 1, sc around post of first sc, ch 10, (sc around post of first sc on next petal, ch 10) around, join.

Rnd 15: For **petals,** (sc, 15 dc, sc) in each ch sp around, join.

Rnd 16: Working behind petals, ch 1, sc around post of first sc, ch 11, (sc around post of first sc on next petal, ch 11) around, join.

Rnd 17: For **petals,** (sc, 15 dc, sc) in each ch sp around, join.

Rnd 18: Working behind petals, ch 1, sc around post of first sc, ch 12, (sc around post of first sc on next petal, ch 12) around, join.

Rnd 19: For **petals,** (sc, 15 dc, sc) in each ch sp around, join.

Rnd 20: Working behind petals, ch 1, sc around post of first sc, ch 13, (sc around post of first sc on next petal, ch 13) around, join.

Rnd 21: For **petals,** (sc, 16 dc, sc) in each ch sp around, join.

Rnd 22: Working behind petals, ch 1, sc around post of first sc, ch 14, (sc around post of first sc on next petal, ch 14) around, join.

Rnd 23: For **petals,** (sc, 17 dc, sc) in each ch sp around, join.

Rnd 24: Working behind petals, ch 1, sc around post of first sc, ch 15, sc in second ch from hook, hdc in next 3 chs, dc in next 6 chs, hdc in next 3 chs, sc in last ch, sl st around post of same sc *(first half of leaf made),* ch 15, (sl st around post of first sc on next petal, ch 15, sc in second ch from hook, hdc in next 3 chs, dc in next 6 chs, hdc in next 3 chs, sc in last chs, sl st around post of same sc, ch 15) around, join.

Rnd 25: *Working on opposite side of ch-15, sc in first ch, hdc in next 3 chs, dc in next 6 chs, hdc in next 3 chs, sc in last ch *(second half of leaf made),* ch 2, sl st in second ch from hook *(tip of leaf),* sl st in **back lps** *(see Stitch Guide)* of next 14 sts on first half of leaf, sl st in next sl st, (sc, 15 dc, sc) in next ch-15 sp, sl st in next sl st; repeat from * around, join with sl st in joining sl st.

Rnd 26: Sl st in each st across to tip of leaf, (sl st, ch 1, sc) in tip, ch 9, (**ttr**—*see Special Stitch*—ch 3, ttr, ch 3, ttr, ch 3, ttr, ch 6, sl st in fifth ch from hook—*ch-5 sp made,* ch 1, ttr, ch 3, ttr, ch 3, ttr, ch 3, ttr) in center dc of next petal, ch 9, *sc in tip of next leaf, ch 9, (ttr, ch 3, ttr, ch 3, ttr, ch 3, ttr, ch 6, sl st in fifth ch from hook, ch 1, ttr, ch 3, ttr, ch 3, ttr, ch 3, ttr) in center dc of next petal, ch 9; repeat from * around, join with sl st in first sc.

Rnd 27: Ch 1, sc in first st, ch 15; for **scallop bottom,** (dc, ch 3, sl st in top of dc just made, dc) 3 times in next ch-5 sp; ch 15, *sc in next sc, ch 15, (dc, ch 3, sl st in top of dc just made, dc) 3 times in next ch-5 sp, ch 15; repeat from * around, join. Fasten off.

Back

Work same as Front. At end of last rnd, **do not fasten off.**

Edging

With wrong sides of Front and Back held together, working through both thicknesses around outer edge, ch 1, sc in first st, *(ch 5, sc) 5 times in same st *(will curve into circle forming flower foundation);* for **petals,** working into ch-5 sps of foundation just made, (sc, 5 dc, sc) in next ch-5 sp; (sc, 3 dc, 5 tr, 3 dc, sc) in next ch-15 sp; ch 3; for **scallop top,** (yo, insert hook in next ch-3 sp, yo, pull through sp, yo, pull through 2 lps on hook) 2 times, yo, pull through all 3 lps on hook, ch 3, [yo, insert hook in same ch-3 sp, yo, pull through sp, yo, pull through 2 lps on hook, yo, insert hook in next ch-3 sp, yo, pull through sp, yo, pull through 2 lps on hook, yo, pull through all 3 lps on hook, ch 3] 2 times *(center ch-3 sp is corner of Pillow);* (sc, 3 dc, 5 tr, 3 dc, sc) in next ch-15 sp, sc in next st; repeat from * 7 more times inserting Pillow Form before closing and *continued on page 80*

continued on page 80

continued from page 79

leaving off sc at end of last repeat, join with sl st in first sc. Fasten off.

Tack corners of pillow form to corners of crocheted piece.

Tassel (make 4)

Cut 100 strands yarn each 15" long. Hold all strands together and tie a separate 10" strand of yarn around the center of all strands. Fold strands in half at center tie *(see Stitch Guide)*. Leaving center tie strands loose, wrap another separate 10" strand of yarn several times around all strands 1" from fold and tie ends securely, leaving long enough ends to hide inside the Tassel. Trim ends. Use center tie strands to attach each Tassel to center ch-3 sp of each corner on Pillow.

Cut ribbon in four equal lengths. Tie in bow around 1" wrap of each Tassel.

With sewing thread and needle, sew one bead to center of rnd 1 on Front. Sew eight beads evenly spaced around sts of rnd 1. Sew one bead between each petal of rnds 7 and 15. Sew a bead in the center of each petal and at bottom of each leaf on rnd 26. Tack one bead to center of each flower on Edging, to center ch-3 on scallop top and on each scallop bottom.

Sweetheart Pillow

Finished Size: 19" square with Ruffle.

Materials:
- ❏ 18 oz. pink worsted yarn
- ❏ ½ yd. matching satin fabric
- ❏ 4 yds. pink ¼" ribbon
- ❏ 8 yds. 3mm strung pearls
- ❏ 98 pearl 6mm beads
- ❏ 1" filigree heart-shaped jewelry finding
- ❏ 14" square pillow form
- ❏ White sewing thread
- ❏ Sewing and tapestry needles
- ❏ F hook or hook needed to obtain gauge

Gauge: 26 dc = 4"; 9 dc rows = 4".

Basic Stitches: Ch, sl st, sc, dc, tr.

Special Stitches: For **beginning mesh (beg mesh)**, ch 5, dc in next st.
For **mesh**, ch 2, skip next 2 chs or sts, dc in next st.
For **ending mesh (end mesh)**, ch 2, dc in third ch of ch-5.
For **double mesh**, ch 5, skip next lacet, dc in next st.
For **block**, dc in next 3 sts, **or,** 2 dc in next ch sp, dc in next st.
For **double block**, 5 dc in next double mesh, dc in next st.
For **lacet**, ch 3, skip next 2 chs or sts, sc in next st, ch 3, skip next 2 chs or sts, dc in next st, **or,** ch 3, sc in ch sp of next double mesh, ch

3, dc in next st.
For **triple treble (ttr),** yo 4 times, insert hook in st, yo, pull loop through, (yo, pull through 2 loops on hook) 5 times.

Pillow Form Cover

Cut two pieces each 15" square from satin. With right sides together, allowing ½" seams, sew three sides together. Clip corners and turn right side out. Insert pillow form. Sew last side closed.

Pillow Side (make 2)

Row 1: Ch 98, dc in eighth ch from hook, (ch 2, skip next 2 chs, dc in next ch) across, turn. *(31 ch sps made)*

Row 2: See Special Stitches to work this row; beg mesh, 6 blocks, 17 mesh, 6 blocks, end mesh, turn.

Rows 3–32: Work according to graph on page 81, turn. At end of last row, fasten off. Lay one piece aside to use as Back.

Inner Heart Ruffle

Rnd 1: For **Front,** working around center heart on one Pillow Side, in sides of sts and in tops of sts, join with sl st according to dot on graph, ch 3, evenly space 189 dc stitches around, join with sl st in top of ch-3. *(190 dc)*

Rnds 2–3: Ch 3, dc in each st around, join. At end of last rnd, fasten off.

Outer Heart Ruffle

Rnd 1: Working around outer heart, in sides of sts and in tops of sts, join with sl st according to star on graph, ch 3, evenly space 324 dc sts around, join with sl st in top of ch-3. *(325 dc)*

Rnds 2–3: Ch 3, dc in each st around, join. At end of last rnd, fasten off.

Pillow Ruffle

Rnd 1: With wrong sides of Front and Back together and Pillow Form between, working around entire outer edge, join with sl st in first st in top right corner on Front, ch 3, dc in same st, 6 dc in end of each row and in each ch sp around with 2 dc in each corner st, join with sl st in top of ch-3.

Rnd 2: Ch 4, tr in each st around, join with sl st in top of ch-4.

Rnd 3: Ch 5, ttr *(see Special Stitches)* in each st around, join with sl st in top of ch-5. Fasten off.

Finishing

1: With sewing thread and needle, sew strung beads around outer edge of each corner heart making curlicues in center *(see photo)*. Sew one 6mm pearl bead to center and ends of curlicues. Sew one bead to point at bottom of each heart.

2: Sew strung beads around outer edge of Inner Heart Ruffle, Outer Heart Ruffle and Pillow Ruffle.

3: Starting at top of Inner Heart Ruffle, weave ribbon through stitches below rnd 1, cut ribbon leaving 6" at each end. Tie in bow. Sew filigree heart below center of bow. String three 6mm beads on sewing thread, sew above filigree heart over center of bow. Sew sixty-four 6mm beads evenly spaced over center of Inner Heart.

4: Starting at top of Outer Heart Ruffle, weave ribbon through stitches below rnd 1, cut ribbon leaving 6" at each end. Tie in bow. String three 6mm beads on sewing thread and sew to point at bottom of Outer Heart Ruffle.

5: Cut remaining ribbon into four equal lengths. Weave one through ch sps on each edge of

Pillow, tie ends in bows at corners. String three 6mm beads on sewing thread and sew to center of each bow. ⚏

= Block
= Double Block
= Beg Mesh, Mesh or End Mesh
= Double Mesh
= Lacet
● = Inner Heart Ruffle Joining
★ = Outer Heart Ruffle Joining

Rose Trellis Bedspread

continued from page 75

Next Rows

Repeat Second Row 6 more times, repeating pattern as established in first 2 rows.

Border

Row 1: Working on one long edge of Bedspread, with right side facing you, join with sl st in st above second cl on corner, beg block, (mesh, block) 18 times, turn.

Rows 2–17: Ch 3, skip next 2 sts, dc in next st, block, (mesh, block) across leaving last block unworked, turn.

Row 18: Ch 3, skip next 2 sts, dc in next st, block, mesh, block leaving last block unworked. Fasten off.

Repeat on each Motif across each long edge and across one short edge.

Edging

Join with sl st in first st on first Border, [ch 2; working in ch-3 sps at end of rows and mesh, *for **shell**, **(5 tr, for picot, ch 3, sc in third ch from hook, 5 tr)** in next ch sp, ch 2, (sc, picot, sc) in next ch sp, ch 2*; repeat between first and second * 3 more times, sc in next st on last row of Border; repeat between first and second * 5 more times, 2 sc in end of first row on Border, sc in each sc on Motifs across to next Border, 2 sc in end of

first row on next Border]; repeat between [ ] around to last Border, ch 2; repeat between first and second * 4 more times, sc in next st on last row of Border; repeat between first and second * 4 more times, shell, ch 2, sl st in last ch sp. Fasten off. ⚏

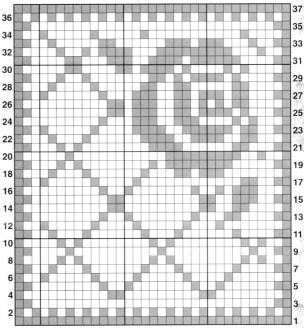

= Block or Beg Block
= Mesh

Lady's Fan Set

by Lavon Mincey

Finished Sizes: Coverlet is 53" × 66". Pillow is 15½" square.

Materials:

- ❑ Fuzzy worsted yarn:
    - 40 oz. white
    - 30 oz. lt. pink
    - 3½ oz. silver
- ❑ Two 12" square pillow forms
- ❑ 176 crystal 5mm beads
- ❑ 5 yds. pink ⅛" satin ribbon
- ❑ 16 yds. pink 1"-wide tulle ribbon
- ❑ Pink sewing thread
- ❑ Tapestry and sewing needles
- ❑ I hook or hook needed to obtain gauge

Gauge: 5 sts = 2"; 5 sc rows = 2", 4 dc rows = 3", 2 tr rows = 2". Motif is 12" square.

Basic Stitches: Ch, sl st, sc, hdc, dc, tr.

Coverlet

Motif (make 20)

Row 1: With silver, ch 4, 4 dc in fourth ch from hook, turn. *(5 dc made)*

Row 2: (Ch 3, dc) in first st, dc in next 3 sts, 2 dc in last st, turn. *(7) Front of row 2 is right side of work.*

Row 3: (Ch 3, dc) in first st, (dc in next st, 2 dc in next st) 3 times, turn. *(11)*

Row 4: (Ch 3, dc) in first st, 2 dc in next st, (dc in next 3 sts, 2 dc in next st) 2 times, 2 dc in last st, turn. *(16)*

Row 5: Ch 1, sc in each st across, turn. Fasten off.

Row 6: Join pink with sl st in **back lp** *(see Stitch Guide)* of first st, ch 21, tr in sixth ch from hook, tr in next 3 chs, dc in next 5 chs, hdc in next 5 chs, sc in last 2 chs, sl st in **back lp** of next 2 sts on row 5, turn. *(17 sts—sl sts are not used or counted as sts.)*

Row 7: Ch 1, skip first 2 sl sts, sc in next 2 sts, hdc in next 5 sts, dc in next 5 sts, tr in last 5 sts, turn.

Row 8: Ch 4 *(counts as tr)*, tr in next 4 sts, dc in next 5 sts, hdc in next 5 sts, sc in next 2 sts, sl st in **back lp** of next 2 sts on row 5, turn.

Rows 9–19: Repeat rows 7 and 8 alternately, ending with row 7.

Row 20: Ch 4, tr in next 4 sts, dc in next 5 sts, hdc in next 5 sts, sc in next 2 sts, sl st in **back lp** of last st on row 5, turn.

Row 21: Ch 1, skip first sl st, sc in next 2 sts, hdc in next 5 sts, dc in next 5 sts, tr in last 5 sts, **do not turn.**

Row 22: Working in ends of rows, skip row 21, 7

continued on page 84

tr in top of st at end of next row, (sl st in top of st at end of next row, 7 tr in top of st at end of next row) 7 times, sl st in next unworked lp on opposite side of ch-21 at base of row 6, turn. *(8 tr groups, 8 sl sts)*

Row 23: (Ch 3, 2 dc) in same ch as last sl st made, (sc in center st of next 7-tr group, 5 dc in next sl st) 3 times, sc in center st of next 7-tr group, 5 tr in next sl st, (sc in center st of next 7-tr group, 5 dc in next sl st) 3 times, sc in center st of last 7-tr group, 3 dc in top of last st on row 21, turn. Fasten off. *Push tr groups to front of work.*

Row 24: Join white with sl st in first st, ch 3, skip next 2 sts, sl st in next sc, ch 2, sl st in center st of next 5-dc group, ch 2, sc in next sc, ch 2, sc in center st of next 5-dc group, ch 2, hdc in next sc, ch 2, 3 dc in center st of next 5-dc group, ch 2, 3 tr in next sc, (3 tr, ch 3 for corner, 3 tr) in center st of next 5-tr group, 3 tr in next sc, ch 2, 3 dc in center st of next 5-dc group, ch 2, hdc in next sc, ch 2, sc in center st of next 5-dc group, ch 2, sc in next sc, ch 2, sl st in center st of next 5-dc group, ch 2, sl st in next sc, ch 3, skip next 2 sts, sl st in last st, turn. *(15 ch sps, 12 tr)*

Row 25: Ch 1, sc in first st, 3 sc in each of first 3 ch sps, 3 hdc in each of next 2 ch sps, 3 dc in next ch sp, 3 tr in next ch sp, tr in next 6 sts, (3 tr, ch 2, 3 tr) in next ch sp at corner, tr in next 6 sts, 3 tr in next ch sp, 3 dc in next ch sp, 3 hdc in each of next 2 ch sps, 3 sc in each of next 3 ch sps, sc in last st, turn. *(62 sts)*

Rnd 26: Working around outer edge, ch 1, (sc, ch 2 for corner, sc) in first st, sc in next 30 sts, (3 sc, ch 1 for corner, 3 sc) in next ch sp at corner, sc in next 30 sts, (sc, ch 2 for corner, sc) in next st, 2 sc in end of next row; working in remaining lps on opposite side of ch on row 6, sc in next 17 chs; working in ends of rows, sc in next row, 3 sc in each of next 4 rows, (sc, ch 2 for corner, sc) in remaining lp on opposite side of row 1; working in ends of rows, 3 sc in each of next 4 rows, sc in next row, sc in next 17 sts, 2 sc in next row, join with sl st in first sc. *(34 sc on each side, 4 ch sps)*

Rnd 27: Ch 3, (2 dc, ch 1, 2 dc) in first ch sp, *dc in next st, skip next st, dc in next 30 sts, skip next st, dc in next st, (2 dc, ch 1, 2 dc) in next ch sp; repeat from * 2 more times, dc in next st, skip next st, dc in next 30 sts, skip last st, join with sl st in top of ch-3. Fasten off. *(36 dc on each side, 4 ch sps)*

Finishing

With right side of Motif facing you, with sewing needle and thread, sew one bead to bottom of each 7-tr group on row 22.

Cut one 4" piece and one 22" piece from tulle ribbon. Fold 22" piece into 4"-wide multi-loop bow, tie 4" piece around center of bow. Trim ends. Cut 8" from satin ribbon. Tie in bow around tulle ribbon bow. Sew bow to center of row 1 on Motif.

Assembly

Matching sts, with tapestry needle and white, sew Motifs together four Motifs wide and five Motifs long. *(144 sts on each short edge; 180 sts on each long edge)*

Edging

Rnd 1: With right side of work facing you, join white with sl st in corner ch sp at beginning of one short edge, (ch 3, 2 dc, ch 2, 3 dc) in same ch sp; skipping each seam, *ch 2, skip next 3 sts, dc in next 5 sts, (ch 2, skip next 2 sts, dc in next 5 sts) across to last 3 sts before next corner, ch 2, skip last 3 sts, (3 dc, ch 2, 3 dc) in corner ch sp; working across long edge, (ch 2, skip next 3 sts, dc in next 5 sts) 2 times, (ch 2, skip next 2 sts, dc in next 5 sts) across to last 3 sts before next corner, ch 2, skip last 3 sts*, (3 dc, ch 2, 3 dc) in corner ch sp; repeat between first and second *, join with sl st in top of ch-3.

Rnds 2–3: Sl st in next 2 sts, (sl st, ch 3, 2 dc, ch 2, 3 dc) in first corner ch sp, ch 2, *(3 dc, ch 2, 3 dc) in next ch sp, ch 2; repeat from * around, join. At end of last rnd, fasten off.

Pillow (make 2)

Back

Row 1: With white, ch 38, dc in fourth ch from hook, dc in each ch across, turn. *(36 dc made)*

Rows 2–19: Ch 3, dc in each st across, turn. At end of last row, fasten off.

Front

Work and finish same as Coverlet Motif.

Edging

Rnd 1: Hold Front and Back wrong sides together, with Front facing you; matching sts on Front to row 1 and row 19 on Back and spacing sts evenly across ends of rows on Back to match Front, join white with sc in any corner ch sp, sc in same ch sp, sc in each st and 2 sc in each corner ch sp around inserting pillow form before closing, join with sl st in first sc. *(38 sts on each side)*

Rnd 2: Ch 1, sc in first st, *ch 2, sc in next 4 sts, (ch 2, skip next 2 sts, sc in next 3 sts, ch 2, skip next 3 sts, sc in next 3 sts) 3 times, sc in next st; repeat from * 2 more times, ch 2, sc in next 4 sts, (ch 2, skip next 2 sts, sc in next 3 sts, ch 2, skip next 3 sts, sc in next 3 sts) across, join.

Rnd 3: Sl st in first corner ch sp, (ch 3, 2 dc, ch 2, 3 dc) in same ch sp, ch 2, *(3 dc, ch 2, 3 dc) in next ch sp, ch 2; repeat from * around, join with sl st in top of ch-3. Fasten off. ⚷

Beautiful Bath

Soothe your worries away in the bath of your dreams—one that is replete with ribbons, bedecked with bows. Relish the knowledge that it was by your hands and your hooks that this relaxing retreat was created, for you and by you. Whether you're after a fast facelift for your bath or a classic look that will be as fresh years from now as it is today, we have several sets from which to choose. You might find that one look is not enough, so change the styles with the seasons!

Swan Lake

by Frances Hughes & Elizabeth Ann White

Hand Towel Edging

Finished Size: Edging is ¾" wide.

Materials:
- ❑ 25 yds. white size 5 pearl cotton
- ❑ 16" × 31" hand towel
- ❑ No. 4 steel hook or hook needed to obtain gauge

Gauge: 6 dc = 1"; 1 dc row = ¼".

Basic Stitches: Ch, sc, dc.

Edging

Row 1: Place slip knot on hook, working across bottom edge of towel, inserting hook over the bound edge and through the cloth, evenly space 85 sc across, turn. *(85 sc made)*

Row 2: Ch 3, dc in each st across, turn.

Row 3: Ch 4, skip next st, dc in next st, (ch 1, skip next st, dc in next st) across, **do not turn.**

Row 4: Ch 1, reverse sc *(see Stitch Guide),* working from left to right, insert hook in next st to the right, complete as sc; reverse sc in each st and each ch sp across. Fasten off. ❑❑

Swan

Finished Size: 11½" long.

Materials:
- ❑ 1½ oz. white cotton sport yarn
- ❑ 3 white chenille stems
- ❑ 24" of 2"-wide satin raffia ribbon
- ❑ Fabric stiffener
- ❑ Polyester fiberfill
- ❑ Tapestry needle
- ❑ No. 1 steel hook or hook needed to obtain gauge

Gauge: Rnds 1–2 = 2" across.

Basic Stitches: Ch, sl st, sc, dc, tr, dtr.

Body

Rnd 1: Ch 4, sl st in first ch to form ring, ch 3, 13 dc in ring, join with sl st in top of ch-3. *(14 dc made)*

Rnd 2: (Ch 3, dc) in first st, 2 dc in each st around, join. *(28)*

Rnd 3: (Ch 3, dc) in first st, dc in next st, (2 dc in next st, dc in next st) around, join. *(42)*

Rnd 4: (Ch 3, dc) in first st, dc in next 2 sts, (2 dc in next st, dc in next 2 sts) around, join. *(56)*

Rnd 5: Working in **back lps** *(see Stitch Guide),* ch 3, dc in each st around, join.

Rnds 6–7: Ch 3, dc in each st around, join.

Rnd 8: (Ch 3, dc) in first st, dc in next 3 sts, (2 dc in next st, dc in next 3 sts) around, join. *(70)*

Rnd 9: Ch 3, dc in each st around, join.

Rnd 10: (Ch 3, dc) in first st, dc in next 4 sts, (2 dc in next st, dc in next 4 sts) around, join. *(84)*

Rnd 11: (Ch 3, dc) in first st, dc in next 39 sts; for **Tail,** (dc, tr) in next st, 3 dtr in next st, (tr, dc) in next st, dc in next 41 sts, join. *(89)*

Rnd 12: Ch 3, dc in next 43 sts, 3 dc in next st, dc in next 44 sts, join. *(91)*

Rnd 13: Ch 1, sc in each st around, join with sl st in first sc.

Rnd 14: Ch 1, **reverse sc** *(see Stitch Guide),* working from left to right, insert hook in next st to the right, complete as sc; reverse sc in each st around, join with sl st in first st. Fasten off.

Rnd 15: Working in remaining **front lps** of rnd 4, join with sc in first st, reverse sc in each st around, join. Fasten off.

Neck & Head

Rnd 1: Starting at bottom of Neck, ch 14, sl st in first st to form ring, ch 3, dc in each ch around, join with sl st in top of ch-3. *(14 dc made)*

Rnds 2–3: Ch 3, dc in each st around, join.

Rnd 4: Ch 1, sc in first st, sc next 2 sts tog, (sc in next st, sc next 2 sts tog) 3 times, sc in last 2 sts, join with sl st in first sc. *(10 sc)*

Rnds 5–48: Ch 1, sc in each st around, join.

Rnd 49: For **Head,** ch 1, sc in first 6 sts, 2 sc in each of next 4 sts, join. *(14)*

Rnds 50–53: Ch 1, sc in each st around, join. Stuff Head lightly.

Rnd 54: Ch 1, sc first 2 sts tog, (sc in next st, sc next 2 sts tog) around, join. *(9)*

Rnd 55: Ch 1, sc in each st around, join.

Row 56: For **Beak,** working in rows, flatten last rnd, working through both thicknesses, ch 1, evenly space 5 sc across, turn.

Row 57: Ch 1, sc in first 5 sts, turn.

Rows 58–59: Skip first st, sc in each st across, turn. *(4, 3)*

Row 60: Sc next 3 sts tog. Fasten off.

Finishing

1: Dip Body in fabric stiffener shaping point of Tail. Dip Neck & Head in fabric stiffener, insert two chenille stems, flatten and shape Neck to form an "S".

2: Pin bottom of Neck to Body *(opposite Tail)* on bottom of rnd 5 just above reverse sc of last rnd; with tapestry needle, sew to secure. Tack curved edge on back of Neck to last round of Body. Let dry.

continued on page 93

Ribbon 'n' Bows Bath

An Original by Annie

Contour Rug

Finished Sizes: 25½" × 38".

Materials:
- ❑ Worsted yarn:
    - 22 oz. pink
    - 7 oz. white
- ❑ Tapestry needle
- ❑ G and H hooks or hooks needed to obtain gauges

Gauges: G hook, 4 hdc = 1"; ribbon = ½"-wide.
H hook, 7 hdc = 2"; 5 hdc rows = 2".

Basic Stitches: Ch, sl st, sc, hdc, dc.

Rug

Row 1: With pink, ch 32; working in **back bar of ch** *(see illustration),* hdc in third ch from hook, hdc in each ch across to last ch, 5 hdc in last ch; working in remaining lps on opposite side of starting ch in **back lps** *(see Stitch Guide),* hdc in each ch across with last st in bottom of ch-2, turn. *(64 hdc made)*

Row 2: Working in **front lps,** ch 2, hdc in next 29 sts, 2 hdc in each of next 5 sts, hdc in last 30 sts, turn. *(70)*

Row 3: Working in **back lps,** ch 2, hdc in next 29 sts, (2 hdc in next st, hdc in next st) 5 times, hdc in last 30 sts, turn. *(75)*

Note: *Work all rows alternating **front** and **back lps.** All unworked lps should be on same side of piece.*

Row 4: Ch 2, hdc in next 29 sts, (2 hdc in next st, hdc in each of next 2 sts) 5 times, hdc in last 30 sts, turn. *(80)*

Row 5: Ch 2, hdc in next 29 sts, (2 hdc in next st, hdc in each of next 3 sts) 5 times, hdc in last 30 sts, turn. *(85)*

Row 6: (Ch 2, hdc) in first st, hdc in next 29 sts, (2 hdc in next st, hdc in next 4 sts) 5 times, hdc in next 29 sts, 2 hdc in last st, turn. *(92)*

Row 7: (Ch 2, hdc) in first st, hdc in next 30 sts, (2 hdc in next st, hdc in next 5 sts) 5 times, hdc in next 30 sts, 2 hdc in last st, turn. *(99)*

Row 8: (Ch 2, hdc) in first st, hdc in next 31 sts, (2 hdc in next st, hdc in next 6 sts) 5 times, hdc in next 31 sts, 2 hdc in last st, turn. *(106)*

Row 9: (Ch 3, 2 hdc) in first st, hdc in next 32 sts, (2 hdc in next st, hdc in next 7 sts) 5 times, hdc in next 32 sts, (2 hdc, dc) in last st, turn. *(113 hdc, 2 dc)*

Row 10: (Ch 3, 2 hdc) in first st, hdc in next 34 sts, (2 hdc in next st, hdc in next 8 sts) 5 times, hdc in next 34 sts, (2 hdc, dc) in last st, turn. *(122 hdc, 2 dc)*

Row 11: (Ch 3, 2 hdc) in first st, hdc in next 36 sts, (2 hdc in next st, hdc in next 9 sts) 5 times, hdc in next 36 sts, (2 hdc, dc) in last st, turn. Fasten off. *(122 hdc, 2 dc)*

Row 12: For **first extension,** with pink, ch 23, (dc, hdc) in first st on row 10, 2 hdc in next st, hdc in next 37 sts, (2 hdc in next st, hdc in next 10 sts) 5 times, hdc in next 37 sts, 2 hdc in next st, (hdc, dc) in last st; for **second extension,** ch 24, turn. *(142 sts, 47 chs)*

Row 13: Hdc in third ch from hook, hdc in next 21 chs, hdc in next 41 sts, (2 hdc in next st, hdc in next 11 sts) 5 times, hdc in next 41 sts, hdc in last 23 chs, turn. *(193 hdc)*

Row 14: Ch 2, hdc in next 63 sts, (2 hdc in next st, hdc in next 12 sts) 5 times, hdc in last 64 sts, turn. *(198)*

Row 15: Ch 2, hdc in next 63 sts, (2 hdc in next st, hdc in next 13 sts) 5 times, hdc in last 64 sts, turn. *(203)*

Row 16: Ch 2, hdc in next 63 sts, (2 hdc in next st, hdc in next 14 sts) 5 times, hdc in last 64 sts, turn. *(208)*

Row 17: Ch 2, hdc in next 63 sts, (2 hdc in next st, hdc in next 15 sts) 5 times, hdc in last 64 sts, turn. *(213)*

Row 18: Ch 2, hdc in next 63 sts, (2 hdc in next st, hdc in next 16 sts) 5 times, hdc in last 64 sts, turn. *(218)*

Row 19: Ch 1, sc in first st, hdc in next 66 sts, (2 hdc in next st, hdc in next 20 sts) 4 times, hdc in next 66 sts, sc in last st, turn. *(220 hdc, 2 sc)*

Row 20: Ch 1, sc in first 2 sts, hdc in next 65 sts, (2 hdc in next st, hdc in next 21 sts) 4 times, hdc in next 65 sts, sc in last 2 sts, turn. *(222 hdc, 4 sc)*

Row 21: Ch 1, sc in first 3 sts, hdc in next 64 sts, (2 hdc in next st, hdc in next 22 sts) 4 times, hdc in next 64 sts, sc in last 3 sts. Fasten off. *(224 hdc, 6 sc)*

Chain Loops

Starting at center of row 1 and working in unworked **front** and **back lps,** join pink with sc in lp at rounded end, (ch 7, sc in next lp) across, *ch 1, sc in first lp of next row, (ch 7, sc in next lp) across; repeat from * across to last row. Leaving **both lps** of last row unworked, fasten off.

Lace

Row 1: With front of Rug facing you, working in **both lps** of last row, join white with sl st in first st, ch 3, dc in next 82 sts, (2 dc in next st, dc in next 20 sts) 3 times, 2 dc in next st, dc in last 83 sts, turn. *(234 dc made)*

continued on page 90

Ribbon 'n' Bows Bath

continued from page 89

Row 2: Ch 1, sc in first 2 sts, ch 3, skip next 2 sts, (sc in next 2 sts, ch 3, skip next 2 sts) across to last 2 sts, sc in last 2 sts, turn. *(118 sc, 58 ch sps)*

Row 3: Ch 3, dc in next st, (ch 3, skip next ch sp, dc in next 2 sts) across, turn.

Row 4: Ch 1, sc in first st, sc in sp between first 2 dc, (ch 4, skip next ch sp, sc in sp between next 2 dc) across to last st, sc in last st, turn. *(61 sc, 58 ch sps)*

Row 5: Ch 1, sc in first st, skip next st, 5 sc in next ch sp, (sc in next st, 5 sc in next ch sp) across to last 2 sts, skip next st, sc in last st, turn. *(349 sc)*

Row 6: Ch 1, sc in first st, ch 1, skip next 2 sts, (dc, ch 2, dc) in next st, ch 1, skip next 2 sts, *sc in next st, ch 1, skip next 2 sts, (dc, ch 2, dc) in next st, ch 1, skip next 2 sts; repeat from * across to last st, sc in last st, turn. *(59 sc, 58 ch sps)*

Row 7: Ch 1, sc in first sc, 6 dc in next ch-2 sp, sc in next sc, (6 dc in next ch-2 sp, sc in next sc) across. Fasten off.

Ribbon

With pink, ch 350; working in **back bar of ch,** hdc in third ch from hook, hdc in each ch across. Fasten off.

Weave over and under 2 dc at a time through sps of row 3 on Lace. Sew ends to back of st at ends of row 3.

Bow

With G hook and pink, ch 53; working in **back bar of ch,** hdc in third ch from hook, hdc in each ch across. Fasten off.

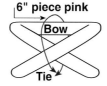

Fold according to diagram. Tie 6" piece pink in knot around center of folded bow.

Center Loop

With G hook and pink, ch 9; working in **back bar of ch,** hdc in third ch from hook, hdc in each ch across. Fasten off.

Wrap center loop around center of bow, sew ends together.

Sew to ribbon at center front of Rug.

Lid Cover

Finished Size: Fits standard or oval toilet lid.

Materials:
- ❏ 14 oz. pink worsted yarn
- ❏ 1 yd. ⅛" elastic
- ❏ White sewing thread
- ❏ Sewing and tapestry needles
- ❏ H hook or hook needed to obtain gauge

Gauge: 7 hdc = 2"; 5 hdc rows = 2".

Basic Stitches: Ch, sl st, sc, hdc, dc.

Cover

Row 1: With pink, ch 28; working in **back bar of ch** *(see illustration on page 89),* hdc in third ch from hook, hdc in each ch across to last ch, 5 hdc in last ch; working in remaining lps on opposite side of starting ch in **back lps** *(see Stitch Guide),* hdc in each ch across with last st in bottom of ch-2, turn. *(57 hdc made)*

Row 2: Working in **front lps,** ch 2, hdc in next 25 sts, 2 hdc in each of next 5 sts, hdc in last 26 sts, turn. *(62)*

Row 3: Working in **back lps,** ch 2, hdc in next 25 sts, (2 hdc in next st, hdc in next st) 5 times, hdc in last 26 sts, turn. *(67)*

Note: *Work all rows alternating **front** and **back lps.** All unworked lps should be on same side of piece.*

Row 4: Ch 2, hdc in next 25 sts, (2 hdc in next st, hdc in next 2 sts) 5 times, hdc in last 26 sts, turn. *(72)*

Row 5: Ch 2, hdc in next 25 sts, (2 hdc in next st, hdc in next 3 sts) 5 times, hdc in last 26 sts, turn. *(77)*

Row 6: Ch 2, hdc in next 25 sts, (2 hdc in next st, hdc in next 4 sts) 5 times, hdc in next 26 sts, turn. *(82)*

Row 7: Ch 2, hdc in next 25 sts, (2 hdc in next st, hdc in next 5 sts) 5 times, hdc in last 26 sts, turn. *(87)*

Row 8: Ch 2, hdc in next 25 sts, (2 hdc in next st, hdc in next 6 sts) 5 times, hdc in last 26 sts, turn. *(92)*

Row 9: Ch 1, sc in first st, hdc in next 25 sts, (2 hdc in next st, hdc in next 7 sts) 5 times, hdc in next 25 sts, sc in last st, turn. *(96 hdc, 2 sc)*

Row 10: Sl st in first 2 sts, sc in next st, hdc in next 23 sts, (2 hdc in next st, hdc in next 8 sts) 5 times, hdc in next 23 sts, sc in next st, sl st in next st leaving last st unworked, turn. *(96 hdc, 2 sc, 3 sl sts)*

Row 11: Skip first sl st, sl st in next 2 sts, sc in next st, hdc in next 21 sts, (2 hdc in next st, hdc in next 9 sts) 5 times, hdc in next 21 sts, sc in next st, sl st in next st leaving last 3 sts unworked, turn. *(97 hdc, 2 sc, 3 sl sts)*

Row 12: Skip first sl st, sl st in next 3 sts, sc in next st, hdc in next 18 sts, (2 hdc in next st, hdc in next 10 sts) 5 times, hdc in next 18 sts, sc in next st, sl st in next st leaving last 4 sts unworked, turn. *(96 hdc, 2 sc, 4 sl sts)*

Row 13: Skip first sl st, sl st in next 3 sts, sc in next st, hdc in next 32 sts, 2 hdc in next st, (hdc in next 12 sts, 2 hdc in next st) 2 times, hdc in next 31 sts, sc in next st, sl st in next st leaving last 5 sts unworked, turn. *(93 hdc, 2 sc, 4 sl sts)*

Row 14: Skip first sl st, sl st in next 3 sts, sc in next st, hdc in next 32 sts, 2 hdc in next st, (hdc in next 10 sts, 2 hdc in next st) 2 times, hdc in next 32 sts, sc in next st, sl st in next st leaving last 5 sts unworked, turn. *(90 hdc, 2 sc, 4 sl sts)*

Row 15: Skip first sl st, sl st in next 3 sts, sc in next st, hdc in next 31 sts, 2 hdc in next st,

(hdc in next 9 sts, 2 hdc in next st) 2 times, hdc in next 32 sts, sc in next st, sl st in next st leaving last 5 sts unworked, turn. Fasten off. *(90 hdc, 2 sc, 4 sl sts)*

Rnd 16: Working around outer edge, join pink with sc in end of row 9 at right back corner, sc in end of each row and in each st around, join with sl st in first sc. *(139 sc)*

Rnd 17: Ch 1, sc in each st around, join, **turn.**

Row 18: Working in rows through **both lps** of sts, ch 1, sc in first 121 sts leaving last 18 sts unworked, turn. *(121)*

Row 19: Ch 1, sc in first 23 sts, sc next 2 sts tog, (sc in next 16 sts, sc next 2 sts tog) 4 times, sc in last 24 sts, turn. *(116)*

Row 20: Leaving excess elastic extended at each end, hold elastic over sts of last row; working over elastic *(see Stitch Guide),* ch 1, sc in each st across, turn. Fasten off.

For **tie,** join pink with sl st in one end of row 20, ch 43, sl st in second ch from hook, sl st in each ch across, join with sl st in same row. Fasten off. Repeat on opposite end of row 20.

Chain Loops

Work same as Contour Rug Chain Loops on page 89.

Finishing

Place Cover on lid of toilet, pull ends of elastic, gathering edge of Cover to fit lid. Leaving ¾", cut off excess ends; fold each end under, sew to back of last row on Cover to secure. ✏

Tank Set

Finished Size: Cover fits up to 6½" × 12½" ×19½" tank bottom and 1½" × 7½" × 21" tank top.

Materials:
- ❏ Worsted yarn:
    - 14 oz. pink
    - 3 oz. white
- ❏ White elastic:
    - 1½ yds. ⅛"-wide
    - 16" of ½"-wide
- ❏ 1½" of ½"-wide Velcro® strip
- ❏ White sewing thread
- ❏ Sewing and tapestry needles
- ❏ G and H hooks or hooks needed to obtain gauges

Gauges: G hook, 4 hdc = 1"; ribbon is ½" wide. H hook, 7 sc = 2"; 4 slanted V sts = 3"; 5 slanted V st rows = 2".

Basic Stitches: Ch, sl st, sc, hdc, dc.

Bottom Cover

Row 1: With pink, ch 152; working over elastic *(see Stitch Guide),* sc in second ch from hook, sc in each ch across, turn. *(151 sc made)*

Row 2: Ch 1; for **slanted V st (sv), (sc, ch 1, dc)** in first st, (skip next 2 sts, sv in next st) across, turn. *(51 sv)*

Rows 3–28: Or to desired length needed to reach bottom of handle; ch 1, sv in each ch-1 sp across, turn.

Row 29: For **first side,** ch 1, sv in first 15 ch-1 sps leaving last 36 ch-1 sps unworked, turn. *(15 sv)*

Rows 30–31: Ch 1, sv in each ch-1 sp across, turn. At end of last row, fasten off.

Row 29: For **handle opening,** skip next 2 ch-1 sps on row 28; for **second side,** join pink with sc in next ch-1 sp, (ch 1, dc) in same ch-1 sp, sv in each ch-1 sp across, turn. *(34 sv)*

Rows 30–31: Ch 1, sv in each ch-1 sp across, turn.

Row 32: Ch 1, sv in each ch-1 sp across second side, ch 8, sv in each ch-1 sp across first side, turn. *(49 sv, 8 chs)*

Row 33: Ch 1, sv in first 15 ch-1 sps, (skip next 2 chs, sv in next ch) 2 times, skip next 2 chs, sv in last 34 ch-1 sps, turn. *(51 sv)*

Row 34: Or to length needed to fit lid on tank, ch 1, sv in each ch-1 sp across, turn.

Row 35: Ch 1, sc in each st and in each ch-1 sp across. Fasten off.

Finishing

1: For edging on handle opening, join pink with sc in unworked sc at bottom right corner, sc in next ch-1 sp, sc in next 2 sts, sc in next ch-1 sp, sc next st and top of dc at end of next row tog, 2 hdc in end of next row, sc top of dc at end of next row and next ch on opposite side of ch-8 tog, skip next ch, sc in next 5 chs, sc last ch and top of dc at end of next row tog, 2 hdc in end of next row, sc in top of dc at end of next row, join with sl st in first sc. Fasten off.

2: For **back fasteners,** from ½"-wide elastic, cut 2 pieces each 3" long and 4 pieces each 2½" long. Cut Velcro® into 3 pieces ½"-square.

3: Sew ½" of each 3" piece of elastic to top of Cover *(see illustration).* Sew loopy side of one Velcro® square to one piece of elastic. Sew fuzzy side of one Velcro® square to opposite piece of elastic. Repeat with 2½" pieces at center and bottom of Cover.

Top Cover

Row 1: With pink, ch 80, sv in second ch from hook, (skip next 2 chs, sv in next ch) across, turn. *(27 sv made)*

Rows 2–20: Ch 1, sv in each ch-1 sp across, turn. At end of last row, **do not turn.**

Rnd 21: Working around outer edge, ch 1, (2 sc in side of dc at end of next row, hdc in ch-1 sp of sv at end of next row) 10 times; working on opposite side of starting ch, 2 sc in first ch, sc in each ch across; repeat between ( ) 10 more times, sc in each st and in each ch-1 sp across to last st, skip last st, join with sl st in

Ribbon 'n' Bows Bath

continued from page 91

back lp *(see Stitch Guide)*, of first sc. *(219 sc)*

Rnd 22: Working in **back lps**, ch 1, sc in each st around, join.

Rnd 23: Ch 1, sv in first st, skip next 2 sts, (sv in next st, skip next 2 sts) around, join, **turn.** *(73 sv)*

Rnds 24–28: Ch 1, sv in each ch-1 sp around, join, **turn.** At end of last rnd, fasten off.

Lace

Rnd 1: Working in **front lps** of rnd 21 on Top Cover, join white with sc in first st, sc in each st around with 2 sc in last st, join with sl st in **back lp** of first sc. *(220 sc made)*

Rnd 2: Working in **back lps**, ch 1, sc in first 2 sts, ch 2, skip next 2 sts, (sc in next 2 sts, ch 2, skip next 2 sts) around, join. *(110 sc, 55 ch sps)*

Rnd 3: Ch 3, dc in next st, ch 2, skip next ch sp, (dc in next 2 sts, ch 2, skip next ch sp) around, join with sl st in top of ch-3. *(110 dc, 55 ch sps)*

Rnd 4: Ch 1, sc in sp between ch-3 and next dc, ch 3, skip next ch sp, (sc in sp between next 2 dc, ch 3, skip next ch sp) around, join. *(55 sc, 55 ch sps)*

Rnd 5: Ch 1, sc in first st, 2 sc in next ch sp, (sc in next st, 2 sc in next ch sp) around, join. *(165 sc)*

Rnd 6: Ch 1, sc in first st, ch 1, skip next 2 sts, (dc, ch 2, dc) in next st, *ch 1, skip next 2 sts, sc in next st, ch 1, skip next 2 sts, (dc, ch 2, dc) in next st; repeat from * around to last 5 sts, ch 1, skip next st, sc in next st, ch 1, skip next st, (dc, ch 2, dc) in next st, ch 1, skip last st, join.

Rnd 7: Ch 1, sc in first sc, 6 dc in next ch-2 sp, (sc in next sc, 6 dc in next ch-2 sp) around, join. Fasten off.

Trim

With top of piece facing you, working in **front lps** of rnd 1 on Lace, join white with sl st in any st, 3 sc in next st, (sl st in next st, 3 sc in next st) around, join with sl st in first sl st. Fasten off.

Ribbon

With pink, ch 240; working in **back bar of ch,** hdc in third ch from hook, hdc in each ch across. Fasten off.

Beginning at center back, weave under and over 2 dc at a time through sps of rnd 3 on Lace. Sew ends together. Hide seam behind first 2 and last 2 dc of rnd. ⚷

Towel Trim

Finished Size: 3½" × 27".

Materials:
- ❏ Worsted yarn:
    - 2½ oz. white
    - ½ oz. pink
- ❏ White sewing thread
- ❏ Sewing and tapestry needles
- ❏ G and H hooks or hooks needed to obtain gauges

Gauges: G hook, 4 hdc = 1"; ribbon = ½"-wide. H hook, 7 hdc = 2"; 5 hdc rows = 2".

Basic Stitches: Ch, sl st, sc, hdc, dc.

Lace

Row 1: With H hook and white, ch 99, sc in second ch from hook, sc in each ch across, turn. *(98 sc made)*

Row 2: Ch 1, sc in first 2 sts, ch 3, skip next 2 sts, (sc in next 2 sts, ch 3, skip next 2 sts) across to last 2 sts, sc in last 2 sts, turn.

Row 3: Ch 3, dc in next st, (ch 3, skip next ch sp, dc in next 2 sts) across, turn.

Row 4: Ch 1, sc in first st, sc in sp between first 2 dc, (ch 4, skip next ch sp, sc in sp between next 2 dc) across to last st, sc in last st, turn. *(27 sc, 24 ch sps)*

Row 5: Ch 1, sc in first st, skip next st, 3 sc in next ch sp, (sc in next st, 3 sc in next ch sp) across to last 2 sts, skip next st, sc in last st, turn. *(97 sc)*

Row 6: Ch 1, sc in first st, ch 1, skip next 2 sts, (dc, ch 2, dc) in next st, ch 1, skip next 2 sts, *sc in next st, ch 1, skip next 2 sts, (dc, ch 2, dc) in next st, ch 1, skip next 2 sts; repeat from * across to last st, sc in last st, turn.

Row 7: Ch 1, sc in first sc, 6 dc in next ch-2 sp, sc in next sc, (6 dc in next ch-2 sp, sc in next sc) across. Fasten off.

Row 8: Working in remaining lps on opposite side of starting ch, with H hook, join white with sl st in first ch, sc in next ch, *ch 1, skip next 2 chs, (dc, ch 2, dc) in next ch, ch 1, skip next 2 chs, sc in next ch; repeat from * across, turn.

Row 9: Ch 1, sc in first sc, 6 dc in next ch-2 sp, sc in next sc, (6 dc in next ch-2 sp, sc in next sc) across. Fasten off.

Ribbon

With pink, ch 116; working in **back bar of ch,** hdc in third ch from hook, hdc in each ch across. Fasten off.

Weave over and under 2 dc at a time through sps of row 3 on Lace. Sew ends to back of st at ends of row 3.

Bow

Work same as Contour Rug Bow on page 90.

Sew ribbon at center of Lace.

Placing bottom edge 2½" from end of towel, sew ends of Lace to edges. Tack each sc of rows 7 and 9 to towel. ⚷

3: For Bow, fold ribbon to form five loops and tie around Neck above Body with chenille stem. ⚬━

Sweetheart Swans

Finished Size: 21½" long.

Materials:
- ❏ 300 yds. white size 20 crochet cotton thread
- ❏ No. 8 steel hook or hook needed to obtain gauge

Gauge: 10 dc = 1"; 4 dc rows = 1".

Basic Stitches: Ch, sl st, sc, dc.

Special Stitches: For **mesh,** ch 2, skip next 2 sts or ch, dc in next st or ch.

For **beginning block (beg block),** ch 3, dc in next 3 sts, **or,** ch 3, 2 dc in next ch sp, dc in next st.

For **block,** 2 dc in next ch sp, dc in next st or ch, **or,** dc in next 3 sts.

For **lacet,** ch 3, skip next 2 ch or sts, sc in next st, ch 3, skip next 2 ch or sts, dc in next st, **or,** ch 3, sc in ch sp of next bar, ch 3, dc in next st.

For **bar,** ch 5, skip next lacet, dc in next st.

For **V stitch (V st),** (dc, ch 5, dc) in next st or end of row.

Swans

Row 1: Ch 123, dc in fourth ch from hook, dc in next 2 chs, mesh 38 times *(see Special Stitches)*, dc in last 3 sts, turn. *(38 mesh, 7 dc made)*

Rows 2–31: Work according to graph across, turn.

Row 32: For **beginning decrease (beg dec),** sl st in first st and in next 2 chs and in next st; work according to graph across to last mesh; for **end decrease (end dec), leave last mesh unworked,** turn.

Rows 33–40: Work according to graph across, turn. At end of last row, fasten off.

Row 41: Working in remaining lps on opposite side of starting ch on row 1, join with sl st in first ch, beg block, lacet 5 times, mesh, block 3 times, mesh, block 4 times, mesh, lacet, mesh 2 times, block 5 times, mesh, lacet 4 times, block, turn.

Rows 42–79: Repeat rows 3-40. At end of last row, **do not turn or fasten off.**

Rnd 80: *See Special Stitches for working V sts on this rnd;* working in ends of rows and in sts, ch 8, dc in last st on row 79 *(first V st made),* V st in next 10 rows, (skip next row, V st in next row) 29 times, V st in next 9 rows, V st in first st on row 40, skip next 3 sts, V st in next st, skip next 4 sts, V st in next st, (skip next 5 sts, V st in next st) 9 times, skip next 2 sts, V st in last st, V st in next 10 rows, (skip next row, V st in next row) 29 times, V st in next 9 rows, V st in first st on row 79, skip next 3 sts, V st in next st, skip next 4 sts, V st in next st, (skip next 5 sts, V st in next st) 9 times, skip next 2 sts, join with sl st in third ch of ch-8.

Rnd 81: Ch 1, (4 sc, ch 3, 4 sc) in ch sp of each V st around, join with sl st in first sc. Fasten off. ⚬━

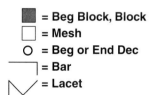

- ▥ = **Beg Block, Block**
- ☐ = **Mesh**
- ○ = **Beg or End Dec**
- ⌐ = **Bar**
- ⋁ = **Lacet**

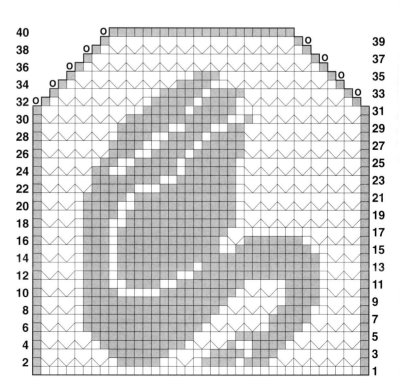

Tissue Hanger

by Sara Romo

Finished Size: 24" long.

Materials:
- ❏ 4 oz. white worsted yarn
- ❏ 30" pink 1" lace-edged ribbon
- ❏ 5 pink silk flowers with leaves
- ❏ White sewing thread
- ❏ 1" plastic ring
- ❏ Sewing and tapestry needles
- ❏ H hook or hook needed to obtain gauge

Gauge: 7 dc = 2"; 7 dc rows = 4".

Basic Stitches: Ch, sl st, sc, hdc, dc.

Holder

Row 1: Ch 13, dc in fourth ch from hook, dc in each ch across, turn. *(11 dc made)*

Rows 2–36: Ch 3, dc in each st across, turn.

Row 37: (Ch 3, 2 dc) in first st, ch 3, 3 dc in next st, ch 6, skip next 7 sts, 3 dc in next st, ch 3, 3 dc in last st, turn.

Row 38: Ch 3; for **shell, (3 dc, ch 3, 3 dc) in next ch-3 sp;** ch 6, skip next ch-6 sp, shell in next ch-3 sp, dc in last st, turn.

Rows 39–41: Ch 3, shell in ch sp of first shell, ch 6, shell in ch sp of last shell, dc in last st, turn.

Row 42: Ch 3, shell in first shell, ch 4, sc around ch-6 sps of last 3 rows at same time, ch 4, shell in last shell, dc in last st, turn.

Rows 43–47: Ch 3, shell in first shell, ch 6, shell in last shell, dc in last st, turn.

Rows 48–73: Repeat rows 42–47 consecutively, ending with row 43.

Row 74: Ch 3, shell in first shell, ch 5, shell in last shell, dc in last st, turn.

Row 75: Ch 3, shell in first shell, skip next ch sp, shell in last shell, dc in last st. Fasten off.

Row 76: For **Border,** join with sl st in top of st at end of row 36, sc in row 37, *(sc, hdc, dc, hdc, sc) in end of next row, sc in end of next row*; repeat between first and second * 18 more times, sc in next 3 sts, 3 sc in next ch sp, sc in next 6 sts, 3 sc in next ch sp, sc in next 3 sts, sc in end of same row; repeat between first and second * 19 more times, sl st in top of st at end of row 36. Fasten off.

Finishing

1: Sew row 1 centered at top of row 75.

2: For **Hanger** at top, tack plastic ring to center of row 1.

3: Tack five silk flowers to top five sc worked around ch-6 sps *(see photo);* leave bottom sc unworked around ch-6 sps without flower.

4: Weave ribbon through ch-6 sps, working over unworked ch-6 sps and under sc worked around ch-6 sps; tack ends in place on inside.

5: Sew row 16 to center of row 64 and row 30 to center of row 53. ⚷

Cameo Bath Set

by Sandee Stuhmer-Zalenski

Finished Sizes: Bath Mat is 24" × 26". Tissue Purse is 9" high. Toilet Seat Cover fits standard toilet seat.

Materials:
- ❏ Worsted yarn:
    - 17 oz. blue
    - 5 oz. gold
    - 3 oz. off-white
- ❏ 2 oz. off-white sport yarn
- ❏ 200 yds. ecru size 10 crochet cotton
- ❏ Spray-on non-slip rug backing *(optional)*
- ❏ Tapestry and embroidery needles
- ❏ H hook for worsted yarn, G hook for sport yarn and No. 4 steel hook for crochet cotton or hooks needed to obtain gauges

Gauges: H hook and worsted yarn: 7 sts = 2". **G hook and sport yarn:** 9 sts = 2". **No. 4 hook and crochet cotton:** 8 sts = 1".

Basic Stitches: Ch, sl st, sc, hdc, dc, tr.

Bath Mat

Rnd 1: With H hook and blue yarn, ch 14, dc in fourth ch from hook, dc in next ch, tr in next 6 chs, dc in next 2 chs, 5 dc in last ch; working on opposite side of ch, dc in next 2 chs, tr in next 6 chs, dc in next 2 chs, 4 dc in next ch, join with sl st in top of ch-3. *(30 sts made)*

Rnd 2: Ch 1, sc in first st, *hdc in next st, dc in next st, 2 dc in next st, tr in next st, 2 tr in each of next 2 sts, tr in next st, 2 dc in next st, dc in next st, hdc in next st, sc in next 2 sts, 3 sc in next st*, sc in next 2 sts; repeat between first and second *, sc in next st, join with sl st in first sc. *(42 sts)*

Rnd 3: Ch 3, dc in next st, 2 dc in next st, (dc in next 2 sts, 2 dc in next st) around, join in top of ch-3. *(56)*

Rnd 4: Ch 2, hdc in next 4 sts, sc in next 12 sts, hdc in next 5 sts, sc in next 6 sts, hdc in next 5 sts, sc in next 12 sts, hdc in next 5 sts, sc in next 6 sts, join in top of ch-2.

Rnd 5: Ch 3, dc in next 2 sts, 2 dc in next st, (dc in next 3 sts, 2 dc in next st) around, join. *(70)*

Rnd 6: Ch 3, dc in next st, 2 dc in next st, (dc in next 4 sts, 2 dc in next st) around, end with dc in last 2 sts, join. *(84)*

Rnd 7: (Ch 3, dc) in first st, (dc in next 3 sts, 2 dc in next st) around, end with dc in last 3 sts, join. *(105)*

Rnd 8: Ch 3, dc in next st, 2 dc in next st, (dc in next 4 sts, 2 dc in next st) around, end with dc in last 2 sts, join. *(126)*

Rnds 9–10: Ch 3, dc in each st around, join.

Rnd 11: Ch 3, dc in next 3 sts, 2 dc in next st, dc in next 6 sts, 2 dc in next st, *hdc in next 4 sts, 2 hdc in next st, sc in next 18 sts, 2 hdc in next st, hdc in next 4 sts*, (dc in next 6 sts, 2 dc in next st) 5 times; repeat between first and second *, (dc in next 6 sts, 2 dc in next st) 3 times, sc in last 2 sts, join. *(140)*

Rnd 12: Ch 3, dc in next 12 sts, 2 dc in next st, (dc in next 13 sts, 2 dc in next st) around, join. *(150)*

Rnd 13: Ch 3, dc in next 4 sts, 2 dc in next st, (dc in next 9 sts, 2 dc in next st) around, end with dc in last 4 sts, join. *(165)*

Rnd 14: Ch 3, dc in next 9 sts, 2 dc in next st, (dc in next 10 sts, 2 dc in next st) around, join. *(180)*

Rnd 15: Ch 3, dc in next 3 sts, 2 dc in next st, (dc in next 8 sts, 2 dc in next st) around, end with dc in last 4 sts, join. *(200)*

Rnd 16: Repeat rnd 9.

Rnd 17: Ch 3, dc in next 8 sts, 2 dc in next st, dc in next 9 sts, 2 dc in next st, *dc in next 2 sts, hdc in next 7 sts, (hdc, sc) in next st, (sc in next 9 sts, 2 sc in next st) 2 times, sc in next 6 sts, hdc in next 3 sts, 2 hdc in next st, hdc in next 4 sts, dc in next 5 sts, 2 dc in next st*, (dc in next 9 sts, 2 dc in next st) 5 times; repeat between first and second *, (dc in next 9 sts, 2 dc in next st) 3 times, join. *(220)*

Rnd 18: Repeat rnd 9.

Rnd 19: Ch 3, dc in next 4 sts, 2 dc in next st, (dc in next 10 sts, 2 dc in next st) around to last 5 sts, dc in last 5 sts, join. *(240)*

Rnd 20: Ch 3, dc in next 10 sts, 2 dc in next st, (dc in next 11 sts, 2 dc in next st) around, join. *(260)*

Rnd 21: Ch 3, dc in next 5 sts, 2 dc in next st, (dc in next 12 sts, 2 dc in next st) around to last 6 sts, dc in last 6 sts, join. Fasten off. *(280)*

Rnd 22: Join gold yarn with sc in first st, sc in each st around, join in first sc.

Rnd 23: Ch 1, sc in first st, skip next st, 5 dc in next st, skip next st, (sc in next st, skip next st, 5 dc in next st, skip next st) around, join. Fasten off.

If desired, spray wrong side of Bath Mat with non-slip backing.

Cameo

With H hook and off-white worsted yarn, make Basic Cameo on page 103 and 104; sew to center of Bath Mat.

Toilet Seat Cover

Note: *Cover will not lay flat until stretched over toilet seat lid.*

continued on page 102

Shells 'n' Bows

by Dorothy Helms

Instructions on page 100

Shells 'n' Bows

Photo on page 98

Fan

Finished Size: 12" wide.

Materials:
- ❑ 50 yds. each of white, dk. blue and lt. blue 1"-wide nylon craft ribbon *(or 2 yds. each netting cut into 1"-wide strips and sew end-to-end)*
- ❑ Sewing thread
- ❑ Sewing and tapestry needles
- ❑ G hook or hook needed to obtain gauge

Gauge: 1 shell = 1"; 3 shell rows = 2¼".

Basic Stitches: Ch, sl st, sc, hdc, dc.

Special Stitch: For **shell**, (2 hdc, ch 2, 2 hdc) in next ch sp.

Fan
Note: *Hold two strands of craft ribbon together as one throughout.*

Row 1: With white, ch 6, sl st in first ch to form ring, ch 1, 6 sc in ring, turn. *(6 sc made)*

Row 2: Ch 1, sc in first st, 2 sc in each of next 4 sts, sc in last st, turn. *(10)*

Row 3: Ch 1, sc in first st, 2 sc in next st, (sc in next st, 2 sc in next st) 3 times, sc in last 2 sts, turn. *(14)*

Row 4: Ch 1, sc in first st, (2 sc in next st, sc in next st) 6 times, sc in last st, turn. *(20)*

Row 5: Ch 2 *(counts as first hdc)*, *(sc, ch 2, sc) in next st, skip next st; repeat from * 8 more times, hdc in last st, turn. *(9 ch sps, 2 hdc)*

Rows 6–7: Ch 2, **shell** *(see Special Stitch)* in first ch sp, shell in each ch sp across, hdc in last st, turn. *(9 shells, 2 hdc)*

Row 8: Ch 4 *(counts as first hdc and ch-2 sp)*, (shell, ch 2) 9 times, hdc in last st, turn.

Row 9: Ch 4, skip first ch sp, shell in next shell, (ch 3, skip next ch sp, shell in next shell) 8 times, ch 2, skip last ch sp, hdc in last st, turn.

Row 10: Ch 3 *(counts as first dc)*, skip next ch sp, (3 hdc, ch 2, 3 hdc) in next shell, *ch 2, skip next ch sp, (3 hdc, ch 2, 3 hdc) in next shell; repeat from * 7 more times, dc in last st, turn. Fasten off. *(54 hdc, 2 dc, 17 ch sps)*

Rnd 11: For **Edging**, hold one strand each of dk. blue and lt. blue together as one, join with sc in first st of first shell, sc in next 2 sts, 2 sc in next ch sp, skip next st, sc in next 2 sts, sc in next ch sp, (sc in next 2 sts, skip next st, 2 sc in next ch sp, skip next st, sc in next 2 sts) 8 times, sc in next ch sp, sc in next st; working in ends of rows, 2 sc in end of next 6 rows, sc in end of next 4 rows, 2 sc in ring, sc in end of next 4 rows, 2 sc in end of next 6 rows, join with sl st in first sc.

Row 12: Sl st in next 4 sts, (skip next 2 sts, 5 dc in next st, skip next 2 sts, sc next 2 sts tog) 7 times, skip next 2 sts, 5 dc in next st, skip next 2 sts, sl st in next 5 sts leaving remaining sts unworked. Fasten off.

Cut a 14" long strand each of dk. blue and lt. blue.

Hold two strands together as one, tie in bow, trim ends. With sewing needle and thread, sew bow to center bottom of row 1 over ring. ⚷

Potpourri Hat

Finished Size: 11" across.

Materials:
- ❑ 50 yds. each white, dk. blue and lt. blue 1"-wide nylon craft ribbon *(or 2 yds. each netting cut into 1"-wide strips and sew end-to-end)*
- ❑ Two 4½" white tulle circles
- ❑ Potpourri
- ❑ Sewing thread
- ❑ Sewing and tapestry needles
- ❑ G hook or hook needed to obtain gauge

Gauge: Rnds 1–2 = 2" across.

Basic Stitches: Ch, sl st, sc, hdc, dc.

Special Stitches: For **beginning shell (beg shell)**, sl st in next st, (sl st, ch 2, hdc, ch 2, 2 hdc) in first ch sp.
For **shell**, (2 hdc, ch 2, 2 hdc) in next ch sp.

Hat
Note: *Hold two strands of craft ribbon together as one throughout.*

Rnd 1: Starting at top, with white, ch 6, sl st in first ch to form ring, ch 1, 12 sc in ring, join with sl st in first sc. *(12 sc made)*

Rnd 2: Ch 1, 2 sc in each st around, join. *(24 sc)*

Rnd 3: Ch 1, sc in first st, 2 sc in next st, (sc in next st, 2 sc in next st) around, join. *(36 sc)*

Rnds 4–5: Ch 1, sc in each st around, join.

Rnd 6: For **Brim**, working in **back lps** *(see Stitch Guide)*, ch 2 *(counts as first hdc)*, hdc in next st, ch 2, (hdc in next 2 sts, ch 2) 17 times, join with sl st in top of first ch-2. *(18 ch sps)*

Rnds 7–9: Beg shell *(see Special Stitches)*, **shell** *(see Special Stitches)* in each ch sp around, join.

Rnd 10: Sl st in next st, (sl st, ch 2, hdc, ch 1, 2 hdc) in first ch sp, ch 1, *(2 hdc, ch 1, 2 hdc) in next shell, ch 1; repeat from * around, join. Fasten off. *(18 shells, 18 ch-1 sps)*

Rnd 11: Hold one strand each of dk. blue and lt. blue together as one, join with sc in last ch sp, sc in each st and each ch sp around, join with sl st in first sc. *(108 sc)*

Rnd 12: Ch 1, sc in first st, skip next 2 sts, 5 dc in next st, skip next 2 sts, (sc in next st, skip next 2 sts, 5 dc in next st, skip next 2 sts) around, join. Fasten off.

Bottom
Rnd 1: With white, ch 6, sl st in first ch to form ring, ch 1, 12 sc in ring, join with sl st in first sc. *(12 sc made)*

Rnd 2: Ch 1, 2 sc in each st around, join. *(24 sc)*

Rnd 3: Ch 1, sc in first st, 2 sc in next st, (sc in next st, 2 sc in next st) around, join. Fasten off. *(36 sc)*

Finishing

1: For **Bag**, hold two 4½" tulle circles together, with sewing needle and thread, sew around outer edge allowing ¼" seam, leaving opening for turning. Turn right side out. Place enough potpourri inside bag so top of Hat will stand up. Sew opening closed.

2: With white craft ribbon and tapestry needle, sew Bottom to wrong side of rnd 4 with Bag between.

3: For **Band**, hold one strand each of dk. blue and lt. blue together as one, leaving 10" end, working in **front lps** on rnd 5, join with sl st in first st, sl st in each st around, join with sl st in first sl st, leaving 10" end. Fasten off. Tie ends in bow ☞

Tissue Box Cover

Finished Size: Fits boutique tissue box.

Materials:
- ❑ 50 yds. each of white, dk. blue and lt. blue 1"-wide nylon craft ribbon *(or 2 yds. each netting cut into 1"-wide strips and sew end-to-end)*
- ❑ Sewing thread
- ❑ Sewing and tapestry needles
- ❑ G hook or hook needed to obtain gauge

Gauge: 6 dc = 2"; 2 dc rows = 1¼"; 1 shell = 1"; 3 shell rows = 2¼".

Basic Stitches: Ch, sl st, sc, hdc, dc.

Special Stitches: For **beginning shell (beg shell)**, sl st in next st, (sl st, ch 3, dc, ch 2, 2 dc) in first ch sp.

For **shell**, (2 dc, ch 2, 2 dc) in next ch sp.

Cover

Note: Hold two strands of craft ribbon together as one throughout.

Rnd 1: With white, ch 20, sl st in first ch to form ring, ch 3 *(counts as first dc)*, dc in next 3 chs, (dc, ch 2, dc) in next ch, *dc in next 4 chs, (dc, ch 2, dc) in next ch; repeat from * 2 more times, join with sl st in top of ch-3. *(24 dc, 4 ch sps made)*

Rnd 2: Ch 3, dc in next 4 sts, (dc, ch 2, dc) in next ch sp, *dc in next 6 sts, (dc, ch 2, dc) in next ch sp; repeat from * 2 more times, dc in last st, join. *(32 dc, 4 ch sps)*

Rnd 3: Ch 3, dc in next 5 sts, (dc, ch 2, dc) in next ch sp, *dc in next 8 sts, (dc, ch 2, dc) in next ch sp; repeat from * 2 more times, dc in last 2 sts, join. *(40 dc, 4 ch sps)*

Rnd 4: Working in **back lps** *(see Stitch Guide)*, ch 3, dc in each st and in each ch around, join. *(48 dc)*

Rnd 5: Ch 3, dc in next 3 sts, ch 2, (dc in next 4 sts, ch 2) around, join. *(12 ch sps)*

Rnd 6: Sl st in next 3 sts, (sl st, ch 3, dc, ch 2, 2 dc) in first ch sp, **shell** *(see Special Stitches)* in each ch sp around, join.

Rnds 7–10: Beg shell *(see Special Stitches)*, shell in ch sp of each shell around, join.

Rnd 11: Beg shell, ch 1, (shell, ch 1) around, join. Fasten off.

Rnd 12: Hold one strand dk. blue and one strand lt. blue together as one, join with sc in last ch sp made, sc in each st and in each ch sp around, join with sl st in first sc. *(72 sc)*

Rnd 13: (Ch 3, 4 dc) in first st, skip next 2 sts, sc in next st, skip next 2 sts, (5 dc in next st, skip next 2 sts, sc in next st, skip next 2 sts) around, join with sl st in top of ch-3. Fasten off.

For **Trim**, hold one strand each of white and dk. blue together as one, working in **front lps** on rnd 3, join with sl st in any st, sl st in each st and in each ch around, join with sl st in first sl st. Fasten off.

For **Opening Trim**, hold one strand each of white and dk. blue together as one, working in remaining lps on opposite side of starting ch on rnd 1, join with sc in any ch; for **reverse sc** *(see Stitch Guide)*, working from left to right, insert hook in next st to the right, complete as sc; reverse sc in each ch around, join with sl st in first sc. Fasten off.

Cut four strands each 10" long dk. blue and four lt. blue. Hold all eight strands together as one. Tie in bow. Trim ends. With sewing needle and thread, sew bow to one side of Cover. ☞

Tissue Roll Cover

Finished Size: Fits standard size tissue roll.

Materials:
- ❑ 50 yds. each of white, dk. blue and lt. blue 1"-wide nylon craft ribbon *(or 2 yds. each netting cut into 1"-wide strips and sew end-to-end)*
- ❑ G hook or hook needed to obtain gauge

Gauge: Rnds 1–2 = 3" across.

Basic Stitches: Ch, sl st, sc, dc.

Special Stitches: For **beginning shell (beg shell)**, sl st in next st, (sl st, ch 3, dc, ch 2, 2 dc) in first ch sp.

For **shell**, (2 dc, ch 2, 2 dc) in next ch sp.

Cover

Note: Hold two strands of craft ribbon together as one throughout.

Rnd 1: With white, ch 6, sl st in first ch to form ring, ch 3 *(counts as first dc)*, 11 dc in ring, join with sl st in top of ch-3. *(12 dc made)*

continued on page 102

Shells 'n' Bows

continued from page 101

Rnd 2: (Ch 3, dc) in first st, 2 dc in each st around, join. *(24 dc)*

Rnd 3: Ch 3, 2 dc in next st, (dc in next st, 2 dc in next st) around, join. *(36 dc)*

Rnd 4: Working in **back lps** *(see Stitch Guide),* ch 3, dc in each st around, join.

Rnd 5: Ch 3, dc in next st, (ch 2, dc in next 4 sts) 8 times, ch 2, dc in last 2 sts, join. *(9 ch sps, 36 dc)*

Rnd 6: Beg shell *(see Special Stitches),* *skip next 4 sts, **shell** *(see Special Stitches)* in next ch sp; repeat from * 7 more times, skip last 2 sts, join. *(9 shells)*

Rnds 7–9: Beg shell, shell in ch sp of each shell around, join.

Rnd 10: Beg shell, ch 1, (shell, ch 1) around, join. Fasten off.

Rnd 11: Hold one strand each of dk. blue and lt. blue together as one, join with sc in last ch sp made, sc in each st and in each ch sp around, join with sl st in first sc. *(54 sc)*

Rnd 12: Ch 1, sc in first st, skip next 2 sts, 5 dc in next st, skip next 2 sts, (sc in next st, skip next 2 sts, 5 dc in next st, skip next 2 sts) around, join. Fasten off.

Fold last 2 rnds up.

Cut two strands each 10" long from dk. blue and two strands lt. blue. Hold all four strands together as one. Tie in bow. Trim ends. Tie separate strand of ribbon around center of all bows. Tie bow to center of rnd 1 on Cover.

Cameo Bath Set

continued from page 97

Rnd 1: With H hook and blue yarn, ch 11, dc in fourth ch from hook, dc in next 3 chs, hdc in next 3 chs, 3 sc in end ch; working on opposite side of ch, hdc in next 3 chs, dc in next 3 chs, 4 dc in next ch, join with sl st in top of ch-3. *(21 sts made)*

Rnd 2: Ch 3, (2 dc in next st, dc in next st) 2 times, 2 dc in next st, hdc in next 3 sts, 3 sc in next st, hdc in next 3 sts, (2 dc in next st, dc in next st) 3 times, 2 dc in next st, 3 dc in last st, join. *(32 sts)*

Rnd 3: Ch 1, sc in first 3 sts, 2 sc in next st, (sc in next 3 sts, 2 sc in next st) around, join with sl st in first sc. *(40)*

Rnd 4: Ch 1, sc in first 4 sts, hdc in next st, (dc in next st, 2 dc in next st) 2 times, dc in next st, hdc in next 2 sts, sc in next 5 sts, 2 sc in next st, sc in next 5 sts, hdc in next 2 sts, (dc in next st, 2 dc in next st) 2 times, dc in next st, hdc in next st, sc in next 4 sts, (2 sc in next st, sc in next st) 2 times, 2 sc in last st, join. *(48)*

Rnd 5: Repeat rnd 3. *(60)*

Rnd 6: Ch 1, sc in first 5 sts, 2 sc in next st, (sc in next 5 sts, 2 sc in next st) 2 times, hdc in next 2 sts, dc in next st, 2 dc in next st, hdc in next st, sc in next 4 sts, hdc in next st, 2 dc in next st, dc in next st, hdc in next 2 sts, sc in next 3 sts, 2 sc in next st, (sc in next 5 sts, 2 sc in next st) around, join. *(70)*

Rnd 7: Ch 1, sc in first 6 sts, 2 sc in next st, (sc in next 6 sts, 2 sc in next st) 2 times, sc in next 4 sts, (sc, ch 1, sc) in next st, sc in next 6 sts, (sc, ch 1, sc) in next st, sc in next 8 sts, 2 sc in next st, (sc in next 6 sts, 2 sc in next st) 2 times, sc in next 4 sts, (sc, hdc) in next st, dc in next st, 2 dc in next st, dc in next st, hdc in next st, sc in last 5 sts, join. *(80 sts, 2 ch sps)*

Rnd 8: Ch 1, sc in first 4 sts, 2 sc in next st, (sc in next 9 sts, 2 sc in next st) 2 times, hdc in next 2 sts, dc in next 2 sts, (dc, ch 2, dc) in next ch sp, dc in next 8 sts, (dc, ch 2, dc) in next ch sp, dc in next 2 sts, hdc in next 2 sts, sc in next st, 2 sc in next st, (sc in next 9 sts, 2 sc in next st) 3 times, sc in last 7 sts, join. *(91 sts, 2 ch sps)*

Rnds 9–10: Ch 1, sc around with (sc, ch 2, sc) in each ch sp, join. *(95 sts, 99 sts)*

Rnd 11: Ch 1, *sc across to 2 sts before next ch sp, sc next 2 sts tog, (sc, ch 2, sc) in ch sp, sc next 2 sts tog; repeat from *, sc around, join.

Rnd 12: Ch 1, sc in first 4 sts, 2 sc in next st, (sc in next 8 sts, 2 sc in next st) 3 times, hdc in next 2 sts, sc in next st, (sc, ch 2, sc) in next ch sp, sc next 2 sts tog, sc in next 10 sts, sc next 2 sts tog, (sc, ch 2 sc) in next ch sp, (sc in next 8 sts, 2 sc in next st) 4 times, hdc in next 9 sts, sc in last 5 sts, join. *(109)*

Rnd 13: Repeat rnd 11.

Rnd 14: Ch 1, sc in first 3 sts, 2 sc in next st, (sc in next 9 sts, 2 sc in next st) 3 times, sc in next 4 sts, sc next 2 sts tog, (sc, ch 2, sc) in next ch sp, sc next 2 sts tog, sc in next 10 sts, sc next 2 sts tog, (sc, ch 2, sc) in next ch sp, sc next 2 sts tog, sc in next 5 sts, 2 sc in next st, (sc in next 9 sts, 2 sc in next st) 4 times, sc in last 7 sts, join. *(118)*

Rnds 15–16: Repeat rnd 11.

Rnd 17: Ch 1, sc in first 18 sts, hdc in next 2 sts, dc in next 23 sts, hdc in next st, (hdc, ch 2, hdc) in next ch sp, hdc in next 14 sts, (hdc, ch 2, hdc) in next ch sp, hdc in next st, dc in next 23 sts, hdc in next 2 sts, sc in next 22 sts, hdc in next 2 sts, dc in next 3 sts, 2 dc in each of next 2 sts, dc in next 3 sts, hdc in last 2 sts, join. *(124)*

Rnd 18: Ch 1, sc in first 25 sts, hdc in next 2 sts, dc in next 18 sts, (hdc, ch 2, hdc) in next ch sp, hdc in next 16 sts, (hdc, ch 2, hdc) in next ch sp, dc in next 18 sts, hdc in next 2 sts, sc

around, join. *(128)*

Rnd 19: Ch 1, sc in first 36 sts, hdc in next st, dc in next 9 sts, (dc, ch 2, dc) in next ch sp, hdc in next 18 sts, (dc, ch 2, dc) in next ch sp, **mark last dc made,** dc in next 9 sts, hdc in next st, sc around, join. Fasten off. *(132)*

Rnd 20: For **border,** join gold yarn with sc in marked st, (2 sc in next st, sc in next 5 sts) 18 times, sc in next 3 sts, (sc, ch 1, sc) in next ch sp, sc in next 20 sts, (sc, ch 1, sc) in next ch sp, join. *(156 sts and chs)*

Rnd 21: Working in **front lps** *(see Stitch Guide)* of sts and chs, ch 1, sc in first st, skip next st, 5 dc in next st, skip next st, (sc in next st, skip next st, 5 dc in next st, skip next st) around, join.

Rnd 22: Working behind last rnd in **back lps** of sts and chs on rnd before last, sl st in first st, ch 1, sc in each st around, join.

Row 23: Working in **both lps,** ch 1, sc in first 132 sts leaving last 24 sts unworked, **turn.** *(132 sts)*

Row 24: Ch 1, sc in each st across, turn.

Row 25: Ch 1, sc in first 9 sts, sc next 2 sts tog, (sc in next 9 sts, sc next 2 sts tog) across, turn. *(120)*

Row 26: Ch 4, dc in next st, (ch 1, skip next st, dc in next st) across. Fasten off.

For **Tie,** with H hook and gold yarn, ch to measure 56", sc in 2nd ch from hook, sc in each ch across. Fasten off. Weave through row 26.

Cameo

With G hook and off-white sport yarn, make Basic Cameo on pages 103 and 104; sew centered on rnds 1–18.

Tissue Purse

Note: Do not join or turn unless otherwise stated. Mark first st of each rnd.

Rnd 1: With H hook and blue yarn, ch 2, 6 sc in second ch from hook. *(6 sc made)*

Rnd 2: 2 sc in each st around. *(12)*

Rnd 3: (Sc in next st, 2 sc in next st) around. *(18)*

Rnd 4: (Sc in next 2 sts, 2 sc in next st) around. *(24)*

Rnd 5: Sc in first st, 2 sc in next st, (sc in next 3 sts, 2 sc in next st) around, end with sc in last 2 sts. *(30)*

Rnd 6: Sc in each st around.

Rnd 7: (2 sc in next st, sc in next 4 sts) around. *(36)*

Rnd 8: (Sc in next 5 sts, 2 sc in next st) around. *(42)*

Rnd 9: Sc in first 3 sts, 2 sc in next st, (sc in next 6 sts, 2 sc in next st) around, end with sc in last 3 sts. *(48)*

Rnd 10: (Sc in next 7 sts, 2 sc in next st) around. *(54)*

Rnd 11: Working this rnd in **back lps,** sc in each st around.

Rnds 12–27: Sc in each st around.

Rnd 28: (Sc in next 7 sts, sc next 2 sts tog) around. *(48)*

Rnds 29–30: Sc in each st around.

Rnd 31: (Sc in next 10 sts, sc next 2 sts tog) around. *(44)*

Rnds 32–34: Sc in each st around; at end of rnd 34, sl st in next st.

Rnd 35: Ch 3, dc in next st, (ch 1, skip next st, dc in next st) around, join with sl st in top of ch-3.

Rnd 36: Ch 1, sc in each st and in each ch around. *(44)*

Rnd 37: (Sc in next 10 sts, 2 sc in next st) around. *(48)*

Rnd 38: (Sc in next 5 sts, 2 sc in next st) around. *(56)*

Rnds 39–41: Sc in each st around. At end of rnd 41, sl st in next st. Fasten off.

Rnd 42: Join gold yarn with sc in first st, sc in each st around, join with sl st in next st.

Rnd 43: Ch 1, sc in first st, skip next st, 5 dc in next st, skip next st, (sc in next st, skip next st, 5 dc in next st, skip next st) around, join. Fasten off.

For **Tie,** with H hook and blue yarn, ch to measure 24", sc in second ch from hook, sc in each ch across. Fasten off. Weave through rnd 35.

Cameo

With No. 4 steel hook and size 10 crochet cotton, make Basic Cameo below; sew over rnds 13–34 centered under ends of Tie.

Basic Cameo

Row 1: Beginning at neck, ch 22, sc in second ch from hook, sc in each ch across, turn. *(21 sc made)*

Row 2: Ch 1, sc in each st across, turn.

Rows 3–4: Ch 1, skip first st, sc in each st across to last 2 sts, sc last 2 sts tog, turn. *(19, 17)*

Rows 5–6: Ch 1, sc in each st across to last 2 sts, sc last 2 sts tog, turn. *(16, 15)*

Row 7: Ch 1, sc in each st across with 2 sc in last st, turn. *(16)*

Row 8: Ch 1, sc in each st across, turn.

Row 9: Ch 1, skip first st, sc in each st across with 2 sc in last st, turn.

Row 10: Ch 1, 2 sc in first st, sc in each st across, turn. *(17)*

Row 11: Ch 1, sc in each st across, ch 9 for **chin,** turn. *(26 sts and chs)*

Row 12: Sc in second ch from hook and in next 7 chs, sc in each st across, turn. *(25 sc)*

Row 13: Ch 1, sc in each st across with 2 sc in last st, turn. *(26)*

Rows 14–15: Ch 1, sc in each st across, turn.

Row 16: Repeat row 9.

Rows 17–18: Ch 1, 2 sc in first st, sc in each st across, turn. *(27, 28)*

Row 19: Ch 1, 2 sc in first st, sc in each st across with 2 sc in last st, turn. *(30)*

Row 20: Ch 1, sc in each st across with 2 sc in last st, ch 4 for **back of head,** turn. *(35 sts and chs)*

Row 21: Sc in second ch from hook and in next 2 chs, sc in each st across to last 2 sts, leave last 2 sc unworked for **bottom lip,** ch 3 for **top**

continued on page 104

Cameo Bath Set

continued from page 103

lip, turn. *(35 sts and chs)*

Row 22: Sc in second ch from hook and in next ch, sc in each st across with 2 sc in last st, turn. *(35 sc)*

Row 23: Repeat row 5. *(34)*

Row 24: Ch 1, sc in each st across with 2 sc in last st, turn. *(35)*

Row 25: Ch 1, sc in each st across with 2 sc in last st, ch 3, turn. *(39 sts and chs)*

Row 26: Repeat row 22. *(39 sc)*

Row 27: Ch 1, sc in each st across, turn.

Row 28: Ch 1, skip first st, sc in each st across, ch 3, turn. *(41 sts and chs)*

Row 29: Sc in second ch from hook and in next ch, sc across to last 2 sts, sc last 2 sts tog, turn. *(39 sc)*

Row 30: Ch 1, skip first st, sc in each st across, turn. *(38)*

Row 31: Ch 1, 2 sc in first st, sc in each st across, turn. *(39)*

Row 32: Repeat row 30. *(38)*

Rows 33–34: Ch 1, sc in each st across, turn.

Row 35: Ch 1, sc in each st across with 2 sc in last st, turn. *(39)*

Row 36: Ch 1, 2 sc in first st, sc in each st across, turn. *(40)*

Row 37: Repeat row 35. *(41)*

Rows 38–40: Ch 1, sc in each st across, turn.

Row 41: Repeat row 25. *(45 sts and chs)*

Row 42: Sc in second ch from hook, sc in next ch, sc in each st across, turn. *(44 sc)*

Row 43: Repeat row 36. *(45)*

Rows 44–46: Ch 1, sc in each st across, turn.

Row 47: Repeat row 30. *(44)*

Rows 48–49: Ch 1, skip first st, sc across to last 2 sts, sc last 2 sts tog, turn. *(42, 40)*

Row 50: Ch 1, skip first st, sc in next 35 sts, sc next 2 sts tog, sl st in next st, skip last st, turn. *(36 sc)*

Row 51: Ch 1, skip sl st, sc in next 33 sts, sc next 2 sts tog, sl st in next st, turn. *(34 sc)*

Row 52: Ch 1, skip sl st, sc in next 30 sts, sc next 2 sts tog, sl st in next st, skip last st, turn. *(31 sc)*

Row 53: Ch 1, skip sl st, sc in next 20 sts, sc next 2 sts tog, sl st in next st, skip last 8 sts, turn. *(21 sc)*

Row 54: Ch 1, skip sl st, sc in next 17 sts, sc next 2 sts tog, sl st in next st, skip last 2 sts, turn. *(18 sc)*

Row 55: Ch 1, sc in each st across, turn.

Rows 56–58: Repeat row 3. *(16, 14, 12)* At end of last row, leave a long strand for sewing and fasten off. ⚷

Kid's Stuff

Where does it say that only grown-ups get the good stuff? Certainly not here! We've chosen clowns and kitties, accents and accessories to please even the most choosy child! Dress up the little darling's domain with their own favorite colors, so they'll be extra appreciative to know that you made these creative, kid-pleasing projects especially with them in mind! And while you're at it, why not make up a few extras to keep in reserves? After all, these fast-and-fun favorites make perfect presents for the new babies that the stork is bringing, too!

Sparkler Rug

by Kathleen Garen

Finished Size: 30½" across.

Materials:
- ❑ Worsted yarn:
  - 22 oz. tan
  - 15½ oz. red
  - 15½ oz. white
  - 7 oz. blue
- ❑ H and J hooks or hook needed to obtain gauge

Gauge: J hook, with 2 strands held together, 3 sc = 1"; 7 sc rows = 2½".

Basic Stitches: Ch, sl st, sc.

Backing
Notes: Work in continuous rnds. Do not join or turn unless otherwise stated. Mark first st of each rnd.

Work in **back lps** *(see Stitch Guide) unless otherwise stated.*

Use 2 strands tan held together throughout.

Rnd 1: With J hook, ch 2, 8 sc in second ch from hook. *(8 sc made)*

Rnd 2: 2 sc in each st around. *(16)*

Rnd 3: Sc in first st; for **increase (inc), 2 sc in next st;** (sc in next st, inc) around. *(24)*

Rnd 4: (Sc in next 2 sts, inc) around. *(32)*

Rnds 5–35: (Sc in each st around to inc, sc in first st of inc, inc) around. At end of last rnd *(280)*.

Rnd 36: Sc in each st around to last 4 sts, sl st in next st leaving last 3 sts unworked. Fasten off.

Front
Starting at center of rnd 1, working in **front lps,** with H hook and single strand blue, join with sc in first st; for **ch lp, (ch 6, sc in next st)** around; ch 6, sc in first st of next rnd, ch lp around; *for **strip,** ch lp in sts of rnd 3 and in increase sts down to edge of Backing and back up to rnd 3; repeat from * around, join with sl st in first st of rnd 3. Fasten off.

Working in rows in sections between strips from rnd 4 to rnd 36, with H hook and single strand, alternating white and red, ch lp each section.

Tassel (make 8)
Cut 50 strands blue each 12" long; tie separate 12" strand around center of all strands held together leaving ends for tying *(see Stitch Guide).* Fold strands in half, tie separate strand around all strands 1½" from fold.

Tie one Tassel to end of each blue strip around Rug.

Happy Hangers

by Cynthia Harris

Basic Hanger

Caution: Use discretion when making toys with parts which could be swallowed or are sharp or otherwise potentially harmful for small children.

Note: Use the following basic instructions as specified in each individual Hanger.

Head Side (make 2)

Row 1: Ch 11, sc in second ch from hook, sc in each ch across, turn. *(10 sc made)*

Rows 2–8: Ch 1, 2 sc in first st, sc in each st across to last st, 2 sc in last st, turn. At end of last row *(24).*

Rows 9–17: Ch 1, sc in each st across, turn.

Rows 18–24: Ch 1, sc first 2 sts tog, sc in each st across to last 2 sts, sc last 2 sts tog, turn. At end of last row, **do not turn.** *(10)*

Rnd 25: Working around outer edge, ch 1, sc in end of each row and in each st around, join with sl st in first sc. Fasten off.

Frame

1: Cut plastic hanger according to cutting illustration.

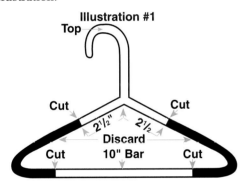

Illustration #1

2: Using crocheted Head Side as pattern, cut two pieces cardboard.

3: Holding both cardboard pieces together, using paper punch, punch holes ¼" from outer edge and ½" apart around edge.

4: With two strands of white yarn, whip-stitch pieces together through holes with plastic hanger between according to assembly illustration.

Illustration #2

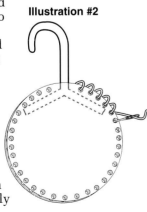

Hanger Bar

Row 1: Ch 41, sc in second ch from hook, sc in each ch across, turn. *(40 sc made)*

Rows 2–8: Ch 1, sc in each st across, turn. At end of last row, fasten off.

Neck

Row 1: Ch 29, sc in second ch from hook, sc in each ch across, turn. *(28 sc made)*

Rows 2–4: Ch 1, sc in each st across, turn. At end of last row, fasten off.

Assembly

1: Hold Head Sides together with row 24 at top and cardboard between with hook at top. Sew together, stuffing lightly between one Side and cardboard before closing for front.

2: Sew ends of rows together on each end of Hanger Bar. Insert 10" plastic bar in Hanger Bar. Sew first and last rows tog, stuffing lightly before closing.

3: Fold Neck in half crosswise. Sew ends of rows together. Sew row 1 to bottom of Head. Sew last row centered to Hanger Bar, stuffing before closing. ⌇

Cow Hanger

Finished Size: 10" tall including hook; 6½" across Head.

Materials:
- ❑ Worsted yarn:
  - 3 oz. white
  - 1 oz. each black and peach
  - Small amount each red, green and yellow
- ❑ Small amount each black, white and red felt
- ❑ Polyester fiberfill
- ❑ 2 pieces 7"-square cardboard
- ❑ Hot glue or craft glue
- ❑ Small saw
- ❑ Paper punch
- ❑ Child's tubular plastic clothes hanger
- ❑ Tapestry needle
- ❑ G hook or hook needed to obtain gauge

Gauge: 4 sc = 1"; 4 sc rows = 1".

Basic Stitches: Ch, sl st, sc, hdc, dc.

Hanger

With white, work Basic Hanger.

Horn (make 2)

Note: *Work in continuous rnds. Do not join or turn unless otherwise stated. Mark first st of each rnd.*

Rnd 1: Starting at tip, with peach, ch 2, 4 sc in second ch from hook. *(4 sc made)*

Rnd 2: Sc in each st around.

Rnd 3: (Sc in next st, 2 sc in next st) around. *(6)*

Rnd 4: Sc in each st around.

Rnd 5: (2 sc in next st, sc in next 2 sts) around. *(8)*

continued on page 116

Stork Wall Art

by Michele Wilcox

Finished Size: Stork is 27" tall.

Materials:
- ❏ 4-ply cotton yarn:
    - 5¼ oz. white
    - 1¾ oz. yellow
    - Small amount black
    - Small amount blue
- ❏ Sheet 7-mesh plastic canvas
- ❏ 2" plastic canvas circle
- ❏ Two 1" plastic rings
- ❏ Polyester fiberfill
- ❏ Tapestry needle
- ❏ G hook or hook needed to obtain gauge

Gauge: 4 sc = 1"; 4 sc rows = 1".

Basic Stitches: Ch, sl st, sc, hdc, dc.

Body Side (make 2)
Row 1: With white, ch 16, sc in second ch from hook, sc in each ch across, turn. *(15 sc made)*

Rows 2–13: Ch 1, 2 sc in first st, sc in each st across with 2 sc in last st, turn. *(Last row will have 39 sts.)*

Rows 14–24: Ch 1, sc in each st across, turn.

Row 25: Ch 1, sc in each st across to last 2 sts, sc last 2 sts tog, turn. *(38)*

Row 26: Ch 1, sc first 2 sts tog, sc in each st across, turn. *(37)*

Rows 27–28: Repeat rows 25 and 26. *(36, 35)*

Row 29: For **Tail,** ch 1, sc in first 10 sts, sc next 2 sts tog leaving remaining 23 sts unworked, turn. *(11)*

Row 30: Ch 1, sc first 2 sts tog, sc in last 9 sts, turn. *(10)*

Row 31: Ch 1, sc in first 8 sts, sc last 2 sts tog, turn. *(9)*

Row 32: Ch 1, sc first 2 sts tog, sc in last 7 sts, turn. *(8)*

Rows 33–34: Ch 1, sc first 2 sts tog, sc in each st across to last 2 sts, sc last 2 sts tog, turn. At end of last row, fasten off. *(6, 4)*

Row 29: Skip next 9 unworked sts on row 28; for **Neck,** join white with sc in next st, sc in last 13 sts, turn. *(14)*

Row 30: Ch 1, sc first 2 sts tog, sc in each st across to last 2 sts, sc last 2 sts tog, turn. *(12)*

Row 31: Ch 1, sc in each st across, turn.

Row 32: Ch 1, sc first 2 sts tog, sc in each st across to last 2 sts, sc last 2 sts tog, turn. *(10)*

Rows 33–46: Ch 1, sc in each st across, turn.

Rows 47–48: For **Head,** ch 1, 2 sc in first st, sc in each st across with 2 sc in last st, turn. *(12, 14)*

Rows 49–53: Ch 1, sc in each st across, turn.

Rows 54–57: Ch 1, sc first 2 sts tog, sc in each st across to last 2 sts, sc last 2 sts tog, turn. *(Last row will have 6 sts.)*

Rnd 58: Working around outer edge, ch 1, sc in each st and in end of each row around, join with sl st in first sc. Fasten off.

Using one crochet Body as pattern, cut piece from plastic canvas ¼" smaller than crochet piece.

Matching sts, hold Body Sides together with plastic canvas between, working in **back lps** *(see Stitch Guide),* join white with sl st in any st on rnd 58, sl st in each st around, stuffing on one side of canvas only before closing, join with sl st in first sl st. Fasten off.

Leg (make 2)
Notes: *Work in continuous rnds; do not join or turn unless otherwise stated. Mark first st of each rnd.*

When changing colors (see Stitch Guide), drop first color to wrong side of work. Always change colors in last st made. Fasten off dropped color when no longer needed.

Rnd 1: Starting at top, with white, ch 12, sl st in first ch to form ring, ch 1, sc in each ch around. *(12 sc made)*

Rnds 2–4: Sc in each st around.

Rnd 5: (Sc in next st, sc next 2 sts tog) around changing to yellow in last st made *(see Notes).* *(8)*

Rnds 6–23: Sc in each st around. Stuff firmly. Continue stuffing as you work.

Rnd 24: For **Knee,** 2 sc in each st around. *(16)*

Rnds 25–26: Sc in each st around.

Rnd 27: (Sc next 2 sts tog) around. *(8) (Knee completed)*

Rnds 28–46: Sc in each st around. At end of last rnd, join with sl st in first sc. Fasten off.

Foot (make 2)
Rnd 1: Starting at back, with yellow, ch 2, 6 sc in second ch from hook, **do not join,** continue working in rnds. *(6 sc made)*

Rnds 2–7: Sc in each st around.

Rnd 8: 2 sc in each st around. *(12)*

Rnd 9: (Sc in next st, 2 sc in next st) around. *(18)*

Rnd 10: For **First Toe,** sc in next 6 sts leaving last 12 sts unworked, **do not join,** continue working in rnds. Stuff. Continue stuffing as you work. *(6)*

Rnds 11–14: Sc in next 6 sts. At end of last rnd, join with sl st in first sc. Fasten off. Sew opening closed.

Rnd 10: For **Second Toe,** join yellow with sc in next unworked st on rnd 9, sc in next 2 sts, skip next 6 sts, sc in next 3 sts, **do not join,**

continued on page 115

Kitty Caddy

by Dawn Kemp

Finished Size: 17½" tall.

Materials:
- ❏ Worsted yarn:
    - 10 oz. lt. blue
    - 1 oz. pink
    - Small amount each med. blue, rose and white
- ❏ 4 oz. white bulky yarn
- ❏ Lt. blue, white and brown six-strand embroidery floss
- ❏ 22" of 1⅜" ribbon
- ❏ 54" of ⅜" ribbon
- ❏ Sewing thread to match
- ❏ 12" Styrofoam® cone
- ❏ 5⅞" Styrofoam® disc
- ❏ Craft glue
- ❏ Polyester fiberfill
- ❏ Sewing, embroider and tapestry needles
- ❏ F, G, H, I and J hooks or hooks needed to obtain gauges

Gauges: F hook and worsted yarn, 9 sc = 2"; 9 sc rows = 2". **H hook and bulky yarn,** 7 sc = 2"; 7 sc rows = 2". **I hook and 2 strands worsted yarn held tog,** 3 sc rows = 1"; 3 dc = 1"; 3 dc rows = 2".

Basic Stitches: Ch, sl st, sc, hdc, dc.

Notes: Center bottom of cone over disc, glue in place. Let dry.

Work in continuous rnds. Do not join unless otherwise stated. Mark first st of each rnd.

Head

Rnd 1: Starting at **top,** with H hook and white bulky, ch 2, 8 sc in second ch from hook. *(8 sc made)*

Rnd 2: 2 sc in each st around. *(16)*

Rnd 3: (Sc in next st, 2 sc in next st) around. *(24)*

Rnd 4: (Sc in next 2 sts, 2 sc in next st) around. *(32)*

Rnd 5: (Sc in next 3 sts, 2 sc in next st) around. *(40)*

Rnds 6–16: Sc in each st around.

Rnd 17: (Sc in next 3 sts, sc next 2 sts tog) around. *(32)*

Rnds 18–19: (Sc in next 2 sts, sc next 2 sts tog) around. At end of last rnd, fasten off. *(24, 18)*

Muzzle

Row 1: With H hook and white bulky, ch 12, sc in second ch from hook, sc in each ch across, turn. *(11 sc made)*

Rows 2–4: Ch 1, 2 sc in first st, sc in each st across to last st, 2 sc in last st, turn. At end of last row *(17).*

Rows 5–9: Ch 1, sc in each st across, turn.

Row 10: Sc first 2 sts tog, sc in each st across to last 2 sts, sc last 2 sts tog. Fasten off. *(15)*

Sew over rnds 11–17 of Head, stuffing before closing.

Facial Features

With rose, using satin stitch *(see Stitch Guide),* embroider nose over rows 8–9 of Muzzle as shown in photo. Using straight stitch *(see Stitch Guide),* embroider mouth over rows 5–7.

With med. blue, using satin stitch, embroider eyes above nose over rnds 9–10 of Head 1½" apart *(see photo).*

With white floss, using french knot *(see Stitch Guide),* embroider sparkle in each eye; with brown and straight stitch, embroider eyebrows and eyelashes according to photo; with lt. blue and straight stitch, embroider whiskers.

Outer Ear (make 2)

Rnd 1: With H hook and white bulky, ch 2, 6 sc in second ch from hook. *(6 sc made)* Front of rnd 1 is right side of work.

Rnd 2: 2 sc in each st around. *(12)*

Row 3: Working in rows, sc in each st across, turn.

Row 4: Sc in first 5 sts, (sc, hdc, sc) in next st, sc in next 5 sts, sl st in last st. Fasten off. *(13 sts)*

Inner Ear (make 2)

Rnds 1–3: With G hook and pink, repeat rnds 1–3 of Outer Ear. Fasten off.

Sew wrong side to right side of row 3 on Outer Ear. Sew over rnds 5–9 of Head 3½" apart.

Curls (make 2)

For **first curl,** with J hook and pink, leaving 4" end, ch 7; *working in **back lps** (see Stitch Guide), 3 sc in second ch from hook, 3 sc in each ch across; sl st in same ch as last sc*; for **second curl,** ch 9; repeat between first and second *; for **third curl,** ch 9; repeat between first and second *. Leaving 4" for sewing, fasten off.

Sew over rnds 1–3 on front of Head. Tie 1⅜" ribbon in bow, sew behind Curls.

Body

Rnd 1: For **dress,** with I hook and 2 strands lt. blue held tog, join with sl st in first st on rnd 19 of Head, ch 3, dc in each st around, join with sl st in top of ch-3. *(18 dc made)*

Rnd 2: Ch 3, dc in next 4 sts, 2 dc in next st, (dc *continued on page 114*

continued on page 114

Kitty Caddy
continued from page 113

in next 5 sts, 2 dc in next st) around, join. *(21)*

Rnd 3: Ch 3, dc in next st, 2 dc in next st, (dc in next 2 sts, 2 dc in next st) around, join. *(28)*

Rnd 4: Ch 3, dc in next 12 sts, 2 dc in next st, dc in next 13 sts, 2 dc in last st, join. *(30)*

Rnd 5: Ch 3, dc in next st, 2 dc in next st, (dc in next 2 sts, 2 dc in next st) around, join. *(40)*

Rnd 6: Ch 3, dc in next 18 sts, 2 dc in next st, dc in next 19 sts, 2 dc in last st, join. *(42)*

Rnd 7: Ch 3, dc in next 19 sts, 2 dc in next st, dc in next 20 sts, 2 dc in last st, join. *(44)*

Rnds 8–9: Ch 3, dc in each st around, join.

Rnd 10: Ch 3, dc in next 2 sts, (2 dc in next st, dc in next 3 sts) around to last st, 2 dc in last st, join. *(55)*

Rnds 11–18: Ch 3, dc in each st around, join. At end of last rnd, **turn.**

Rnd 19: For **pocket,** working in **back lps,** ch 3, (2 dc in next st, dc in next st) around, join. *(82)*

Rnd 20: Working in **back lps,** ch 3, dc in each st around, join.

Rnds 21–23: Ch 3, dc in each st around, join. At end of last rnd, fasten off.

Rnd 24: For **pocket trim,** with F hook and white worsted, join with (sc, ch 3, sc) in first st, skip next st, *(sc, ch 3, sc) in next st, skip next st; repeat from * around, join with sl st in first sc. Fasten off.

Rnd 25: For **bottom ruffle,** working in remaining **front lps** of rnd 19, with F hook and white worsted, join with (sl st, ch 3, 2 dc) in first st, 3 dc in each st around, join with sl st in top of ch-3. *(246)*

Rnd 26: Ch 1, (sc, ch 3, sc) in first st, skip next st, *(sc, ch 3, sc) in next st, skip next st; repeat from * around, join. Fasten off.

Dividing pocket into six equal sections, tack rnd 23 to rnd 14. Cut six pieces ⅜" ribbon each 9" long. Tie each piece in bow, sew to pockets where tacked.

Arm (make 2)
Rnd 1: For **hand,** with H hook and white bulky, ch 2, 6 sc in second ch from hook, join with sl st in first sc. *(6 sc made)*

Rnd 2: Ch 1, 2 sc in each st around, join. *(12)*

Rnds 3–6: Ch 1, sc in each st around, join. At end of last rnd, fasten off.

Rnd 7: For **arm,** working in **back lps,** with I hook and 2 strands lt. blue held tog, join with sl st in first st, ch 3, dc in each st around, join with sl st in top of ch-3. *(12 dc)*

Rnd 8: Ch 3, 2 dc in next st, (dc in next st, 2 dc in next st) around, join. *(18)*

Rnds 9–10: Ch 3, dc in each st around, join.

Rnd 11: Ch 3, dc in next st, dc next 2 sts tog, (dc in next 2 sts, dc next 2 sts tog) 3 times, dc in last 2 sts, join. *(14)*

Rnds 12–14: Ch 3, dc in each st around, join. At end of last rnd, fasten off.

Rnd 15: For **ruffle,** working in **front lps** of rnd 6, with H hook and white worsted, join with sl st in first st, ch 3, 2 dc in same st, 3 dc in each st around, join. Fasten off. *(36)*

Rnd 16: For **ruffle trim,** repeat rnd 24 of Body. Stuff lightly.

Flatten rnd 14, sew to rnd 2 on side of Body.

Heart Pocket
Rnd 1: With F hook and pink, ch 2, 6 sc in second ch from hook. *(6 sc made)*

Rnd 2: 2 sc in each st around. *(12)*

Rnd 3: (Sc in next st, 2 sc in next st) around. *(18)*

Rnd 4: Sc in next 2 sts, 3 sc in next st, sc in next st, sl st in next st, sc in next st, 3 sc in next st, sc in next 6 sts, 3 sc in next st, sc in last 4 sts. *(24 sts)*

Rnd 5: Sc in next 2 sts, 2 sc in each of next 3 sts, hdc in next st, sl st in next sl st, hdc in next st, 2 sc in each of next 3 sts, sc in next 7 sts, (sc, hdc, sc) in next st, sc in last 5 sts, join with sl st in first sc. Fasten off. *(32)*

Sew to center front of dress leaving top unsewn.

Collar
Row 1: With I hook and 2 strands lt. blue held together, ch 28, sc in second ch from hook, sc in each ch across, turn. *(27 sc made)*

Row 2: (Ch 3, 2 dc) in first st, 3 dc in each st across, turn. *(81 dc)*

Row 3: Ch 3, (dc in next st, 2 dc in next st) across, turn. *(121)*

Row 4: Ch 3, dc in each st across, turn. Fasten off.

Row 5: For **trim,** with F hook and white worsted, join with (sc, ch 3, sc) in first st, *skip next st, (sc, ch 3, sc) in next st; repeat from * across. Fasten off.

Place around neck, sew ends of rows 1–5 together. Sew row 1 of Collar to rnd 1 of Dress. Insert cone in Body.

Bottom Cover
Rnd 1: With I hook and 2 strands lt. blue held tog, ch 2, 8 sc in second ch from hook. *(8 sc made)*

Rnd 2: 2 sc in each st around. *(16)*

Rnd 3: (2 sc in next st, sc in next st) around. *(24)*

Rnd 4: (2 sc in next st, sc in next 2 sts) around. *(32)*

Rnd 5: Sc in each st around.

Rnd 6: (2 sc in next st, sc in next 3 sts) around. *(40)*

Rnd 7: (2 sc in next st, sc in next 4 sts) around. *(48)*

Rnd 8: (2 sc in next st, sc in next 5 sts) around. *(56)*

Rnd 9: (2 sc in next st, sc in next 6 sts) around. *(64)*

Rnd 10: (2 sc in next st, sc in next 7 sts) around, join with sl st in first sc. Fasten off. *(72)*

Hold over bottom of disc; sew to rnd 19 on Body.

continue working in rnds. *(6)*

Rnds 11–14: Sc in next 6 sts. At end of last rnd, join with sl st in first sc. Fasten off. Sew opening closed.

Rnd 10: For **Third Toe,** join yellow with sc in next unworked st on rnd 9, sc in last 5 sts, **do not join,** continue working in rnds. *(6)*

Rnds 11–14: Sc in next 6 sts. At end of last rnd, join with sl st in first sc. Fasten off. Sew opening closed.

Sew opening between each Toe closed.

Sew center of each Foot to bottom of each Leg. Flatten top of each Leg and sew flattened edge centered to bottom of Body. Cross one Leg at Knee, tack in place to secure *(see photo).*

Wing Side *(make 2)*

Row 1: Starting at top, with white, ch 21, sc in second ch from hook, sc in each ch across, turn. *(20 sc made)*

Row 2: Ch 1, sc in each st across to last 2 sts, sc last 2 sts tog, turn. *(19)*

Row 3: Ch 1, sc first 2 sts tog, sc in each st across, turn. *(18)*

Rows 4–7: Repeat rows 2 and 3 alternately. *(Last row will have 14 sts.)*

Rows 8–11: Ch 1, sc first 2 sts tog, sc in each st across to last 2 sts, sc last 2 sts tog, turn. *(Last row will have 6 sts.)*

Rnd 12: Working around outer edge, ch 1, sc in each st and in end of each row around, join with sl st in first sc. Fasten off.

Matching sts, hold Wing Sides together; working in **back lps** *(see Stitch Guide),* join white with sl st in any st on rnd 12, sl st in each st around, stuffing before closing, join with sl st in first sl st. Fasten off.

Center and sew Wing to front of Body.

Beak Side *(make 2)*

Row 1: Starting at tip, with yellow, ch 2, 3 sc in second ch from hook, turn. *(3 sc made)*

Row 2: Ch 1, 2 sc in first st, sc in each st across with 2 sc in last st, turn. *(5)*

Row 3: Ch 1, sc in each st across, turn.

Rows 4–7: Repeat rows 2 and 3 alternately. *(Last row will have 9 sts.)*

Rows 8–10: Ch 1, sc in each st across, turn.

Rnd 11: Working around outer edge, ch 1, sc in each st and in end of each row around with 3 sc in each corner, join with sl st in first sc. Fasten off.

Matching sts, hold Beak Sides together; working in **back lps,** skip first 9 sts on rnd 11 at wide end of piece, join yellow with sl st in next st, sl st in each st across to other end of rnd 11 at wide end of piece. Fasten off.

Stuff and sew Beak to Head over rows 47–55 *(see photo).*

With black, embroider satin stitch *(see Stitch Guide)* over rows 52–54 on stuffed side of Body about ¾" from edge of Beak for eye *(see photo).*

Hat

Rnd 1: With blue, ch 2, 6 sc in second ch from hook, **do not join,** continue working in rnds. *(6 sc made)*

Rnd 2: 2 sc in each st around. *(12)*

Rnd 3: (Sc in next st, 2 sc in next st) around. *(18)*

Rnd 4: (Sc in next 2 sts, 2 sc in next st) around. *(24)*

Rnd 5: (Sc in next 3 sts, 2 sc in next st) around. *(30)*

Rnd 6: Working in **back lps,** sc in each st around.

Rnds 7–9: Working in **both lps,** sc in each st around.

Rnd 10: Sc in each st around changing to black in last st made, sc in each st around.

Rnds 11–12: Sc in each st around. At end of last rnd, join with sl st in first sc. Fasten off.

Brim

Row 1: With blue, ch 5, sc in second ch from hook, sc in next 2 chs, 3 sc in last ch; working in remaining lps on opposite side of starting ch, sc in next 3 chs, turn. *(9 sc made)*

Row 2: Ch 1, sc in first 3 sts, 2 sc in each of next 3 sts, sc in last 3 sts, turn. *(12)*

Row 3: Ch 1, sc in first 4 sts, 2 sc in each of next 4 sts, sc in last 4 sts, turn. *(16)*

Row 4: Ch 1, sc in first 6 sts, 2 sc in each of next 4 sts, sc in last 6 sts. Fasten off. *(20)*

Sew straight edge on Brim to last rnd on Hat. Insert plastic canvas circle inside Hat. Tack center st on row 2 of Brim to center front on rnd 7 of Hat; push front and sides of Hat down over Brim. Stuff. Sew Hat on top of Head.

Sling

Row 1: With white, ch 2, 3 sc in second ch from hook, turn. *(3 sc made)*

Rows 2–4: Ch 1, 2 sc in first st, sc in each st across with 2 sc in last st, turn. *(5, 7, 9)*

Rows 5–8: Ch 1, sc in each st across, turn.

Rows 9–11: Ch 1, sc first 2 sts tog, sc in each across to last 2 sts, sc last 2 sts tog, turn. *(7, 5, 3)*

Rows 12–19: Ch 1, sc in each st across, turn.

Row 20: Ch 1, 2 sc in first st, sc in each st across with 2 sc in last st, turn. *(5)*

Rows 21–46: Repeat rows 19 and 20 alternately. *(Last row will have 31 sts.)*

Rows 47–81: Ch 1, sc in each st across, turn.

Row 82: Ch 1, sc first 2 sts tog, sc in each st across to last 2 sts, sc last 2 sts tog, turn. *(29)*

Row 83: Ch 1, sc in each st across, turn.

Rows 84–109: Repeat rows 82 and 83 alternately. *(Last row will have 3 sts.)*

Rows 110–116: Ch 1, sc in each st across, turn.

Rows 117–119: Ch 1, 2 sc in first st, sc in each st across with 2 sc in last st, turn. *(5, 7, 9)*

Rows 120–123: Ch 1, sc in each st across, turn.

Rows 124–126: Ch 1, sc first 2 sts tog, sc in each st across to last 2 sts, sc last 2 sts tog, turn. *(7, 5, 3)*

Row 127: Ch 1, sc first 3 sts tog, turn. *(1)*

Rnd 128: Working around outer edge, ch 1, sc in each st, in end of each row around with 3 sc in each point, join with sl st in first sc. Fasten

continued on page 116

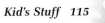

Stork Wall Art

continued from page 115

off. Tie narrow sections at ends together in a knot *(see photo)*.

Heart

Row 1: With blue, ch 2, 3 sc in second ch from hook, turn. *(3 sc made)*

Row 2: Ch 1, sc in first st, 2 sc in next st, sc in last st, turn. *(4)*

Row 3: Ch 1, 2 sc in first st, sc in each st across with 2 sc in last st, turn. *(6)*

Row 4: Ch 1, sc in each st across, turn.

Rows 5–6: Ch 1, 2 sc in first st, sc in each st across with 2 sc in last st, turn. *(8, 10)*

Row 7: Ch 1, sc in each st across, turn.

Row 8: Ch 1, 2 sc in first st, sc in each st across with 2 sc in last st, turn. *(12)*

Row 9: Ch 1, sc in each st across, turn.

Rnd 10: Working around outer edge, ch 1, sc in first st, (hdc, dc) in next st, 2 dc in next st, hdc in next st, sl st in next 2 sts, hdc in next st, dc in next st, 2 dc in next st, (dc, hdc) in next st, sc in last st; working in ends of rows, skip first row, sc in end of next 8 rows, 3 sc in opposite side of ch-2 on row 1, sc in end of next 8 rows, join with sl st in first sc. Fasten off.

Sew Heart to one side of Sling leaving top edge unsewn *(see photo)*.

Sew one plastic ring to back of Sling just below knot. Sew other plastic ring to center back of Stork's Head directly below Hat. ☞

Happy Hangers

continued from page 109

Rnd 6: (Sc in next 3 sts, 2 sc in next st) around. *(10)*

Rnd 7: (2 sc in next st, sc in next 4 sts) around. *(12)*

Rnd 8: (Sc in next 5 sts, 2 sc in next st) around. *(14)*

Rnd 9: Sc in each st around, join with sl st in first sc. Fasten off. Stuff.

Sew to top of Head 2½" apart. Curve tips inward slightly.

Ear (make 2)

Row 1: With white, ch 4, sc in second ch from hook, sc in each ch across, turn. *(3 sc made)*

Row 2: Ch 1, sc in each st across, turn.

Row 3: Ch 1, 2 sc in first st, sc in next st, 2 sc in last st, turn. *(5)*

Rows 4–5: Ch 1, sc in each st across, turn.

Row 6: Ch 1, 2 sc in first st, sc in each st across to last st, 2 sc in last st, turn. *(7)*

Rows 7–9: Ch 1, sc in each st across, turn.

Row 10: Ch 1, sc first 2 sts tog, sc in each st across to last 2 sts, sc last 2 sts tog, turn. *(5)*

Row 11: Ch 1, sc in each st across, turn.

Row 12: Ch 1, sc first 2 sts tog, sc in each st across to last 2 sts, sc last 2 sts tog, turn. *(3)*

Rnd 13: Working around outer edge, ch 1, sc in each st and in end of each row around, join with sl st in first sc. Fasten off.

Sew to sides of Head ¼" below each Horn.

Muzzle

Row 1: Starting at top, with peach, ch 13, sc in second ch from hook, sc in each ch across, turn. *(12 sc made)*

Rows 2–3: Ch 1, 2 sc in first st, sc in each st across to last st, 2 sc in last st, turn. *(14, 16)*

Rows 4–7: Ch 1, sc in each st across, turn.

Rows 8–9: Ch 1, sc first 2 sts tog, sc in each st across to last 2 sts, sc last 2 sts tog, turn. *(14, 12)*

Rnd 10: Working around outer edge, ch 1, sc in each st and in end of each row around, join with sl st in first sc. Fasten off.

Sew centered over rows 5–12 on front of Head, stuffing before closing.

Mouth

Row 1: With peach, ch 5, sc in second ch from hook, sc in each ch across, turn. *(4 sc made)*

Rnd 2: Working around outer edge, ch 1, 2 sc in first st, sc in next 2 sts, 2 sc in last st; working in remaining lps on opposite side of starting ch, 2 sc in first ch, sc in next 2 chs, 2 sc in last ch, join with sl st in first sc. Fasten off.

Sew center 3 sts centered to bottom of Muzzle *(see photo)*.

Patch No. 1

Row 1: With black, ch 5, sc in second ch from hook, sc in each ch across, turn. *(4 sc made)*

Row 2: Ch 1, 2 sc in first st, sc in each st across to last st, 2 sc in last st, ch 3, turn. *(6 sc, 3 chs)*

Row 3: Sc in second ch from hook, sc in next ch, sc in each st across, turn. *(8)*

Row 4: Ch 1, sc in each st across, turn.

Row 5: Ch 1, sc first 2 sts tog, sc in each st across, ch 3, turn. *(7 sc, 3 chs)*

Row 6: Sc in second ch from hook, sc in next ch, sc in each st across, turn. *(9)*

Row 7: Ch 1, sc first 2 sts tog, sc in next 5 sts, sc last 2 sts tog, turn. *(7)*

Row 8: Ch 1, sc in first 6 sts leaving last st unworked, turn. *(6)*

Row 9: Ch 1, sc in first 4 sts leaving last 2 sts unworked. Fasten off. *(4)*

Patch No. 2

Row 1: With black, ch 3, sc in second ch from hook, sc in last ch, turn. *(2 sc made)*

Row 2: Ch 1, 2 sc in first st, sc in last st, turn. *(3)*

Row 3: Ch 1, sc in first 2 sts, 2 sc in last st, turn. *(4)*

Rows 4–5: Ch 1, 2 sc in first st, sc in each st across to last st, 2 sc in last st, turn. *(6, 8)*

Row 6: Ch 1, sc first 2 sts tog, sc in each st across to last st, 2 sc in last st, turn.

Row 7: Ch 1, sc in first 4 sts, (sc next 2 sts tog) 2 times, turn. *(6)*

Row 8: Ch 1, sc first 2 sts tog, (sc next 2 sts tog) 2 times. Fasten off. *(3)*

Patch No. 3

Row 1: With black, ch 2, 2 sc in second ch from hook, turn. *(2 sc made)*

Row 2: Ch 1, sc in each st across, turn.

Row 3: Ch 1, 2 sc in each st across, turn. *(4)*

Row 4: Ch 1, sc in each st across, turn.

Row 5: Ch 1, 2 sc in first st, sc in each st across, turn. *(5)*

Row 6: Ch 1, sc in each st across to last st, 2 sc in last st, turn. *(6)*

Row 7: Ch 1, sc in each st across to last 2 sts, sc last 2 sts tog, turn. *(5)*

Row 8: Ch 1, sc first 2 sts tog, sc in each st across, turn. *(4)*

Row 9: Ch 1, sc in each st across to last st, 2 sc in last st, turn. *(5)*

Row 10: Ch 1, 2 sc in first st, sc in each st across, turn. *(6)*

Row 11: Ch 1, sc first 2 sts tog, sc in each st across. Fasten off. *(5)*

Patch No. 4

Row 1: With black, ch 3, sc in second ch from hook, sc in last ch, turn. *(2 sc made)*

Row 2: Ch 1, 2 sc in each st across, turn. *(4)*

Row 3: Ch 1, 2 sc in first st, sc in each st across, turn. *(5)*

Row 4: Ch 1, sc in each st across to last st, 2 sc in last st, turn. *(6)*

Row 5: Ch 1, sc in first 4 sts leaving last 2 sts unworked, turn. *(4)*

Row 6: Ch 1, sc in first 2 sts, sc last 2 sts tog. *(3)*

Row 7: Ch 1, sc first 2 sts tog, sc in last st. Fasten off. *(2)*

Patch No. 5

Row 1: With black, ch 6, sc in second ch from hook, sc in each ch across, turn. *(5 sc made)*

Rows 2–3: Ch 1, 2 sc in first st, sc in each st across to last st, 2 sc in last st, turn. *(7, 9)*

Row 4: Ch 1, sc first 2 sts tog, sc in next 5 sts leaving last 2 sts unworked, turn. Fasten off. *(6)*

Flower

Rnd 1: With yellow, ch 2, 5 sc in second ch from hook, join with sl st in first sc. Fasten off. *(5 sc made)*

Rnd 2: For **petals,** join red with sl st in any st, (ch 3, 3 dc, ch 3, sl st) in same st as first sl st, (sl st, ch 3, 3 dc, ch 3, sl st) in each of next 4 sts, join with sl st in first ch of first ch-3. Fasten off.

Leaf

With green, ch 6, dc in third ch from hook, 2 hdc in next ch, 2 sc in next ch, 3 sc in last ch; working in remaining lps on opposite side of starting ch, 2 sc in next ch, 2 hdc in next ch, 3 dc in last ch, join with sl st in top of ch-3. Fasten off.

Assembly

Sew Patches No. 1, 2 and 3, Flower and Leaf on face according to assembly illustration.

Sew Patch No. 4 on one side of Neck and Patch No. 5 over right side of Hanger Bar.

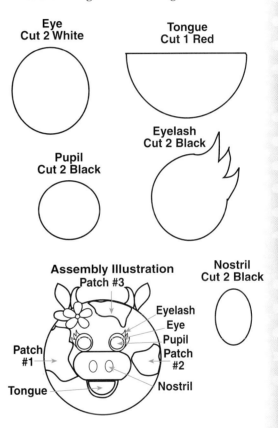

Eye
Cut 2 White

Tongue
Cut 1 Red

Eyelash
Cut 2 Black

Pupil
Cut 2 Black

Nostril
Cut 2 Black

Assembly Illustration
Patch #3

Eyelash
Eye
Pupil
Patch #2

Patch #1

Tongue

Nostril

Facial Features

From felt, trace and cut all pieces according to pattern pieces.

Glue eyelashes, eye and pupil pieces together according assembly illustration. Glue on front of Head above Muzzle ¾" apart.

Glue nostrils centered on Muzzle ½" apart.

Glue tongue centered on Mouth.

Lion Hanger

Finished Size: 10" tall including hook; 6½" across Head.

Materials:

❑ Worsted yarn:

    4 oz. yellow

    1 oz. each brown and orange

❑ Small amount each black, white and red felt

continued on page 118

continued from page 117

- ❑ Polyester fiberfill
- ❑ 2 pieces 7"-square cardboard
- ❑ 2" and 1¼"-squares cardboard
- ❑ Hot glue or craft glue
- ❑ Small saw
- ❑ Paper punch
- ❑ Child's tubular plastic clothes hanger
- ❑ Tapestry needle
- ❑ G and K hooks or hooks needed to obtain gauges

Gauges: G hook, 4 sc = 1"; 4 sc rows = 1". **K hook and 3 strands held tog,** 3 chs = 1".

Basic Stitches: Ch, sl st, sc.

Special Stitch: For **loop stitch (lp st—see illustration),** insert hook in st, wrap yarn 2 times around 2 fingers, insert hook from left to right through all lps on fingers, pull lps through st, drop lps from fingers, yo, pull through all lps on hook.

Hanger
With white, work Basic Hanger on page 109.

Ear Front (make 2)
Note: *Work in continuous rnds. Do not join or turn unless otherwise stated. Mark first st of each rnd.*
Rnd 1: With G hook and orange, ch 2, 6 sc in second ch from hook. *(6 sc made)*
Rnd 2: 2 sc in each st around. *(12)*
Rnd 3: (2 sc in first st, sc in next st) around, join with sl st in first sc. Fasten off. *(18)*

Ear Back (make 2)
Rnds 1–3: With G hook and yellow, repeat rnds 1–3 of Ear Front. At end of last rnd, **turn, do not fasten off.**
Rnd 4: With wrong side of one Ear Front and Ear Back tog, matching sts, working through both thicknesses, ch 1, sc in each st around, join with sl st in first sc. Fasten off.
Sew Ears to last rnd on back of Head 5½" apart at top.

Mane
With K hook and one strand each of yellow, brown and orange held tog, ch 61, 2 lp sts *(see Special Stitch)* in second ch from hook, 2 lps sts in each ch across. Fasten off.
With yellow, sew starting ch around last rnd on front of Head.

Nose
Wrap brown around 1¼" cardboard 30 times; slide lps off cardboard, tie separate 6" strand brown around center of all lps; cut lps. Trim ends. Sew centered on front of face.

Cheek (make 2)
Wrap yellow around 2" cardboard 60 times; slide lps off cardboard, tie separate 6" strand yellow around center of all lps; cut lps. Trim ends. Sew one on each side of Nose.

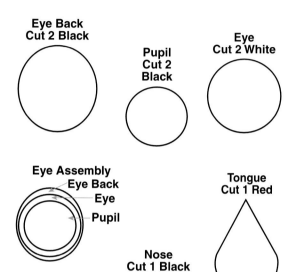

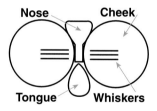

Facial Features
1: From felt, trace and cut all pieces according to pattern pieces.
2: Glue eye pieces together according to assembly illustration. Glue above Cheeks ¾" apart.
3: Glue tongue below Nose with tip pointing upward. 🗝

Clown Hanger
Finished Size: 10" tall including hook; 6½" across Head.
Materials:
- ❑ Worsted yarn:
  - 3 oz. white
  - 1 oz. each yellow, green and orange
  - Small amount each red and blue
- ❑ Small amount each black, red and green felt
- ❑ Polyester fiberfill

- ❏ 2 pieces 7"-square cardboard
- ❏ 2½"-square cardboard
- ❏ Hot glue or craft glue
- ❏ Small saw
- ❏ Paper punch
- ❏ Child's tubular plastic clothes hanger
- ❏ Tapestry needle
- ❏ G hook or hook needed to obtain gauge

Gauge: 4 sc = 1"; 4 sc rows = 1".

Basic Stitches: Ch, sl st, sc, hdc, dc, tr.

Hanger
With white, work Basic Hanger on page 109.

Ear (make 2)
Note: Work in continuous rnds. Do not join or turn unless otherwise stated. Mark first st of each rnd.

Rnd 1: With white, ch 2, 6 sc in second ch from hook. *(6 sc made)*

Rnd 2: 2 sc in each st around. *(12)*

Rnd 3: (2 sc in first st, sc in next st) around. *(18)*

Row 4: Fold in half, matching sts; working through both thicknesses, ch 1, sc in each st across. Fasten off.

Sew folded edge to side of Head 7½" apart.

Nose
Rnd 1: With red, ch 3, sl st in first ch to form ring, ch 1, 2 sc in each ch around. *(6 sc made)*

Rnd 2: 2 sc in each st around. *(12)*

Rnd 3: (2 sc in next st, sc in next st) around. *(18)*

Rnd 4: (2 sc in next st, sc in next 2 sts) around. *(24)*

Rnd 5: (2 sc in next st, sc in next 3 sts) around. *(30)*

Rnd 6: (Sc next 2 sts tog) around, join with sl st in first sc. Fasten off. Stuff. *(15)*

Sew to center of face.

Mouth
With yellow, ch 17, 3 dc in third ch from hook, dc in next 13 chs, (3 dc, ch 2, sl st) in last ch. Fasten off.

Sew below Nose according to facial assembly illustration.

Hair Piece (make 2)
Wrap blue around 2½" cardboard 12 times; slide lps off cardboard, tie separate strand blue around center of all lps. Tie to Head through sts above each Ear.

Bottom Ruffle
With green, ch 40, 3 tr in fourth ch from hook, 3 tr in each ch across to last ch, (3 tr, ch 3, sl st) in last ch. Fasten off.

Wrap around bottom of Neck, tack together in back.

Ruffle (make 1 yellow, 1 orange)
Ch 38, 3 dc in third ch from hook, 3 dc in each ch across to last ch, (3 dc, ch 2, sl st) in last ch. Fasten off.

Wrap yellow Ruffle around Neck above Bottom Ruffle, tack together in back. Repeat with orange Ruffle above yellow Ruffle.

Facial Features
1: From felt, trace and cut all pieces according to pattern pieces.

2: Glue eyebrows, eyes, smile and cheeks to front of face according to facial features illustration.

Eyebrow
Cut 2 Green

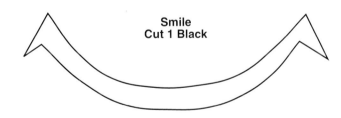

Smile
Cut 1 Black

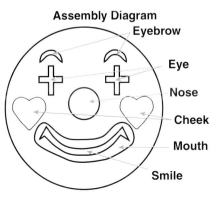

Assembly Diagram

- Eyebrow
- Eye
- Nose
- Cheek
- Mouth
- Smile

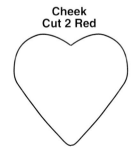

Cheek
Cut 2 Red

Eye
Cut 2 Black

Clown Nursery

by Estella Prudhomme

Doorstop With Balloons

Finished Size: 17" tall with Balloons.

Materials:
- ❑ Worsted yarn:
  - 8 oz. yellow
  - 3 oz. each blue, lt. pink and green
  - 2 oz. white
  - Small amount each black and dk. pink
- ❑ White six-strand embroidery floss
- ❑ 2-liter soft drink bottle
- ❑ 3"-square cardboard
- ❑ Sand or gravel
- ❑ Polyester fiberfill
- ❑ Craft glue
- ❑ Tapestry needle
- ❑ G hook or hook needed to obtain gauge

Gauge: 4 sc = 1"; 4 sc rows = 1".

Basic Stitches: Ch, sl st, sc, hdc, dc.

Note: Work in continuous rnds. Do not join unless otherwise stated. Mark first st of each rnd.

Clown
Rnd 1: Starting at head, with white, ch 2, 6 sc in second ch from hook. *(6 sc made)*
Rnd 2: 2 sc in each st around. *(12)*
Rnd 3: (Sc in next st, 2 sc in next st) around. *(18)*
Rnd 4: (Sc in next 2 sts, 2 sc in next st) around. *(24)*
Rnd 5: (Sc in next 3 sts, 2 sc in next st) around. *(30)*
Rnd 6: (Sc in next 4 sts, 2 sc in next st) around. *(36)*
Rnd 7: (Sc in next 5 sts, 2 sc in next st) around. *(42)*
Rnd 8: (Sc in next 6 sts, 2 sc in next st) around. *(48)*
Rnds 9–13: Sc in each st around.
Rnd 14: (Sc in next 6 sts, sc next 2 sts tog) around. *(42)*
Rnd 15: (Sc in next 5 sts, sc next 2 sts tog) around. *(36)*
Rnd 16: (Sc in next 4 sts, sc next 2 sts tog) around. *(30)*
Rnd 17: (Sc in next 3 sts, sc next 2 sts tog) around. *(24)*
Rnd 18: Sc in each st around.
Rnd 19: (Sc in next 2 sts, sc next 2 sts tog) around. *(18)*
Rnd 20: Sc in each st around.
Rnd 21: (Sc in next st, sc next 2 sts tog) around. *(12)*
Rnd 22: Sc in each st around.
Rnd 23: (Sc in next st, 2 sc in next st) around. *(18)*
Rnd 24: (Sc in next 2 sts, 2 sc in next st) around. *(24)*
Rnd 25: (Sc in next 3 sts, 2 sc in next st) around. Fasten off. *(30)*
Rnd 26: Working in **back lps** *(see Stitch Guide)*, join yellow with sc in first st, sc in next 3 sts, 2 sc in next st, (sc in next 4 sts, 2 sc in next st) around. *(36)*
Rnd 27: (Sc in next 5 sts, 2 sc in next st) around. *(42)*
Rnd 28: (Sc in next 6 sts, 2 sc in next st) around. *(48)*
Rnds 29–35: Sc in each st around. At end of last rnd, join with sl st in first sc.
Rnd 36: Working in **back lps,** ch 3, dc in each st around, join with sl st in top of ch-3. *(48 dc)*
Rnds 37–49: Ch 3, dc in each st around, join, **turn.**
Rnd 50: Working in **back lps,** ch 3, dc in each st around, join.
Rnd 51: Ch 3, dc in each st around, join.
Rnds 52–55: Working in **back lps,** ch 3, dc in each st around, join. At end of last rnd, fasten off.
Rnd 56: Working in **remaining lps** of rnd 51, join yellow with sc in any st, sc in each st around, join with sl st in first sc. Fasten off.
Rnd 57: Working in **remaining lps** of rnd 52, join blue with sl st in any st, (ch 3, 2 dc) in same st, 3 dc in each st around, join with sl st in top of ch-3.

Rnd 58: Ch 3, dc in each st around, join. Fasten off.
Rnd 59: With lt. pink, repeat rnd 57 working in **remaining lps** of rnd 53.
Rnd 60: Ch 3, dc in each st around, join. Fasten off.
Rnd 61: With green, repeat rnd 57 working in **remaining lps** of rnd 54.
Rnd 62: Ch 3, dc in each st around, join. Fasten off.
Rnd 63: With yellow, repeat rnd 57 working in **remaining lps** of rnd 55.
Rnd 64: Ch 3, dc in each st around, join. Fasten off.
Rnd 65: For **shirt trim,** with yellow, repeat rnd 57 working in **front lps** of rnd 35.
Rnd 66: Ch 3, dc in each st around, join. Fasten off.
Rnd 67: For **collar,** with yellow, repeat rnd 57 working in **front lps** of rnd 25. Fasten off.

Bottom
Rnd 1: With yellow, ch 6, sl st in first ch to form ring, ch 3, 12 dc in ring, join with sl st in top of ch-3. *(13 dc made)*
Rnd 2: Ch 3, 2 dc in each st around, join. *(25)*
Rnd 3: Ch 3, dc in each st around, join.
Rnd 4: Ch 3, 2 dc in each st around, join. Fasten off. *(49)*
Stuff head of Clown. Partially fill 2-liter bottle with sand or gravel, replace cap. Place bottle through rnds below neck, making sure neck of bottle is in neck of Clown.
Sew rnd 4 of Bottom to **front lps** of rnd 49 on inside of Clown.
Fold rnds 52–55 up forming a pocket around bottom of body and bringing ruffles to right side of work.

Nose
Rnd 1: With lt. pink, ch 2, 5 sc in second ch from hook. *(5 sc made)*
Rnd 2: 2 sc in each st around. *(10)*
Rnds 3–4: Sc in each st around. At end of last rnd, fasten off. Stuff.
Sew Nose to rnds 14–17 of head.

Mouth
With dk. pink, ch 12, 3 sc in second ch from hook, sc in each ch across to last ch, 6 sc in last ch; working in remaining lps on opposite side of starting ch, (sc in next 2 chs, 2 sc in next ch) 3 times, 2 sc in same ch as first 3 sc, join with sl st in first sc. Fasten off.
With black, using backstitch *(see Stitch Guide),* embroider across center of Mouth *(see photo).*
Sew to head centered below Nose.

Eyes
With black, using straight and fly stitches *(see Stitch Guide),* embroider eyelashes and eyebrows according to photo, with bottom of eyelashes on rnd 14 of head 1¾" apart.
With white floss, using french knot *(see Stitch Guide),* embroider eyes over bottom of eyelashes.

continued on page 122

Clown Nursery

continued from page 121

Arm (make 2)

Rnd 1: Starting at **hand,** with white, ch 2, 6 sc in second ch from hook. *(6 sc made)*

Rnd 2: 2 sc in each st around. *(12 sc)*

Rnd 3: (Sc in next st, 2 sc in next st) around. *(18)*

Rnds 4–5: Sc in each st around.

Rnd 6: (Sc in next st, sc next 2 sts tog) around. *(12)*

Rnd 7: Sc in each st around, join with sl st in first sc. Fasten off.

Rnd 8: Working in **back lps,** join yellow with sl st in any st, ch 3, dc in each st around, join with sl st in top of ch-3. *(12 dc)*

Rnds 9–12: Ch 1, sc in first 2 sts, hdc in next 2 sts, dc in next 4 sts, hdc in next 2 sts, sc in next 2 sts, join with sl st in first sc.

Rnd 13: Ch 3, 2 dc in next st, (dc in next st, 2 dc in next st) around, join. *(18)*

Rnds 14–15: Ch 3, dc in each st around, join. At end of last rnd, fasten off.

Rnd 16: Working in remaining **front lps** of rnd 7, join yellow with sl st in any st, (ch 3, 2 dc) in same st, 3 dc in each st around, join. Fasten off.

Sew Arms across rnds 26–35 on each side of body with sc sts on rnds 9–12 facing upward.

Hat

Rnd 1: With yellow, ch 43, sl st in first ch to form ring, ch 3, dc in each ch around, join with sl st in top of ch-3. *(43 dc made)*

Rnd 2: Ch 3, (dc in next 4 sts, dc next 2 sts tog) around, join. *(36)*

Rnd 3: Ch 3, (dc in next 3 sts, dc next 2 sts tog) around, join. *(29)*

Rnd 4: Ch 3, (dc in next 2 sts, dc next 2 sts tog) around, join. *(22)*

Rnd 5: Ch 3, dc in each st around, join.

Rnd 6: Ch 3, (dc in next st, dc next 2 sts tog) around, join. *(15)*

Rnd 7: Ch 3, dc in each st around, join.

Rnd 8: Ch 3, (dc next 2 sts tog) around, join. *(8)*

Rnd 9: Ch 3, (dc next 2 sts tog) around to last st, dc in last st, join. Fasten off. *(5)*

Rnd 10: Working in remaining lps on opposite side of starting ch on rnd 1, join yellow with sc in any ch, sc in each ch around, join. *(43)*

Rnd 11: (Ch 3, 2 dc) in first st, 3 dc in each st around, join.

Rnd 12: Ch 3, dc in each st around, join. Fasten off. Tack to top of head.

Balloon (make 4 each lt. pink, green & blue)

Rnd 1: Ch 2, 6 sc in second ch from hook. *(6 sc made)*

Rnd 2: 2 sc in each st around. *(12)*

Rnd 3: (Sc in next st, 2 sc in next st) around. *(18)*

Rnds 4–6: Sc in each st around.

Rnd 7: (Sc in next st, sc next 2 sts tog) around. *(12)*

Rnd 8: Sc in each st around.

Rnds 9–10: (Sc next 2 sts tog) around. *(6, 3)*

Rnd 11: Working in **front lps,** 2 sc in each st around. Fasten off. Stuff. *(6)*

Attach 9" matching strand of yarn to each Balloon. Sew or glue Balloons together according to photo, pull six strands through each hand of Clown. Trim ends even. Tack in place on Hat and hands.

Pom-Pom (make 3)

Wrap the following colors side-by-side on cardboard; 30 wraps blue, 30 wraps lt. pink, 30 wraps green. Slide yarn off cardboard, tie a separate 6" strand blue lightly around center of all lps; cut lps. Trim ends.

Sew one to top of Hat. Sew one to each side of head on rnd 13. ⚷

Caddy

Finished Size: 15½" tall without Hat.

Materials:
- ❏ Worsted yarn:
    - 8 oz. yellow
    - 4 oz. each blue, lt. pink and green
    - 2 oz. white
    - Small amount each black and dk. pink
- ❏ White six-strand embroidery floss
- ❏ Three 2-liter soft drink bottles *(type with black liners)*
- ❏ 3"-square cardboard
- ❏ Polyester fiberfill
- ❏ Tapestry needle
- ❏ G hook or hook needed to obtain gauge

Gauge: 4 sc = 1"; 4 sc rows = 1".

Basic Stitches: Ch, sl st, sc, hdc, dc.

Notes: Work in continuous rnds. Do not join unless otherwise stated. Mark first st of each rnd.

Clown

Rnds 1–35: Work rnds 1–35 of Clown from Doorstop on page 121. At end of last rnd, fasten off.

Cut top of one 2-liter bottle 4" from the top. Stuff head of Clown. Place top of bottle in Clown, making sure neck of Clown and neck of bottle match.

Rnd 36: Working in **back lps** of rnd 35, join yellow with sl st in any st, ch 3, dc in each st around, join.

Rnd 37: Ch 3, (dc next 2 sts tog) around to last st, dc in last st, join. *(25)*

Rnds 38–39: Ch 3, (dc next 2 sts tog) around, stuffing bottle before closing. At end of last rnd, fasten off. *(13, 7)*

Rnd 40: Working in **front lps** of rnd 35, join green with sl st in any st, (ch 3, 2 dc) in same st, 3 dc in each st around, join.

Rnd 41: Ch 3, dc in each st around, join. Fasten off.

Rnd 42: Working in **front lps** of rnd 25, join yellow with sl st in any st, (ch 3, 2 dc) in same st, 3 dc in each st around, join. Fasten off.

Nose, Mouth, Eyes, Arm, Hat & Pom-Pom

Work same as Nose, Mouth, Eyes, Arm, Hat and Pom-Pom from Doorstop on page 121.

Sew Arms to each side of Clown across rnds 27–33 with sc on rnds 9–12 facing inward.

Ball (optional—make 1 each lt. pink, green & blue)

Rnd 1: Ch 2, 6 sc in second ch from hook. *(6 sc made)*

Rnd 2: 2 sc in each st around. *(12)*

Rnds 3–6: Sc in each st around.

Rnd 7: (Sc next 2 sts tog) around. Leaving 4" end, fasten off. Stuff and sew opening closed.

Cut an 8" strand of white. Run one end of strand through each ball. Tack ends of strand to hands as shown.

Middle Box (not shown—make 1 with lt. pink ruffle, 1 with blue ruffle)

Rnd 1: With yellow, ch 6, sl st in first ch to form ring, ch 3, 12 dc in ring, join with sl st in top of ch-3. *(13 dc made)*

Rnd 2: Ch 3, 2 dc in each st around, join. *(25)*

Rnd 3: Ch 3, (dc in next st, 2 dc in next st) around, join. *(37)*

Rnd 4: Ch 3, (dc in next 2 sts, 2 dc in next st) around, join. *(49)*

Rnd 5: Working in **back lps,** ch 3, dc in each st around, join.

Rnds 6–8: Ch 3, dc in each st around, join.

Rnds 9–10: Working in **back lps,** ch 1, sc in each st around, join with sl st in first sc. At end of last rnd, fasten off.

Rnd 11: Working in remaining **front lps** of rnd 4, join ruffle color with sl st in any st, (ch 3, 2 dc) in same st, 3 dc in each st around, join.

Rnd 12: Ch 3, dc in each st around, join. Fasten off.

Rnd 13: Working in remaining **front lps** of rnd 8, join yellow with sl st in any st, sl st in each st around, join with sl st in first sl st. Fasten off.

Cut bottom from 2-liter bottle just above black inner liner, place inside Middle Box. Fold rnds 9–10 over top of Box to inside.

Bottom Box

Rnds 1–6: Repeat rnds 1–6 of Middle Box.

Rnd 7: Working in **back lps,** ch 3, dc in each st around, join.

Rnds 8–10: Ch 3, dc in each st around, join.

Rnds 11–12: Working in **back lps,** ch 1, sc in each st around, join. At end of last rnd, fasten off.

Rnd 13: Working in remaining **front lps** of rnd 6, join yellow with sl st in any st, (ch 3, 2 dc) in same st, 3 dc in each st around, join.

Rnd 14: Ch 3, dc in each st around, join. Fasten off.

Rnd 15: Working in remaining **front lps,** of rnd 11, join yellow with sl st in any st, sl st in each st around, join with sl st in first sl st. Fasten off.

Cut bottom from 2-liter bottle 1" above black liner, place inside Bottom Box. Fold rnds 11–12 over top of Box to inside.

Shoe (make 2)

Toe

Rnd 1: With green, ch 2, 6 sc in second ch from hook. *(6 sc made)*

Rnd 2: 2 sc in each st around. *(12)*

Rnd 3: (Sc in next st, 2 sc in next st) around. *(18)*

Rnd 4: Sc in each st around.

Rnd 5: (Sc in next 2 sts, 2 sc in next st) around. *(24)*

Rnds 6–7: Sc in each st around.

Rnd 8: (Sc in next 2 sts, sc next 2 sts tog) around. Fasten off. *(18)*

Sole

Rnd 1: With green, ch 13, dc in third ch from hook, 2 dc in same ch, dc in each ch across to last ch, 7 dc in last ch; working in remaining lps on opposite side of starting ch, dc in each ch across to last ch, 3 dc in last ch, join with sl st in top of ch-3. *(32 dc made)*

Rnd 2: For **toe end,** ch 3, 2 dc in each of next 3 sts, hdc in next st, sc in each st around to last 4 sts, hdc in next st, 2 dc in each of next 3 sts, join. Fasten off. *(38 sts)*

Stuff Toe of Sole. Sew to toe of Sole, tack portion of Sole behind Toe to bottom of Box.

Stack Caddy.

Doll

Finished Size: 15" tall without Hat.

Materials:
- ❑ Worsted yarn:
    - 8 oz. yellow
    - 2 oz. each white and green
    - 1 oz. each lt. pink and blue
    - Small amount each black and dk. pink
- ❑ White six-strand embroidery floss
- ❑ 3"-square cardboard
- ❑ Polyester fiberfill
- ❑ Tapestry needle
- ❑ G hook or hook needed to obtain gauge

Gauge: 4 sc = 1"; 4 sc rows = 1".

Basic Stitches: Ch, sl st, sc, hdc, dc.

Note: Work in continuous rnds. Do not join unless otherwise stated. Mark first st of each rnd.

Doll

Rnds 1–28: Work rnds 1–28 of Clown from Doorstop on page 121. At end of last rnd, join with sl st in first sc. Stuff.

Rnds 29–35: Ch 3, dc in each st around, join with sl st in top of ch-3.

Rnd 36: Working in **back lps,** ch 3, dc in each st around, join. Fasten off. Stuff. Flatten rnd 36 and sew closed.

Rnd 37: Working in remaining **front lps** of rnd 35; for **first leg,** join yellow with sl st in center st, ch 3, dc in next 23 sts leaving

continued on page 124

continued from page 123

remaining sts unworked, join. *(24 dc)*

Rnds 38–43: Ch 3, dc in each st around, join.

Rnds 44–47: Working in **back lps,** ch 1, sc in each st around, join. At end of last rnd, fasten off.

Rnd 48: Join green with sl st in any st, ch 3, dc in each st around, join. Fasten off.

Rnd 49: Working in remaining **front lps** of rnd 46, join yellow with sl st in any st, (ch 3, 2 dc) in same st, 3 dc in each st around, join. Fasten off.

Rnd 50: With blue, repeat rnd 49 working in remaining **front lps** of rnd 45.

Rnd 51: With lt. pink, repeat rnd 49 working in remaining **front lps** of rnd 44.

Rnd 52: With green, repeat rnd 49 working in remaining **front lps** of rnd 43. Stuff.

Rnd 53: Working in unworked **front lps** of rnd 35; for **second leg,** join yellow with sl st in first unworked st, ch 3, dc in each st around, join with sl st in top of ch-3. *(24 dc)*

Rnds 54–68: Repeat rnds 38–52 of first leg. At end of last rnd, fasten off.

Rnd 69: With yellow, repeat rnd 49, working in remaining **front lps** of rnd 25. **Do not fasten off.**

Rnd 70: Ch 3, dc in each st around, join. Fasten off.

Nose, Mouth & Eyes

Work same as Nose, Mouth and Eyes from Doorstop on page 121.

Arm (make 2)

Rnds 1–7: Work same as rnds 1–7 of Arm from Doorstop on page 122. At end of last rnd, **do not fasten off.**

Rnd 8: (Sc in next st, 2 sc in next st) around. Fasten off. *(18)*

Rnd 9: Working in **back lps,** join yellow with sc in first st, sc in each st around, join.

Rnds 10–12: Working in **back lps,** ch 1, sc in each st around, join.

Rnds 13–15: Ch 1, sc in first 2 sts, hdc in next 2 sts, dc in next 10 sts, hdc in next 2 sts, sc in last 2 sts, join.

Rnds 16–17: Ch 3, dc in each st around, join. At end of last rnd, fasten off.

Rnd 18: Working in remaining **front lps** of rnd 11, join green with sl st in any st, (ch 3, 2 dc) in same st, 3 dc in each st around, join. Fasten off.

Rnd 19: With lt. pink, repeat rnd 18 working in **remaining lps** of rnd 10.

Rnd 20: With blue, repeat rnd 18 working in **remaining lps** of rnd 9.

Rnd 21: With yellow, repeat rnd 18 working in **remaining lps** of rnd 8.

Stuff. Sew across rnds 27–31 on each side of body.

Shoe (make 2)

Work same as Shoe from Caddy on page 123.
Stuff Toe of Shoe. Sew to toe of Sole. Tack portion of Sole behind Toe to bottom of leg.

Hat

Rnd 1: With yellow, ch 43, sl st in first ch to form ring, ch 3, dc in each ch around, join with sl st in top of ch-3. *(43 dc made)*

Rnd 2: Ch 3, (dc in next 4 sts, dc next 2 sts tog) around, join. *(36)*

Rnd 3: Ch 3, (dc in next 3 sts, dc next 2 sts tog) around, join. *(29)*

Rnd 4: Ch 3, (dc in next 2 sts, dc next 2 sts tog) around, join. *(22)*

Rnd 5: Ch 3, dc in each st around, join.

Rnd 6: Ch 3, (dc in next st, dc next 2 sts tog) around, join. *(15)*

Rnd 7: Ch 3, dc in each st around, join.

Rnd 8: Ch 3, (dc next 2 sts tog) around, join. *(8)*

Rnd 9: Ch 3, (dc next 2 sts tog) around to last st, dc in last st, join. *(5)*

Rnd 10: Ch 3, (dc next 2 sts tog) around, join. Fasten off.

Rnd 11: Working in remaining lps on opposite side of starting ch on rnd 1, join yellow with sc in any ch, sc in each ch around, join. *(43)*

Rnd 12: (Ch 3, 2 dc) in first st, 3 dc in each st around, join.

Rnd 13: Ch 3, dc in each st around, join. Fasten off. Tack to top of head.

Pom-Pom (make 3)

Work same as Pom-pom from Doorstop on page 122. ⌐☞

Ripple Baby Afghan

Finished Size: 33" × 52".

Materials:
❑ Worsted yarn:
    10 oz. yellow
    4 oz. each green, lt. pink and blue
    2 oz. white
❑ G hook or hook needed to obtain gauge

Gauge: 4 dc = 1"; 6 dc rows = 1".

Basic Stitches: Ch, sl st, dc.

Note: Ch-3 is not used or counted as a stitch.

Afghan

Row 1: With yellow, ch 130, dc in third ch from hook, dc in next 4 chs, 3 dc in next ch, dc in next 5 chs, (skip next 2 chs, dc in next 5 chs, 3 dc in next ch, dc in next 5 chs) across, turn.

Rows 2–6: Ch 3, skip first st, dc in next 5 sts, 3 dc in next st, dc in next 5 sts, (skip next 2 sts, dc in next 5 sts, 3 dc in next st, dc in next 5 sts) across leaving last st unworked, turn.

Next Rows: Repeat row 2 working color sequence of (1 row of white, 2 rows each of green, lt. pink and blue, 1 row of white, 6 rows of yellow) 6 times.

Last Row: Sl st in each st across. Fasten off. ⌐☞

Holiday Home

*Christmas is my favorite time of year,
one that I look forward to all year long.
Therefore, it's my personal belief that it
is simply not possible to have too many
decorations in your holiday home!
I've chosen several of my all-time
favorites to include in this chapter,
almost a dozen projects in all!
Choose from pillows and potholders,
angels and afghans. There are wreaths
from rags and nutcrackers that are not!
So while visions of sugarplums may
dance in others' heads, you'll dream of
nothing but the delightful holiday decor
that you've found here!*

Cardinal Pillow

by Beth Mueller

Finished Size: 15" square.

Materials:

- ❑ Worsted yarn:
  - 7 oz. white
  - 1 oz. each dk. red, red and green
  - Small amount each lt. brown, med. brown and black
- ❑ 14" square pillow form
- ❑ ⅜" brown flat button
- ❑ White acrylic paint
- ❑ Round toothpick
- ❑ 64" of gold ¼" metallic rick-rack
- ❑ Brown and gold sewing thread
- ❑ Sewing and tapestry needles
- ❑ J hook or hook needed to obtain gauge

Gauge: 6 sc = 2"; 6 sc rows = 2".

Basic Stitches: Ch, sl st, sc.

Pillow Front

Row 1: With white, ch 42, sc in second ch from hook, sc in each ch across, turn. *(41 sc made)*

Rows 2–4: Ch 1, sc in each st across, turn.

Notes: *When **changing colors** (see Stitch Guide), drop first color to wrong side of work, pick up next color, always change colors in last st made.*

Use separate ball for each color section.

Each square on graph equals one sc.

Row 5: Ch 1, sc in first 3 sts changing to green *(see Notes)*, sc in next st changing to white, sc in next 33 sts changing to green, sc in next st changing to white, sc in last 3 sts, turn.

Rows 6–51: Ch 1, sc in each st across changing colors according to corresponding row on graph, turn. At end of last row, fasten off.

Pillow Back

Row 1: With white, ch 42, sc in second ch from hook, sc in each ch across, turn. *(41 sc made)*

Rows 2–51: Ch 1, sc in each st across, turn. At end of last row, fasten off.

Assembly

For **eye**, with sewing needle and brown thread, sew button to cardinal according to graph. Using white paint and toothpick, place a small dot at upper right-hand side on button.

Cut four 16" pieces from rick-rack. With sewing needle and gold thread, sew rick-rack to Front according to graph.

Hold Front and Back wrong sides together, with Front facing you; working through both thicknesses, join white with sc in first st on row 51, sc in each st and in end of every other row around with 3 sc in each corner inserting pillow form before closing, join with sl st in first sc. Fasten off. ⚿

Yarn:

☐ = White	■ = Forest Green	**Placements:**
■ = Cardinal	▨ = Warm Brown	◯ = Eye
■ = Country Red	■ = Mid Brown	▭ = Rick-Rack
	☐ = Black	

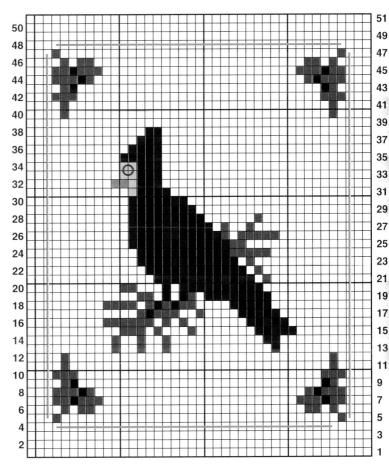

Rag Wreaths

by Tammy Kreimeyer

Large Wreath

Finished Size: 12" across.

Materials:
- ❑ Cotton fabric:
    - 2¾ yds. main color (MC)
    - 1¾ yds. contrasting color (CC)
- ❑ 12" Styrofoam® wreath
- ❑ Tapestry needle
- ❑ J hook or hook needed to obtain gauge

Gauge: 2 sc = 1"; 3 sc rows = 2".

Basic Stitches: Ch, sc.

Note: Tear or cut fabric into 2" strips.

Large Wreath

Row 1: With MC, ch 15, sc in second ch from hook, sc in each ch across, turn. *(14 sc made)*

Row 2: Ch 1, sc in each st across, turn.

Rows 3–12: Ch 1, sc in each st across, turn. At end of last row, fasten off.

Row 13: Join CC with sc in first st, sc in each st across, turn.

Rows 14–18: Ch 1, sc in each st across, turn. At end of last row, fasten off.

Row 19: Join MC with sc in first st, sc in each st across, turn.

Rows 20–30: Ch 1, sc in each st across, turn. At end of last row, fasten off.

Row 31: Join CC with sc in first st, sc in each st across, turn.

Rows 32–36: Ch 1, sc in each st across, turn. At end of last row, fasten off.

Row 37: Join MC with sc in first st, sc in each st across, turn.

Rows 38–48: Ch 1, sc in each st across, turn. At end of last row, fasten off.

Row 49: Join CC with sc in first st, sc in each st across, turn.

Rows 50–54: Ch 1, sc in each st across, turn. At end of last row, fasten off.

Row 55: Join MC with sc in first st, sc in each st across, turn.

Rows 56–66: Ch 1, sc in each st across, turn. At end of last row, fasten off.

Row 67: Join CC with sc in first st, sc in each st across, turn.

Rows 68–72: Ch 1, sc in each st across, turn. At end of last row, fasten off.

Whipstitch row 1 and row 72 together to form circle. Place over Styrofoam® wreath. Matching ends of rows, whipstitch closed. Decorate as desired. ✎

Small Wreath

Finished Size: 10" across.

Materials:
- ❑ Cotton fabric:
    - 1¼ yds. red & white (MC)
    - ½ yd. each white, red, and green
- ❑ 10" Styrofoam® wreath
- ❑ Tapestry needle
- ❑ I hook or hook needed to obtain gauge

Gauge: 2 sc = 1"; 3 sc rows = 2".

Basic Stitches: Ch, sc.

Note: Tear or cut fabric into 2" strips.

Small Wreath

Row 1: With MC, ch 13, sc in second ch from hook, sc in each ch across, turn. *(12 sc made)*

Rows 2–3: Ch 1, sc in each st across, turn. At end of last row, fasten off.

Row 4: Join white with sc in first st, sc in each st across, turn. Fasten off.

Row 5: Join red with sc in first st, sc in each st across, turn. Fasten off.

Row 6: Join white with sc in first st, sc in each st across, turn. Fasten off.

Row 7: Join MC with sc in first st, sc in each st across, turn.

Rows 8–9: Ch 1, sc in each st across, turn. At end of last row, fasten off.

Row 10: Join white with sc in first st, sc in each st across, turn. Fasten off.

Row 11: Join green with sc in first st, sc in each st across, turn. Fasten off.

Row 12: Join white with sc in first st, sc in each st across, turn. Fasten off.

Row 13: Join MC with sc in first st, sc in each st across, turn.

Rows 14–15: Ch 1, sc in each st across, turn. At end of last row, fasten off.

Rows 16–48: Repeat rows 4–15 consecutively, ending with row 12.

Whipstitch row 1 and row 48 together. Place over Styrofoam® wreath. Matching ends of rows, whipstitch closed. Decorate as desired. ✎

Poinsettia Afghan

by Lavon Mincey

Finished Size: 50½" × 63".

Materials:
❑ Worsted yarn:
    35 oz. white
    20 oz. green
    10 oz. burgundy
    1 oz. yellow
❑ Tapestry needle
❑ H hook or hook needed to obtain gauge

Gauge: 3 dc = 1"; 3 V st rows = 1¾".

Basic Stitches: Ch, sl st, sc, hdc, dc, tr, dtr.

Afghan

Motif (make 16)

Rnd 1: With yellow, ch 4, sl st in first ch to form ring, ch 1, 8 sc in ring, join with sl st in first sc. Fasten off. *(8 sc made)*

Rnd 2: Working in **front lps** (see Stitch Guide), join burgundy with sl st in first st, *[ch 10, sc in second ch from hook, hdc in next ch, dc in next 5 chs, dc in next ch, sc in next ch, sl st in same st as last sl st *(long petal made);* for **short petal,** sl st in next st, ch 8, sc in second ch from hook, hdc in next ch, dc in next 3 chs, hdc in next ch, sc in next ch, sl st in same st as last sl st], sl st in next st; repeat from * 2 more times; repeat between [ ], join with sl st in first sl st. Fasten off. *(4 long petals, 4 short petals)*

Rnd 3: With petals in front, working in **back lps** of rnd 1, join green with sl st in any st, *[ch 10, sc in second ch from hook, hdc in next ch, dc in next 5 chs, dc in next ch, sc in next ch, sl st in same st as last sl st *(leaf made)],* sl st in next 2 sts; repeat from * 2 more times; repeat between [ ], sl st in last st, join. Fasten off. *(4 leaves)*

Rnd 4: Join green with sc in tip of any leaf, (ch 5, sc in tip of next petal) 2 times, ch 5, *sc in tip of next leaf, (ch 5, sc in tip of next petal) 2 times, ch 5; repeat from * around, join. *(12 ch sps)*

Rnd 5: (Sl st, ch 3, 5 dc) in first ch sp, 6 dc in each ch sp around, join with sl st in top of ch-3. *(72 dc)*

Rnd 6: (Ch 2, hdc) in first st, hdc in next 5 sts, (2 hdc in next st, hdc in next 5 sts) around, join with sl st in top of ch-2. Fasten off. *(84 hdc)*

Sew **back lps** of 16 sts on two Motifs together, making two strips of eight Motifs each.

Panel (make 2)

Rnd 1: Working around outer edge of one strip, join white with sl st in next st on one end Motif, ch 5, *dtr in next st, tr in next 2 sts, dc in next 2 sts, hdc in next 2 sts, sc in next 9 sts, hdc in next 2 sts, dc in next 2 sts, tr in next 2 sts; for **corner, (dtr, ch 3, dtr)** in next st, tr in next 2 sts, dc in next 2 sts, hdc in next 2 sts, sc in next 8 sts, hdc in next 2 sts, dc in next 2 sts, tr in next 2 sts; for **corner, (dtr, ch 3, dtr)** in next st, tr in next 2 sts, dc in next 2 sts, hdc in next 2 sts, sc in next 9 sts, hdc in next 2 sts, dc in next 2 sts, tr in next 2 sts, dtr in next 2 sts; (on next Motif, work dtr in next 2 sts, tr in next 2 sts, dc in next 2 sts, hdc in next 2 sts, sc in next 10 sts, hdc in next 2 sts, dc in next 2 sts, tr in next 2 sts, dtr in next 2 sts) 6 times*, dtr in next st; repeat between first and second *, join with sl st in top of ch-4.

Rnd 2: Ch 3, dc in each st around with (2 dc, ch 2, 2 dc) in each corner ch sp, join with sl st in top of ch-3. Fasten off.

Row 3: Working in rows across one long edge, for **inner edge,** join white with sl st in one corner ch sp, ch 3, skip next st; *for **V st, (dc, ch 1, dc)** in next st, skip next 2 sts; repeat from * across, dc in last ch sp, turn. *(69 V sts, 2 dc)*

Rows 4–17: Ch 3, V st in each V st across, dc in last st, turn. At end of last row, fasten off.

Row 18: Join green with sc in first st, sc in each st and in each ch sp across, turn.

Row 19: Ch 3, skip next st, (V st in next st, skip next 2 sts) across, dc in last st. Fasten off.

Row 3: Working on opposite long edge of Panel; for **outer edge,** join white with sl st in one corner ch sp, ch 3, skip next st, (V st in next st, skip next 2 sts) across, dc in last ch sp, turn. *(69 V sts, 2 dc)*

Rows 4–11: Ch 3, V st in each V st across, dc in last st, turn. At end of last row, fasten off.

Sew **back lps** of inner edges on Panels together.

Border

Rnd 1: Join white with sc in st at any corner, 2 sc in same st as first sc, sc in each st, in each ch and in each seam around with 2 sc in end of each row and 3 sc in each corner, join with sl st in first sc.

Rnd 2: Sl st in next st, (yo, insert hook in same st as sl st, yo, pull lp through) 4 times, yo, pull through all lps on hook, ch 1, skip next st; *for **puff st,** yo, insert hook in next st, yo, pull lp through, (yo, insert hook in same st, pull lp through) 3 times, yo, pull through all lps on hook, ch 1, skip next st; repeat from * around, join with sl st in top of first puff st. Fasten off.

continued on page 137

Nutcracker Duo

by Karin Strom

Basic Instructions

(Use with instructions for each Nutcracker.)

Finished Sizes: About 14" to 14½" tall.

Materials:
- ❏ You will need the following items plus additional materials listed for individual Nutcracker
- ❏ Acrylic paint:
  - Peach *(for skin)*
  - Lt. pink *(for cheeks)*
- ❏ Fabric paint:
  - Dk. pink *(for lips)*
  - White *(for teeth)*
  - Black *(for eyes and mustache)*
- ❏ Small paint brush
- ❏ Styrofoam® pieces:
  - 4¼" of 3"-diameter pole *(for Red or Green Nutcracker Body)*
  - 2½" egg *(for Head)*
  - 4"-square of ½"-thick sheet *(for Cracker Top)*
  - 1¼" of 3"-diameter pole *(for Base Form)*
- ❏ Scraps of red felt and 9" × 12" sheet of color felt to match Jacket
- ❏ Polyester fiberfill
- ❏ ¼" wooden dowel pieces:
  - 3" long *(for Cracker Pivot)*
  - 4½" long *(for Cracker Handle)*
  - Two 6" pieces *(for Legs)*
- ❏ 8" square of poster board
- ❏ Craft glue
- ❏ Four wooden toothpicks
- ❏ Sharp knife *(to cut Styrofoam)*
- ❏ Bobby pins for markers
- ❏ Tapestry needle
- ❏ G hook or hook needed to obtain gauge

Gauge: 4 sc = 1"; 4 sc rows = 1".

Basic Stitches: Ch, sl st, sc, dc.

Basic Body

1: Cut slot in Styrofoam® **egg** or 4¼" **pole** according to Front and Side View illustrations. Firmly press around the middle of the egg or pole to form an indention at the waist.

2: Cut Jacket-color felt to fit all surfaces of slot and glue in place, cutting a 1"-diameter opening in felt centered on each side of slot for Pivot Dowel to go through.

3: Cut **Cracker Top** from 4" Styrofoam® square according to Full-Size Pattern on page 137. Cut a strip of red felt to fit across top edge according to gray line and glue in place; cover remainder of Cracker Top with Jacket-color felt.

4: For **Cracker Handle,** cut two pieces from poster board each ¾" × 4", glue one on each side of 4½" long dowel *(see Handle illustrations);* glue long edges of poster board together on each side.

5: Cut a ¾" × 8" piece of Jacket-colored felt; glue to

cardboard on each side and around end of Handle.

6: Press extended end of dowel into back of Styrofoam® Cracker Top and glue in place *(see Cracker Top Pattern).*

7: For **Oval Nose,** cut a ⅜" × ⅝" oval from Styrofoam® or for **Round Nose,** cut a ½" ball from Styrofoam® *(see Face Illustration for individual Nutcracker).* Trim Nose flat on one side and glue to Styrofoam® ball.

8: Paint face on Styrofoam® ball according to Face Illustration for individual Nutcracker.

Basic Cracker

Row 1: For **Handle Cover,** with Jacket-color yarn, ch 3, sc in second ch from hook, sc in last ch, turn. *(2 sc made)*

Rows 2–44: Ch 1, sc in each st across, turn. At end of last row, fasten off.

Beginning at triangle on Handle of Body Assembly illustration, glue Handle Cover over felt on both sides and around end of Handle; skipping notch, continue gluing Cover across bottom and front of Cracker Top to edge of red felt at front.

Paint bottom lip and teeth on front end of Cracker Top same as top lip and teeth on Face illustration.

Place assembled Cracker in slot of Body *(see Body Assembly).*

For Cracker **Pivot Dowel,** push 3"-long wooden dowel through both sides of Body and through notch at bottom of Cracker Top 1¼" down from top edge.

Basic Base
Top & Sides

Rnd 1: For **Top,** ch 2, 6 sc in second ch from hook, **do not join.** *(6 sc made) Mark first st of each rnd. Back of rnd 1 is right side of work.*

Rnds 2–3: 2 sc in each st around. *(12, 24)*

Rnd 4: (Sc in next 3 sts, 2 sc in next st) around. *(30)*

Rnd 5: (Sc in next 4 sts, 2 sc in next st) around. *(36)*

Rnd 6: For **Sides,** working this rnd in **back lps** *(see Stitch Guide),* sc in each st around.

Rnds 7–9: Sc in each st around. At end of last rnd, sl st in first sc. Fasten off.

For **Trim,** working in **remaining lps** of rnd 5, with rnd 1 toward you, join with sl st in any st, sl st in each st around, join with sl st in first sl st. Fasten off.

Bottom

Rnds 1–5: Repeat rnds 1–5 of Top & Sides. At end of last rnd, sl st in first st. Fasten off.

For **Trim,** working through both thicknesses of last rnd and rnd 9 on Sides, with Bottom toward you, join with sl st in any st, sl st in each st around, inserting Styrofoam® Base Form before closing, join with sl st in first sl st. Fasten off.

Basic Shoe (make 2)

Row 1: With black, ch 4, sc in second ch from hook, *continued on page 134*

continued on page 134

Nutcracker Duo

continued from page 133

sc in each ch across, turn. *(3 sc made)*

Rows 2–20: Ch 1, sc in each st across, turn. At end of last row, fasten off.

Fold in thirds *(see illustration)* and sew or glue together.

Glue Shoes side-by-side centered on Top of Base.

Basic Lower Leg (make 2)
Row 1: Ch 6, sc in second ch from hook, sc in each ch across, turn. *(5 sc made)*

Rows 2–12: Ch 1, sc in each st across, turn. At end of last row, fasten off.

Basic Upper Leg (make 2)
Row 1: Ch 6, sc in second ch from hook, sc in each ch across, turn. *(5 sc made)*

Rows 2–18: Ch 1, sc in each st across, turn. At end of last row, fasten off.

With Upper and Lower Leg pieces touching, glue row 1 of one Upper and one Lower Leg piece to center of 6" dowel leaving both ends of dowel extended. Repeat on other 6" dowel. Let dry.

When dry, wrap each Leg piece around dowel and sew last rnd in place; sew edges of Upper and Lower Leg pieces together.

Push extended end at bottom of one dowel between stitches on one Shoe *(see arrow on Shoe illustration)* and into Styrofoam® Base; glue edge of Lower Leg to top of Shoe. Repeat with other dowel and Shoe.

Basic Pants
Rnd 1: Ch 2, 6 sc in second ch from hook, **do not join.** *(6 sc made)* Mark first st of each rnd.

Rnd 2: 2 sc in each st around. *(12)*

Rnd 3: Sc in next st, 2 sc in next st) around. *(18)*

Rnd 4: Sc in next 2 sts, 2 sc in next st) around. *(24)*

Rnd 5: 2 sc in next st, sc in next 3 sts) around. *(30)*

Rnd 6: Sc in each st around, **turn.**

Row 7: Working in rows, ch 1, sc in first 28 sts leaving last 2 sts unworked for **slot,** turn. *(28)*

Row 8: Ch 1, 2 sc in each of first 2 sts, sc in next 24 sts, 2 sc in each of last 2 sts, turn. *(32)*

Row 9: Ch 1, 2 sc in first st, sc in each st across with 2 sc in last st, turn. *(34)*

Row 10: Ch 1, sc in each st across. Fasten off.

Glue Pants centered on bottom of Styrofoam® Body with ends of rows 7–10 matching edges of slot at back of Body.

Push extended ends at tops of Leg dowels between stitches on Pants and into bottom of Styrofoam® Body; glue edges of Upper Legs to Pants.

Basic Arm (make 2)
Sleeve
Row 1: With Jacket color, ch 13, sc in second ch from hook, sc in each ch across, turn. *(12 sc made)*

Rows 2–19: Ch 1, sc in each st across, turn. At end of last row, fasten off.

With last row at center, roll Sleeve into a 1" diameter roll and sew starting ch in place.

Hand & Cuff
Rnd 1: For **Hand,** ch 2, 6 sc in second ch from hook, **do not join.** *(6 sc made)* Mark first st of each rnd.

Rnd 2: 2 sc in each st around. *(12)*

Rnd 3: Sc in each st around.

Rnd 4: (Sc next 2 sts tog) around, join with sl st in first sc. Fasten off. *(6)*

Rnd 5: For **Cuff,** join with sc in first st, sc in same st, 2 sc in each st around. *(12)*

Rnd 6: Sc in each st around.

Rnd 7: Sc in each st around, join with sl st in first sc. Fasten off.

Stuff Hand.

Place Cuff over one end of Sleeve, sew or glue in place.

Sleeve Cap
Rnd 1: With gold, ch 2, 6 sc in second ch from hook, **do not join.** *(7 sc made)* Mark first st of each rnd.

Rnd 2: 2 sc in each st around. *(14)*

Rnd 3: Sc in each st around, join with sl st in first sc. Fasten off.

With back of sts facing out, place Sleeve Cap over other end of Sleeve and sew or glue in place. ☞

Red Nutcracker

Materials:
❑ Worsted yarn:
- 3 oz. red *(Jacket color)*
- 1 oz. black
- 1 oz. gold
- 1 oz. off-white

❑ Natural mohair *(for hair)*

❑ Additional materials listed in Basic Instructions on page 133.

Body & Cracker
Make Basic Pole Body and Basic Cracker in Basic Instructions on pages 133.

Base
Using red with gold for Trim, make Basic Base on page 133.

Shoes & Legs
Make Basic Shoes on page 133.

With red, make Basic Lower Legs *(above left)*.

With off-white, make Basic Upper Legs *(above left)*.

Jacket Top (make 2)
Row 1: Beginning at top, with gold, ch 2, 3 sc in second ch from hook, turn. *(3 sc made)*

Rows 2–3: Ch 1, 2 sc in each st across, turn. *(6, 12)*

Row 4: Ch 1, sc in first 2 sts, 2 sc in next st, (sc in next 3 sts, 2 sc in next st) 2 times, sc in last st, turn. *(15)*

Row 5: Ch 1, sc in each st across, turn. Fasten off.

Row 6: Join red with sc in first st, sc in each st across, turn.

Rows 7–11: Ch 1, sc in each st across, turn.

Row 12: Ch 1, sc in first 2 sts, sc next 2 sts tog, (sc in next 3 sts, sc next 2 sts tog) 2 times, sc in last

st, turn. Fasten off. *(12)*

To **join Jacket Tops** at front, with wrong side of both Top pieces facing you, join black with sl st in st at end of last row on one Jacket Top piece, ch 3, sl st in st at end of last row on other Jacket Top piece. Fasten off.

Jacket Bottom

Row 1: With wrong side of both Top pieces facing you, join black with sc in first st on last row of first Top piece, sc in each st across to ch-3, sc in next 3 chs, sc in each st across next Top piece, turn. Fasten off. *(27 sc made)*

Row 2: Join red with sc in first st, sc in next 2 sts, 2 sc in next st, (sc in next 3 sts, 2 sc in next st) 5 times, sc in last 3 sts, turn. *(33)*

Rows 3–7: Ch 1, sc in each st across, turn.

Rnd 8: Working in rnds, ch 1, sc in each st around, **do not turn,** ch 3, join with sl st in first sc, **turn.**

Rnd 9: Ch 1, sc in first 3 chs, sc in each st around, join. Fasten off. *(36)*

Jacket Underside

Rnd 1: With red, ch 2, 6 sc in second ch from hook, **do not join.** *(6 sc made) Mark first st of each rnd.*

Rnds 2–3: 2 sc in each st around. *(12, 24)*

Rnd 4: (Sc in next 3 sts, 2 sc in next st) around. *(30)*

Rnd 5: (Sc in next 4 sts, 2 sc in next st) around, join with sl st in first sc. Fasten off. *(36)*

Jacket Finishing

Sew last rnd of Jacket Underside to **back lps** of last rnd on Jacket Bottom.

Place Jacket on top of Styrofoam® Body with ends of rows matching edges of slot at back and front of Body; glue in place.

Work a French knot *(see Stitch Guide)* on each end of rows 7, 9 and 11 on front leaving a ¾" length of yarn loose; glue each ¾" length of yarn to same row as French knot *(see photo).*

For **Belt Buckle,** place a ¼"-wide × ¾"-long strip of black paint at center front on row 1 of Jacket Bottom just below bottom of slot. Let paint dry.

Glue a strand of gold yarn around outer edge of black paint to outline Buckle.

Arms

Using off-white for Hands and Cuffs, make Basic Arms on page 134.

Make Basic Sleeve Caps.

Sew or glue tops of Arms to sides of Jacket Top over rows 6–9.

Hat Brim

Rnd 1: With black, ch 2, 6 sc in second ch from hook, **do not join.** *(6 sc made) Mark first st of each rnd.*

Rnds 2–3: 2 sc in each st around. *(12, 24)*

Rnd 4: (Sc in next 3 sts, 2 sc in next st) around. *(30)*

Rnd 5: Sc in each st around, join with sl st in first sc. Fasten off.

Hat Band

Rnd 1: With gold, ch 24, sl st in first ch to form ring, ch 1, sc in each ch around, join with sl st in first sc. *(24 sc made)*

Rnd 2: Ch 1, sc in each st around, join.

Row 3: For **First Point,** ch 1, sc in first 3 sts leaving remaining sts unworked, **turn,** ch 1, sc 3 sts tog, **turn,** fasten off; *work the following steps to complete the rnd:*

A: For **Next Point,** join gold with sc in next unworked st on rnd 2 of Band, sc in next 2 sts leaving remaining sts unworked, **turn,** ch 1, sc 3 sts tog, **turn,** fasten off;

B: Repeat step A 5 more times;

C: For **Last Point,** join gold with sc in next unworked st on rnd 2 of Band, sc in last 2 sts, **turn,** ch 1, sc 3 sts tog, **turn, do not fasten off.**

Rnd 4: Ch 1, 2 sc in end of each row and in sc-3-tog at tip of each Point around with sl st in rnd 2 between each pair of Points, join with sl st in first sc. Fasten off.

Hat Crown

Rnd 1: With red, ch 2, 6 sc in second ch from hook, **do not join.** *(6 sc made) Mark first st of each rnd.*

Rnds 2–3: 2 sc in each st around. *(12, 24)*

Rnds 4–9: Sc in each st around. At end of last rnd, join with sl st in first sc. Fasten off.

Button

Rnd 1: With gold, ch 2, 5 sc in second ch from hook, **do not join.** *(5 sc made)*

Rnd 2: Sc in each st around, join with sl st in first sc. Fasten off.

Sew or glue Button to center of Crown.

Matching straight edges, sew or glue Crown to inside of Band; sew or glue Crown and Band to center of Brim.

Head Finishing

To attach **Head,** using toothpicks to hold ball in place, position ball on top of Jacket with face toward front, glue ball to top of Jacket.

For hair, cut several 6" lengths of natural mohair; glue to top of Head framing face and to front of Cracker Top just below teeth for beard *(see photo).*

Trim all hair to desired length.

Stuff Hat and glue to top of Head. ⌐☞

Green Nutcracker

Materials:
❏ Worsted yarn:
   3 oz. green *(Jacket color)*
   1 oz. black
   1 oz. gold
   Small amount beige
   Small amount pink
❏ Curly hair
❏ Additional materials listed in Basic Instructions on page 133.

continued on page 136

Nutcracker Duo

continued from page 135

Body & Cracker
Make Basic Pole Body and Basic Cracker in Basic Instructions on pages 133.

Base
Using green with gold for Trim, make Basic Base on page 133.

Shoes & Legs
Make Basic Shoes on page 133.
With green, make Basic Lower Legs on page 134.
With beige, make Basic Upper Legs on page 134.

Jacket Top (make 2)
Row 1: Beginning at top, with green, ch 2, 3 sc in second ch from hook, turn. *(3 sc made)*
Rows 2–3: Ch 1, 2 sc in each st across, turn. *(6, 12)*
Row 4: Ch 1, sc in first 2 sts, 2 sc in next st, (sc in next 3 sts, 2 sc in next st) 2 times, sc in last st, turn. *(15)*
Rows 5–11: Ch 1, sc in each st across, turn.
Row 12: Ch 1, sc in first 2 sts, sc next 2 sts tog, (sc in next 3 sts, sc next 2 sts tog) 2 times, sc in last st, turn. Fasten off. *(12)*
To **join Jacket Tops** at front, with wrong side of both Top pieces facing you, join black with sl st in st at end of last row on one Jacket Top piece, ch 3, sl st in st at end of last row on other Jacket Top piece. Fasten off.

Jacket Bottom
Row 1: With wrong side of both Top pieces facing you, join black with sc in first st on last row of first Top piece, sc in each st across to ch-3, sc in next 3 chs, sc in each st across next Top piece, turn. Fasten off. *(27 sc made)*
Row 2: Join green with sc in first st, sc in next 2 sts, 2 sc in next st, (sc in next 3 sts, 2 sc in next st) 5 times, sc in last 3 sts, turn. *(33)*
Rows 3–7: Ch 1, sc in each st across, turn.
Rnd 8: Working in rnds, ch 1, sc in each st around, ch 3, join with sl st in first sc, **turn.**
Rnd 9: Ch 1, sc in first 3 chs, sc in each st around, join. Fasten off. *(36)*

Jacket Underside
Rnd 1: With green, ch 2, 6 sc in second ch from hook, **do not join.** *(6 sc made)*
Rnds 2–3: 2 sc in each st around. *(12, 24)*
Rnd 4: (Sc in next 3 sts, 2 sc in next st) around. *(30)*
Rnd 5: (Sc in next 4 sts, 2 sc in next st) around, join with sl st in first sc. Fasten off. *(36)*

Jacket Finishing
Sew last rnds of Jacket Underside and Jacket Bottom together.
Place Jacket on Styrofoam® Body with ends of rows matching edges of slot at back and front of Body; glue in place.
For **Trim** *(make 2)*, with gold, ch 54. Fasten off. Glue one Trim to each side of Jacket Top forming three large loops at lower front and one long double line along front neck edge *(see photo)*.
For **Belt Buckle,** place a ¼"-wide × ½"-long strip of black paint at center front on row 1 of Jacket Bottom just below slot opening. Let paint dry.
Glue a strand of gold yarn around outer edge of black paint to outline Buckle.

Arms
Using pink for Hands and gold for Cuffs, make Basic Arms on page 134.
Make Basic Sleeve Caps on page 134.
Sew or glue tops of Arms to sides of Jacket Top over rows 6–9.

Hat Crown
Rnd 1: With green, ch 2, 6 sc in second ch from hook, **do not join.** *(6 sc made)* Mark first st of each rnd.
Rnds 2–3: 2 sc in each st around. *(12, 24)*
Rnd 4: (Sc in next 3 sts, 2 sc in next st) around. *(30)*
Rnd 5: Working this rnd in **front lps,** sc in each st around.
Rnd 6: Sc in each st around.
Rnd 7: (Sc in next 13 sts, sc next 2 sts tog) around. *(28)*
Rnd 8: Sc in each st around.
Rnd 9: (Sc in next 12 sts, sc next 2 sts tog) around. *(26)*
Rnd 10: Sc in each st around.
Rnd 11: (Sc in next 11 sts, sc next 2 sts tog) around. *(24)*
Rnd 12: Sc in each st around, join with sl st in first sc. Fasten off.

Hat Brim
Row 1: Join black with sc in first st, 2 sc in each of next 10 sts, sc in next st, turn. *(22 sc made)*
Rows 2–3: Ch 1, skip first 2 sts, sc in each st across to last 3 sts, skip next 2 sts, sc in last st, turn. At end of last row, fasten off. *(18, 14)*
For **trim,** glue a strand of gold yarn across bottom of row 1 on Brim.
Make a gold French knot *(see Stitch Guide)* at each end of strand.
With gold, ch 26. Fasten off. Shape into three loops and glue to front of Hat *(see photo)*.

Head Finishing
To attach **Head,** using toothpicks to hold ball in place with face toward front, glue ball to top of Jacket.
For hair, cut several 6" lengths of Curly Hair; glue to top of Head framing face and to front of Cracker Top just below teeth for beard *(see photo)*.
Trim all hair to desired length.
Stuff Hat and glue to top of Head.

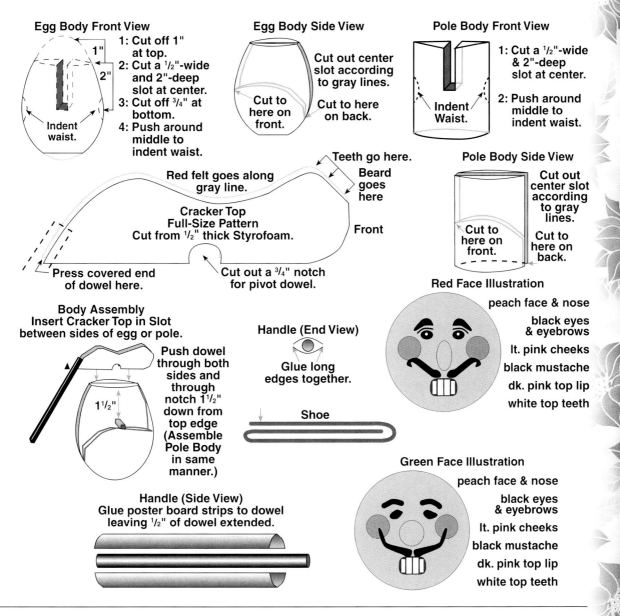

Egg Body Front View

1: Cut off 1" at top.
2: Cut a ½"-wide and 2"-deep slot at center.
3: Cut off ¾" at bottom.
4: Push around middle to indent waist.

Indent waist.

Egg Body Side View

Cut out center slot according to gray lines.

Cut to here on front.

Cut to here on back.

Pole Body Front View

1: Cut a ½"-wide & 2"-deep slot at center.

2: Push around middle to indent waist.

Indent Waist.

Pole Body Side View

Cut out center slot according to gray lines.

Cut to here on front.

Cut to here on back.

Teeth go here.

Beard goes here

Red felt goes along gray line.

Cracker Top Full-Size Pattern
Cut from ½" thick Styrofoam.

Front

Press covered end of dowel here.

Cut out a ¾" notch for pivot dowel.

Body Assembly
Insert Cracker Top in Slot between sides of egg or pole.

Push dowel through both sides and through notch 1½" down from top edge (Assemble Pole Body in same manner.)

1½"

Handle (End View)

Glue long edges together.

Shoe

Red Face Illustration

peach face & nose
black eyes & eyebrows
lt. pink cheeks
black mustache
dk. pink top lip
white top teeth

Green Face Illustration

peach face & nose
black eyes & eyebrows
lt. pink cheeks
black mustache
dk. pink top lip
white top teeth

Handle (Side View)
Glue poster board strips to dowel leaving ½" of dowel extended.

Poinsettia Afghan

continued from page 131

Leaf (make 20)
Row 1: With green, ch 11, sl st in second ch from hook, sl st in next ch, sc in next 7 chs, 2 sc in last ch; working in remaining lps on opposite side of ch, sc in next 8 chs leaving remaining chs unworked, turn.
Row 2: Ch 2, sl st in next st, sc in next 6 sts, 2 sc in each of next 2 sts, sc in next 7 sts leaving remaining sts unworked, turn.
Row 3: Ch 2, sl st in next st, sc in next 6 sts, 2 sc in each of next 2 sts, sc in next 6 sts leaving remaining sts unworked, turn.
Row 4: Ch 2, sl st in next st, sc in next 5 sts, 2 sc in next st, sc in next st, 2 sc in next st, sc in next 5 sts leaving remaining sts unworked, turn.
Row 5: Ch 2, sl st in next st, sc in next 5 sts, sl st in next st leaving remaining sts unworked. Fasten off.

Berry (make 30)
With burgundy, ch 4, sl st in first ch to form ring, ch 1, 5 sc in ring, join with sl st in first sc. Leaving long end, fasten off.
Weave long end through top of sts, pull tight and secure end.
Sew Leaves and Berries to Panels across seam as shown in photo.

Angel Doily

by Nanette Seale

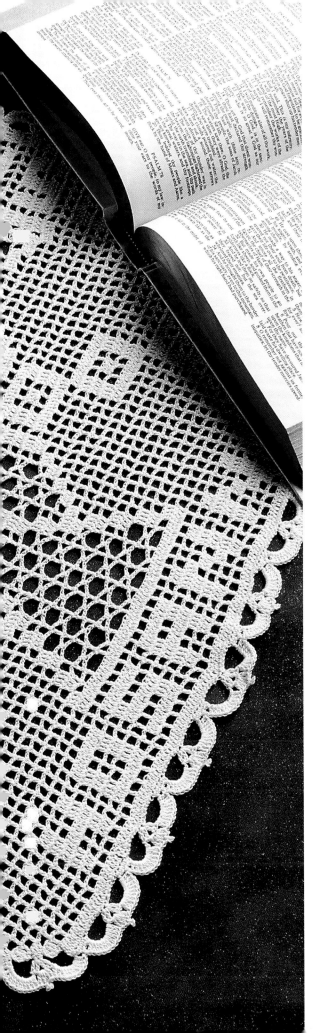

Finished Size: $23\frac{1}{2}$" × $24\frac{1}{2}$".

Materials:
- ❏ 1,000 yds. white size 10 crochet cotton thread
- ❏ No. 8 steel crochet hook or hook needed to obtain gauge

Gauge: 10 sts or chs = 1"; 11 dc rows = 3".

Basic Stitches: Ch, sl st, sc, dc.

Special Stitches: For **mesh**, ch 2, skip next 2 chs or sts, dc in next st or in third ch of next double mesh.

For **beginning (beg) mesh,** ch 5, skip next 2 chs or sts, dc in next dc *(first 3 chs of ch-5 count as first dc).*

For **double mesh,** ch 5, skip next 5 chs or sts, dc in next dc.

For **lacet,** ch 2, skip next 2 chs or sts, sc in next ch or st, ch 2, skip next 2 chs or sts, dc in next dc.

For **beg lacet,** ch 5, skip next 2 chs or sts, sc in next ch or st, ch 2, skip next 2 chs or sts, dc in next dc *(first 3 chs of ch-5 count as first dc).*

For **block,** dc in next 3 dc—**or**—2 dc in next ch sp, dc in next dc—**or**—3 dc in next double mesh *(dc worked at center of double mesh goes in third ch of ch-5).*

For **double block,** 5 dc in ch sp of next double mesh.

For **beg block,** ch 3, dc in next 3 dc—**or**—ch 3, 2 dc in next ch sp, dc in next dc *(first ch-3 counts as first dc).*

For **beg increase (inc) block,** ch 5, skip first 3 chs, dc in fourth ch from hook, dc in next ch *(3 skipped chs count as first dc).*

For **end inc block,** yo, insert hook in base of last dc made, yo, pull through, yo, pull through one lp on hook *(ch-1 made),* (yo, pull through 2 lps on hook) 2 times *(dc made),* *yo, insert hook in last ch-1 made, yo, pull through ch, yo, pull through one lp on hook *(ch-1 made),* (yo, pull through 2 lps on hook) 2 times *(dc made);* repeat from *.

For **beg decrease (dec) block,** skip first dc, sl st in next 3 dc and work beg block.

For **beg inc mesh,** (ch 5, dc) in first st *(first 3 chs of ch-5 count as first dc).*

For **beg double inc mesh,** ch 8, dc in sixth ch from hook, ch 2, skip next 2 chs, dc in next dc.

For **end inc mesh,** (dc, ch 2, dc) in last dc.

For **beg dec mesh,** ch 2, skip next 2 sts or chs, dc in next dc *(ch-2 is not worked into or counted as a st).*

For **end dec mesh,** skipping 2 sts or chs between, dc fourth st from end of row and last st of row tog.

continued on page 143

Snowflake Potholders

by Ann Kirtley

Finished Sizes: Bright Pink is 8" across; Purple is 7½" across; Royal Blue and Emerald Green are 6½" across.

Materials:
- ❑ Worsted yarn:
    ½ oz. bright pink for Bright Pink Doily
    ½ oz. purple for Purple Doily
    ½ oz. green for Emerald Green Doily
    ½ oz. blue for Royal Blue Doily
    Small amount gold for each doily
- ❑ 50 yds. white size 10 crochet cotton thread for each doily
- ❑ One 6mm gold bead for each doily
- ❑ Sewing needle and white thread
- ❑ No. 8 steel and G hooks or hooks needed to obtain gauges

Gauges: No. 8 steel hook, rnds 1–4 = 2½". **G hook,** 1 dc = ½" tall.

Basic Stitches: Ch, sl st, sc, dc, tr, dtr.

Notes: Work **Fronts** with No. 8 steel hook and size 10 thread.
Work **Backs** with G hook and worsted yarn.

Bright Pink Doily
Front
Rnd 1: Ch 6, sl st in first ch to form ring, ch 6 *(counts as dc and ch sp),* (dc in ring, ch 3) 5 times, join with sl st in third ch of ch-6. *(6 dc, 6 ch sps made)*

Rnd 2: Ch 12 *(counts as first tr and ch-7 lp),* (tr in next st, ch 7) around, join with sl st in fourth ch of beginning ch-12.

Rnd 3: Ch 16 *(counts as first dtr and ch-11 lp),* (dtr in next st, ch 11) around, join with sl st in fifth ch of beginning ch-16.

Rnd 4: Ch 1, sc in first st, ch 11, (sc in next dtr, ch 11) around, join with sl st in first sc.

Rnd 5: Ch 1, sc in first st, ch 9, sc around ch-11 lps of rnds 3 and 4 as one, (ch 9, sc in next st, ch 9, sc around ch-11 lps of rnds 3 and 4 as one) around, ch 5, join with dc in fifth ch of beginning ch-9.

Rnd 6: Ch 6, sc in next st, (ch 15, sl st in twelfth ch from hook) 3 times *(three spokes made),* (ch 11, sl st in same ch as last sl st) 2 times *(two more spokes made),* ch 3, (sl st in base of same ch as next spoke, ch 11, sl st in same ch, ch 3) 2 times *(two more spokes made),* sl st in first sc made, ch 6, sl st in next ch-9 lp on previous rnd; *work steps A–E to complete rnd:*

A: Ch 6, sc in next sc, ch 10, sl st in last ch-11 lp of last spoke made, ch 5, sl st in fifth ch of last ch-10 *(spoke made),* (ch 15, sl st in twelfth ch from hook) 2 times, (ch 11, sl st in same ch as last sl st) 2 times, ch 3;

B: (Sl st in base of same ch as next spoke, ch 11, sl st in same ch as last sl st, ch 3) 2 times, sl st in last sc made, ch 6, sl st in next ch-9 lp on previous rnd;

C: Repeat steps A and B ten more times;

D: Repeat step A;

E: Sl st in base of same ch as next spoke, ch 11, sl st in same ch as last sl st, ch 3, sl st in base of same ch as next spoke, ch 6, sl st in first ch-11 lp on first set of spokes, ch 6, sl st in same ch as last sl st on this set of spokes, ch 3, sl st in last sc made, ch 6, join with sl st in first ch of first ch-6. Fasten off.

Rnd 7: Skip first free spoke, join with sl st in next spoke, ch 5, (sl st in next spoke, ch 5) 3 times, skip next sl st *(at base of last spoke),* sl st in next sl st *(between spokes),* [ch 5, (sl st in next spoke, ch 5) 5 times, skip next sl st, sl st in next sl st between spokes] 11 times, ch 5, sl st in next spoke, ch 5, join with sl st in first sl st.

Rnd 8: Ch 1, (5 sc in next 2 ch-5 sps, sl st in next sl st, ch 7, skip next 3 sl sts, sl st in next sl st) around, join with sl st in first sc.

Rnd 9: (Ch 7, skip next 5 sts, sl st in sp between 5–dc groups, ch 10, sl st in same sp, ch 7, skip next 5 sts, sl st in next sl st, 9 sc in next ch-7 lp, sl st in next sl st) around, join. Fasten off.

Back
Rnd 1: With bright pink, ch 5, sl st in first ch to form ring, ch 3, 11 dc in ring, join with sl st in top of ch-3. *(12 dc made)*

Rnd 2: (Ch 3, dc) in first st, 2 dc in each st around, join. *(24)*

Rnd 3: Ch 3, 2 dc in next st, (dc in next st, 2 dc in next st) around, join. *(36)*

Rnd 4: Ch 3, dc in each st around, join.

Rnd 5: Ch 3, dc in next st, 2 dc in next st, (dc in next 2 sts, 2 dc in next st) around, join. *(48)*

Rnd 6: Ch 3, dc in each st around, join.

Rnd 7: Ch 3, dc in next st, 2 dc in next st, (dc in next 2 sts, 2 dc in next st) around, join. *(64)*

Rnd 8: Ch 3, 2 dc in next st, (dc in next st, 2 dc in next st) around, join. *(96)*

Rnd 9: Ch 1, sc in first 3 sts, 2 sc in next st, (sc in next 3 sts, 2 sc in next st) around, join with sl st in first sc. Fasten off. *(120)*

Rnd 10: Join gold with sc in first st; **reverse sc** *(see Stitch Guide)* in each st around, join with sl st in first sc; for **hanger,** ch 8, sl st in joining sl st, ch 1, 10 sc in ch-8 loop, join with sl st in first sc. Fasten off.

Assembly
With needle and thread, tack top of each ch-10 lp of rnd 9 on wrong side of Front to right side of Back as shown in photo. Sew bead to center of rnd 1 on Front.

continued on page 142

Snowflake Potholders

continued from page 141

Purple Doily
Front
Note: Skip each ch sp unless otherwise stated.

Rnd 1: Ch 6, sl st in first ch to form ring, ch 3 *(counts as first dc)*, 23 dc in ring, join with sl st in top of ch-3. *(24 dc made)*

Rnd 2: Working in **back lps** *(see Stitch Guide)*, (ch 5, skip next st, sl st in next st) 11 times, ch 2, dc in last st *(joining ch sp made)*. *(12 ch sps)*

Rnd 3: Ch 3, 2 dc in third ch from hook *(scallop made)*, (sl st in next ch-5 sp, ch 3, 2 dc in third ch from hook) around, join with sl st in joining dc of rnd 2.

Rnd 4: Ch 9 *(first 4 chs count as first tr)*, sl st in fifth ch from hook; working around ch-9, tr back into sl st between last 2 scallops on last rnd, ch 3, (tr in sl st between next 2 scallops, ch 5, sl st in fifth ch from hook; working around last tr, tr in same sl st as tr on last rnd, ch 3) around, join with sl st in first tr.

Rnd 5: Sl st in next ch-5 lp, *ch 4, yo 2 times, insert hook in same lp, yo, pull through lp, (yo, pull through 2 lps on hook) 2 times, yo 2 times, insert hook in next ch-5 lp, yo, pull through lp, (yo, pull through 2 lps on hook) 2 times, yo, pull through 3 lps on hook *(dec made)*, ch 7, sl st in top of st just made, ch 4, sl st in same ch-5 lp as second half of dec; repeat from * 10 more times, ch 4, yo 2 times, insert hook in same ch-5 lp, yo, pull through lp, (yo, pull through 2 lps on hook) 2 times, yo, insert hook in first ch-5 lp already worked into at beginning of rnd, yo, pull through lp, (yo, pull through 2 lps on hook) 2 times, yo, pull through all loops on hook, ch 7, sl st in top of st first made, ch 4, sl st in first lp of rnd.

Rnd 6: Ch 16 *(counts as first tr and ch-10 base)*, *[sl st in third ch from hook, sl st in next 3 chs *(right spoke)*, ch 7, sl st in third ch from hook, sl st in next 4 chs *(center spoke)* sl st in same ch at base of right spoke, ch 6, sl st in third ch from hook, sl st in next 3 chs *(left spoke)*, sl st in next 4 chs on base, ch 6, sl st in next ch-7 lp on last rnd, ch 6], dtr in next sl st, ch 10; repeat from * 10 more times; repeat between [ ], join with sl st in sixth ch of beginning ch-16. Fasten off.

Rnd 7: Join with sl st in end of any right spoke, *[ch 5, sl st in end of center spoke, ch 5, sl st in end of left spoke, ch 5], sl st in next right spoke; repeat from * 10 more times; repeat between [ ], join with sl st in first sl st.

Rnd 8: Ch 1, (5 sc in next ch sp, dc in next sl st, ch 4, sl st in second ch from hook, ch 2, sl st in top of dc just made, 5 sc in next ch sp, 7 sc in next ch sp) around, join with sl st in first sc. Fasten off.

Back
Rnds 1-3: With purple, repeat rnd 1-3 of Bright Pink Back on page 141. *(12 dc made)*

Rnds 4–5: Repeat rnd 5 of Bright Pink Back. *(48, 64)*

Rnd 6: Ch 3, dc in each st around, join.

Rnd 7-8: Repeat rnds 9-10 of Bright Pink Back.

Assembly
With needle and thread, tack top of each ch-4 of rnd 8 on wrong side of Front to right side of Back as shown in photo. Sew bead to center of rnd 1 on Front.

Emerald Green Doily
Front
Rnd 1: Ch 6, sl st in first ch to form ring, ch 3 *(counts as first dc)*, 23 dc in ring, join with sl st in top of ch-3. *(24 dc made)*

Rnd 2: Working in **back lps** *(see Stitch Guide)*, ch 4 *(counts as dc and ch sp)*, (dc in next st, ch 1) around, join with sl st in third ch of ch-4.

Rnd 3: Working in **back lps**, ch 2, dc in next ch, dc next st and ch tog, ch 3, *(dc next st and ch tog) 2 times, ch 3; repeat from * around, join with sl st in top of first dc made. *(24 tr, 12 ch sps)*

Rnd 4: Ch 3, tr in next st, ch 5, sl st in next ch-3 sp, ch 5, (tr next 2 sts tog, ch 5, sl st in next ch-3 sp, ch 5) around, join with sl st in top of first tr. *(12 tr, 24 ch sps)*

Rnd 5: (Ch 10, sl st in third ch from hook—*end loop made*, sl st in next 7 chs, sl st in same st as ch 10, ch 5, dtr in next sl st, ch 5, sl st in top of dtr just made, ch 5, sl st in next decrease) around, join with sl st in first ch of beginning ch-10. Fasten off.

Rnd 6: Join with sl st in any end loop, ch 5, sl st in ch-5 lp made in top of next dtr, ch 5, (sl st in next end loop, ch 5, sl st in ch-5 lp made in top of next dtr, ch 5) around, join with sl st in first sl st.

Rnd 7: (Ch 6, sl st) 3 times in first st, 5 sc in next 2 ch-5 sps, (sl st, ch 15, sl st) in next sl st, 5 sc in next 2 ch-5 sps, *sl st in next sl st, (ch 6, sl st) 3 times in same st, 5 sc in next 2 ch-5 sps, (sl st, ch 15, sl st) in next sl st, 5 sc in next 2 ch-5 sps; repeat from * around, join with sl st in first sl st. Fasten off.

Back
Rnds 1-3: With green, repeat rnd 1-3 of Bright Pink Back on page 141. *(12 dc made)*

Rnds 4–5: Repeat rnd 5 of Bright Pink Back. *(48, 64)*

Rnd 6-7: Repeat rnds 9-10 of Bright Pink Back.

Assembly
With needle and thread, tack top of each ch-15 lp of rnd 7 on wrong side of Front to right side of Back as shown in photo. Sew bead to center of rnd 1 on Front.

Royal Blue Doily
Front
Note: Skip each ch sp unless otherwise stated.

Rnd 1: Ch 6, sl st in first ch to form ring, ch 4 *(counts as first tr)*, 17 tr in ring, join with sl st in top of ch-4. *(18 tr made)*

Rnd 2: Ch 3, tr in next st, ch 1, *yo 2 times, insert

hook in same st as last st, yo, pull through st, (yo, pull through 2 lps on hook) 2 times, yo 2 times, insert hook in next st, yo, pull throush st; repeat between ( ) 2 times, yo, pull through all lps on hook, ch 1; repeat from * around with second half of last repeat worked in same st as ch 3, join with sl st in top of first tr made.

Rnd 3: Ch 3, tr in next st, ch 1, yo 2 times, insert hook in same st, yo, pull through st, (yo, pull through 2 lps on hook) 2 times, yo 2 times, insert hook in next st, yo, pull through st; repeat between ( ) 2 times, yo pull through all lps on hook, ch 5, sl st in next ch sp, ch 5, *[yo, 2 times, insert hook in next st, yo, pull through st; repeat between ( ) 2 times]; repeat between [ ] one more time, yo, pull through all lps on hook, ch 1, yo 2 times, insert hook in same st, yo, pull through st; repeat between ( ) 2 times, yo 2 times, insert hook in same st, yo, pull through st; repeat between ( ) 2 times, ch 5, sl st in next ch sp, ch 5; repeat from * around, join,

Rnd 4: Ch 3, dc in next st, (ch 5, sl st, ch 7, sl st, ch 5, sl st) in top of dc just made, ch 3, sl st in first ch of next ch 5, ch 5, sl st in last ch of next ch 5, *ch 3, dc next 2 sts tog; repeat between ( ) in top of dc decrease just made, ch 3, sl st in first ch of next ch 5, ch 5, sl st in last ch of next ch 5; repeat from * around, ch 3, join with sl st in top of beginning ch 3.

Rnd 5: (Ch 5, sl st in next sl st, ch 7, sl st in next sl st, ch 5, sl st in next sl st, ch 3, sl st in next ch-5 sp, ch 3, sl st in top of next dc decrease) around, ending

last repeat with ch 3, sl st in joining sl st of last rnd.

Rnd 6: (Ch 7, sc in next ch-7 lp, ch 3, sl st in top of sc just made—*end loop made,* ch 7, skip next slst, sl st in next sl st, ch 5, skip next sl st, sl st in next sl st) arund, join with sl st in first ch of beginning ch 7. Fasten off.

Rnd 7: Join with sl st in any end loop, (ch 7, sl st in second ch from hook, sl st in next 5 ch—*spoke made,* ch 15, sl st in next end loop) around, join.

Rnd 8: Sl st in next 3 sl sts up side of spoke, *ch 3, sl st in tip of spoke, ch 3, sl st in next sl st on opposite side of spoke, ch 3, sl st in next ch-15 lp, (Ch 3, dc in third ch from hook, sl st in same ch-15 lp) 4 times, ch 3, skip first 2 ch on side of next spoke, sl st in next sl st on spoke; repeat from * around ending last repeat with sl st in third sl st at beginning of rnd.

Rnd 9: Sl st in next 3 ch, *(sl st, ch 2, sl st) in next sl st made in tip of spoke, ch 5, sl st in next ch-3 sp, (ch 4, sl st in next ch-3 sp) 3 times, ch 5; repeat from * around, join with sl st in first sl st worked into tip of first spoke. Fasten off.

Back

With royal blue, work same a Emerald Green Back on opposite page.

Assembly

With needle and thread, tack top of each ch-2 sp of rnd 9 on worong side of Front to right side of Back as showin photo. Sew bead to center of rnd 1 on Front. ⚷

For **picot,** ch 3, sl st in third ch from hook.
For **shell,** (2 dc, ch 2, 2 dc) in st or ch indicated.
For **V st,** (dc, ch 2, dc) in st or ch indicated.
For **joined V st,** dc in st or ch indicated, ch 1, sl st in ch sp of corresponding V st on adjacent Motif or Panel, ch 1, dc in same st or ch on this Motif or Panel beside last dc made.
For **cluster,** ch 3, (yo, insert hook in first ch of ch-3, yo, pull through ch, yo, pull through 2 lps on hook) 2 times, yo, pull through all 3 lps on hook.

Doily

Row 1: Ch 162, dc in fourth ch from hook, dc in each ch across, turn. *(160 dc made forming 53 blocks.)*
Note: *See Special Stitches for instructions for stitches shown in Doily Key.*
Rows 2–81: Work according to corresponding row of graph on page 144, turn.
Rnd 82: Working around outer edge, ch 1, sc in first 3 sts; *work the following steps to complete the rnd:*

ꓑ𝔫𝔤𝔢𝔩 𝔇𝔬𝔦𝔩𝔶

continued from page 139

A: *Ch 7, skip next 7 sts, **shell** *(see Special Stitches)* in next st, ch 7, skip next 7 sts, sc in next 5 sts; repeat from * 6 more times;
B: Ch 7, skip next 7 sts, shell in next st, ch 7, skip next 7 sts, sc in last 2 sts, sc in end of row 81, sc in 2 sts of block on next row;
C: (Ch 7, skip corner at end of next row, shell in corner at end of next row, ch 7, skip corner at end of next row, 5 sc evenly spaced across end of next row and sts or chs of next block) 2 times, ch 7, skip corner at end of next row, shell in corner at end of next row, ch 7, skip next 2 rows;
D: (5 sc evenly spaced across ends of next 2 rows, ch 7, skip next 3 rows, shell in top of st at end of next row, ch 7, skip same row as shell and next 2 rows) 6 times, 5 sc evenly spaced across ends of next 2 rows;
E: (Ch 7, skip corners at ends of next 2 rows, shell in corner of next row, ch 7, skip next row, 5 sc evenly spaced across sts or chs of

continued on page 144

Angel Doily

continued from page 143

block at end of next row and end of next row) 2 times;

F: Ch 7, skip next row, shell in corner at end of next row, ch 7, skip next row and end of row 1; working on opposite side of starting ch on row 1, sc in first 5 chs;

G: (Ch 7, skip next 7 chs, shell in next ch, ch 7, skip next 7 chs, sc in next 5 chs) 7 times, ch 7, skip next 7 chs, shell in next ch, ch 7, skip last 7 chs, 5 sc evenly spaced across ends of rows 1 and 2;

H: Repeat steps C, D, E;

I: Ch 7, skip next row, shell in corner at end of next row, ch 7, skip next row, 2 sc in end of row 81, join with sl st in first sc.

Rnd 83: Ch 1, sc in first sc, *[10 dc in next ch-7 sp, (3 dc, **picot**—*see Special Stitches*, 2 dc) in ch sp of next shell, 10 dc in next ch-7 sp], sc in third sc of next 5-sc group; repeat from * around to last 2 ch-7 sps; repeat between [ ], join. Fasten off.

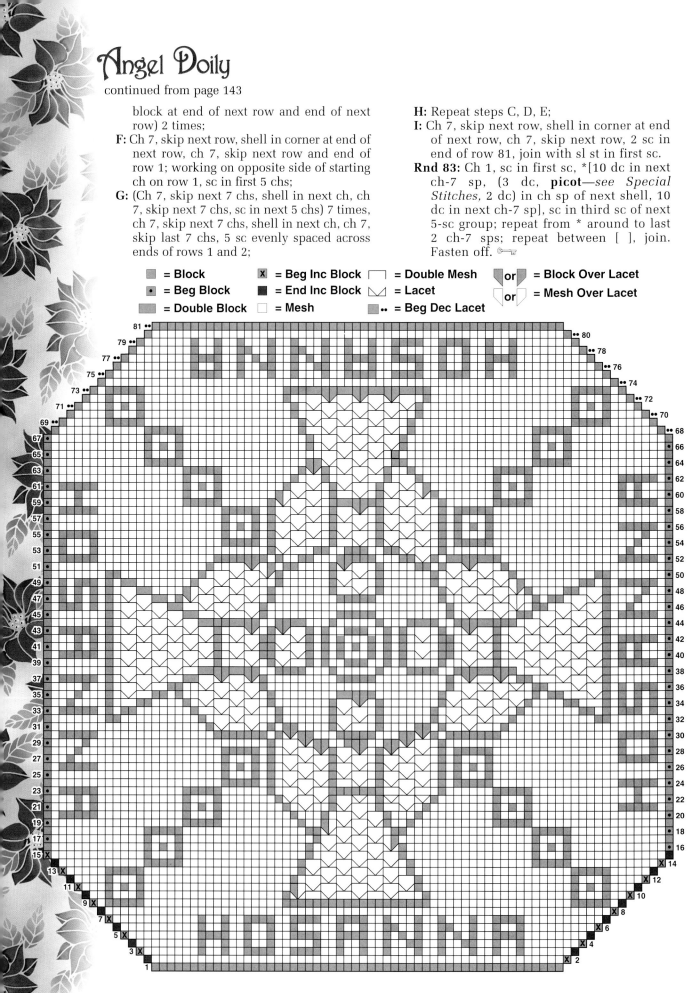

▨ = Block	☒ = Beg Inc Block	⬜ = Double Mesh	◣◥ = Block Over Lacet
• = Beg Block	■ = End Inc Block	◣◥ = Lacet	◣◥ = Mesh Over Lacet
▨ = Double Block	☐ = Mesh	▨•• = Beg Dec Lacet	

Afghans All Around

Nothing completes a room like an afghan! There's something irresistible about curling up with one, no matter where we are in our homes! So I chose these afghans to complete this book. There are ones for him and ones for her. There are fancy florals and filets; afghans with stripes and others with special stitches. No matter which style you choose, it is sure to be the finishing touch to your favorite room!

Lap Afghan

by Kenneth Cormier

Finished Size: 44½" long.

Materials:
- ❑ 30 oz. yellow worsted yarn
- ❑ H hook or hook needed to obtain gauge

Gauge: 3 rows = 1¼".

Basic Stitches: Ch, sl st, sc, dc, tr.

Afghan

Row 1: Ch 122, sc in second ch from hook, sc in each ch across, turn. *(121 sc made)*

Row 2: Ch 5, dc next 5 sts tog, ch 2, dc in next st, (ch 2, dc next 5 sts tog, ch 2, dc in next st) across, turn. *(First ch-5 counts as first dc and ch-2.)*

Row 3: Ch 1, sc in each ch and in each st across, turn.

Row 4: Ch 3, skip next 2 sts, (5 dc in next st, skip next 2 sts, dc in next st, skip next 2 sts) across, turn.

Row 5: Ch 1, sc in each st across, turn.

Rows 6–9: Repeat rows 2–5 consecutively.

Row 10: Ch 1, sc in first st, (tr in next st, sc in next st) across, turn.

Row 11: Ch 1, sc in each st across, turn.

Rows 12–15: Repeat rows 10 and 11 alternately.

Rows 16–23: Repeat rows 2–5 consecutively.

Rows 24–29: Repeat rows 10 and 11 alternately.

Rows 30–107: Repeat rows 16–29 consecutively, ending with row 23. At end of last row, fasten off.

Fringe

For each Fringe *(see Stitch Guide)*, cut four strands each 10" long. With all four strands held together, fold in half, insert hook in first st on one short end of Afghan, pull center fold of strands through to the back, pull ends through fold and gently pull to tighten. Repeat in every sixth st across both short ends.

For second row of knots, divide each Fringe in half using four strands from the first and four from the next Fringe, hold them all together and tie them loosely in a knot.

Repeat across both short ends. Trim ends to desired length. ⚷

Fans Afghan

by Hattie Pulsifer

Finished Size: 37½" × 68" plus Fringe.

Materials:
- ❑ Worsted yarn:
    24 oz. lt. blue
    16 oz. med. blue
- ❑ 12 large safety pins
- ❑ H hook or hook needed to obtain gauge

Gauge: Shell = 3" × 6"; Strip = 7½" wide.

Basic Stitches: Ch, sl st, sc, dc.

Strip (make 3 with lt. blue and 2 with med. blue)
First Fan
Row 1: Ch 10, dc in eighth ch from hook, ch 5, skip next ch, dc in last ch, turn. *(2 large sps made)*

Row 2: Ch 3, 10 dc in ch-5 sp, 10 dc in ch-8 sp, turn. *(21 dc)*

Row 3: Ch 4, dc in next dc, (ch 1, skip next dc, dc in next dc) across, ch 1, dc in top of ch-3, turn. *(12 dc, 11 ch-1 sps)*

Row 4: Ch 3, (3 dc in next ch-1 sp) 5 times, 4 dc in next ch-1 sp, (3 dc in next ch-1 sp) 5 times, turn. *(35)*

Row 5: Ch 4, dc in next dc, (ch 1, skip next dc, dc in next dc) across, ch 1, dc in top of ch-3, turn. **Do not fasten off.** *(19 dc, 18 ch-1 sps)*

Second & Third Fans
Row 1: Ch 5, skip first ch-1 sp, dc in next ch-1 sp, ch 5, skip next ch-1 sp, sl st in next ch-1 sp, sl st in next dc, sl st in next ch-1 sp, turn.

Row 2: (10 dc in next ch-5 sp) 2 times; for **Second Fan,** dc in same sp, turn *(21 dc);* for **Third Fan,** (sl st in next ch-1 sp, sl st in next dc, sl st in next ch-1 sp) on previous Fan, turn *(20 dc).*

Row 3: For **Second Fan,** ch 4 *(counts as first dc and ch-1 sp);* for **Third Fan,** ch 1 *(counts as first ch-1 sp);* for **both Fans,** sc in next dc, (ch 1, skip next dc, dc in next dc) across, ch 1, skip last dc, sl st in next ch-1 sp on previous Fan *(11 ch-1 sps),* (sl st in next dc, sl st in next ch-1 sp) on previous Fan, turn.

Row 4: (3 dc in next ch-1 sp) 5 times, 4 dc in next ch-1 sp, (3 dc in next ch-1 sp) 5 times; for **Second Fan,** dc in same sp, turn *(35 dc);* for **Third Fan,** (sl st in next ch-1 sp, sl st in next dc, sl st in next ch-1 sp) on previous Fan, turn *(34 dc).*

Row 5: For **Second Fan,** ch 4 *(counts as first dc*

and ch-1 sp);* for **Third Fan,** ch 1 *(counts as first ch-1 sp);* for **both Fans,** dc in next dc, (ch 1, skip next dc, dc in next dc) across, ch 1, skip last dc, sl st in next ch-1 sp on previous Fan *(18 ch-1 sps),* turn.
Repeat Third Fan until Afghan is desired length *(Afghan in photo has 35 Fans).*

End of Strip
Row 1: With beginning end of Strip at top and high side to the right, join with sl st in first large sp at center of Fan, ch 5, dc in next sp, ch 5, (sl st in end of row 2, 2 sl st in end of row 3) on First Fan, turn.

Row 2: (10 dc in ch-5 sp) 2 times *(20 dc),* (sl st in end of row 2, 2 sl st in end of row 3) on First Fan, turn.

Row 3: Ch 1 *(counts as first ch-1 sp),* dc in next dc, (ch 1, skip next dc, dc in next dc) across, ch 1, skip last dc, sl st in next ch-1 sp on previous Fan *(11 ch-1 sps),* (sl st in end of row 4, sl st in end of row 5) on First Fan, sl st in end of row 2 on Second Fan, turn.

Row 4: (3 dc in next ch-1 sp) 5 times, 4 dc in next ch-1 sp, (3 dc in next ch-1 sp) 5 times *(34 dc),* (sl st in end of row 4, 2 sl st in end of row 5) on First Fan, turn.

Row 5: Ch 1 *(counts as first ch-1 sp),* dc in next dc, (ch 1, skip next dc, dc in next dc) across, ch 1, skip last dc, sl st in end of row 5 on Second Fan. *(18 ch-1 sps)* Fasten off.

Assembly
1: Lay Strips side by side on floor or bed, alternating colors and reversing direction of Strips so that curves on sides fit together. Pin Strips together one seam at a time with large safety pins as they should be joined.

2: Pick up first two Strips, join med. blue with sl st in first pinned space at bottom on right Strip, ch 3, sl st in corresponding space on left Strip, (ch 3, sl st in next space on right Strip, ch 3, sl st in next space on left Strip) to top.

3: Repeat step 2 to join remaining Strips.

Fringe
For each Fringe *(see Stitch Guide),* cut two 16" strands of each color. Holding all four strands together, fold in half. Insert hook from back to front in space at end of Afghan; pull fold through to back, forming loop. Insert cut ends through loop and pull gently to tighten Fringe. Fringe across ends of Afghan. ⚷

Striped Afghan

by Lorna Hendricks

Finished Size: 50" × 54".

Materials:
- ❑ Worsted yarn:
  - 36 oz. white
  - 36 oz. purple
- ❑ I hook or hook needed to obtain gauge

Gauge: 3 rows = 3".

Basic Stitches: Ch, sl st, sc, dc, tr.

Notes: For **color change** *(see Stitch Guide)*, drop first color to wrong side of work, pick up when needed. Do not carry dropped color along back of work. Always change to next color in last st of last color used.

Afghan

Row 1: With purple, ch 181, dc in third ch from hook, dc in each ch across, turn. *(180 dc made)*

Row 2: Ch 1, sc in each st across, changing to white in last st *(see Note)*, turn.

Rows 3–4: Ch 1, sc in each st across, turn. At end of last row change to purple.

Row 5: Ch 2, dc in next 2 sc, work **treble front post (tr fp**—*see Stitch Guide)*, tr fp around next sc three rows below, *skip sc behind tr fp, dc in next 3 sc, tr fp around next sc three rows below; repeat from * across, ending with dc in last 3 sc, turn.

Rows 6–17: Repeat rows 2–5 consecutively three times.

Rows 18–20: Ch 1, sc in each st across, turn. At end of last row change to white.

Row 21: Ch 2, dc in next 2 sc, tr fp around next sc three rows below, *skip sc behind tr fp, dc in next 3 sc, tr fp around next sc three rows below; repeat from * across, ending with dc in last 3 sc, turn.

Row 22: Ch 1, sc in each st across, changing to purple in last st, turn.

Rows 23–24: Ch 1, sc in each st across, turn. At end of last row change to white.

Row 25: Ch 2, dc in next 2 sc, tr fp around next sc three rows below, *skip sc behind tr fp, dc in next 3 sc, tr fp around next sc three rows below; repeat from * across, ending with dc in last 3 sc, turn.

Row 26: Ch 1, sc in each st across, changing to purple in last st, turn.

Rows 27–28: Ch 1, sc in each st across, turn. At end of last row change to white.

Row 29: Ch 2, dc in next 2 sc, tr fp around next sc three rows below, *skip sc behind tr fp, dc in next 3 sc, tr fp around next sc three rows below; repeat from * across, ending with dc in last 3 sc, turn.

Row 30: Ch 1, sc in each st across, changing to purple in last st, turn.

Rows 31–32: Ch 1, sc in each st across, turn. At end of last row change to white.

Row 33: Ch 2, dc in next 2 sc, tr fp around next sc three rows below, *skip sc behind tr fp, dc in next 3 sc, tr fp around next sc three rows below; repeat from * across, ending with dc in last 3 sc, turn.

Rows 34–36: Ch 1, sc in each st across, turn. Change to purple in last st on last row.

Row 37: Ch 2, dc in next 2 sc, tr fp around next sc three rows below, *skip sc behind tr fp, dc in next 3 sc, tr fp around next sc three rows below; repeat from * across, ending with dc in last 3 sc, turn.

Rows 38–136: Repeat rows 6–37 consecutively three times ending with row 28.

Rows 137–139: Repeat rows 3–5.

Rows 140–147 Repeat rows 2–5 consecutively two times.

Row 148: Ch 1, sc in each st across. **Do not turn or fasten off.**

Edging

Rnd 1: Ch 1, sc in end of each row and in each st around, working 3 sc in each corner st, join with sl st in first sc, changing to white.

Rnd 2: Ch 1, sc in each st around, with 3 sc in each corner st and changing to purple in last st.

Rnd 3: Ch 1, sc in each st around, with 3 sc in each corner st, join with sl st in first sc. Fasten off. ⌐━

Spring Flowers

by Ann Parnell

Finished Size: 38" × 48".

Materials:
- ❑ Acrylic sport yarn:
    - 6 oz. teal
    - 4 oz. white
    - 2 oz. each purple, pink and yellow
- ❑ F hook or hook needed to obtain gauge

Gauge: Rnds 1–4 = 4".

Basic Stitches: Ch, sl st, sc, hdc, dc, tr.

Special Stitches: For **beginning cluster (beg cl)**, ch 3, yo 2 times, insert hook in st, yo, pull through, (yo, pull through 2 lps on hook) 2 times, leaving last lps on hook; *yo 2 times, insert hook in same st, yo, pull through, (yo, pull through 2 lps on hook) 2 times, leaving last lps on hook; yo, pull through all lps on hook.

Treble crochet cluster (tr cl), yo 2 times, insert hook in st, yo, pull through, (yo, pull through 2 lps on hook) 2 times, leaving last lps on hook; *yo 2 times, insert hook in same st, yo, pull through, (yo, pull through 2 lps on hook) 2 times, leaving last lps on hook; repeat from * number of times needed for number of tr in cluster; yo, pull through all lps on hook.

First Motif

Rnd 1: With pink, ch 6, sl st in first ch to form ring, ch 3, 15 dc in ring, join with sl st in top of ch-3. *(16 dc made)*

Rnd 2: (Ch 5, dc) in first st, *skip next st, (dc, ch 2, dc) in next st; repeat from * around to last st, skip last st, join with sl st in third ch of ch-5.

Rnd 3: (Sl st, ch 3, 2 dc, ch 2, 3 dc) in next ch sp, (3 dc, ch 2, 3 dc) in each ch-2 sp around, join with sl st in top of ch-3.

Rnd 4: (Ch 1, sc) in sp between next two 3-dc groups, 9 dc in next ch-2 sp, (sc in sp between next two 3-dc groups, 9 dc in next ch-2 sp) around, join with sl st in first sc. Fasten off.

Rnd 5: Join teal with sl st in any sc, **beg cl** *(see Special Stitches)* in same st, *ch 3, sl st under the two lowest vertical bars in back of fifth dc of next 9-dc group, ch 3, **(3-tr cl**—*see Special Stitches*—ch 5, 3-tr cl) in next sc; repeat from * around ending with ch 3, 3-tr cl in first sc, ch 2, join with dc in top of ch-3.

Rnd 6: For **first corner, beg cl** in same ch sp, *ch 4, (3-tr cl, ch 5, 3-tr cl) in next ch sp, ch 4, skip next ch sp, sc in next ch sp, ch 4, skip next ch sp, (3-tr cl, ch 5, 3-tr cl) in next ch sp, ch 4; for **corner (3-tr cl, ch 4, 3-tr cl)** in next ch sp; repeat from * around ending with 3-tr cl in first corner ch sp, ch 5, join with sl st in top of beg cl. Fasten off.

Rnd 7: Join white with sl st in any ch-5 sp of corner, beg cl in same sp, *ch 2; for **V st (dc, ch 3, dc) in same ch sp;** V st in each ch sp across to corner, ch 2, (3-tr cl, ch 3, 3-tr cl) in corner ch sp; repeat from * around ending with 3-tr cl in first corner ch sp, ch 1, join with hdc in top of beg cl.

Rnds 8–10: Beg cl in corner ch sp, *ch 2, V st in each ch sp across to corner, ch 2, (3-tr cl, ch 3, 3-tr cl) in corner ch sp; repeat from * around ending with 3-tr cl in first corner ch sp, ch 1, join. At end of last rnd, ch 3, join with sl st in beg cl. Fasten off.

Second Motif

Rnds 1–4: With yellow, work rnds 1–4 of First Motif.

Rnds 5–9: Work same as First Motif.

Rnd 10: Beg cl in corner ch sp, ch 2, V st in each ch sp across to corner, ch 2, 3-tr cl in corner ch sp, holding First Motif behind this Motif with wrong sides together, (ch 1, sc, ch 1, 3-tr cl) in corner ch sp, ch 2, (dc in next ch sp, ch 1, sc in next V st on this Motif, ch 1, dc in same ch sp) across to corner, ch 2, (3-tr cl, ch 3, 3-tr cl) in corner sp, *ch 2, V st in each ch sp across to corner, ch 2, (3-tr cl, ch 3, 3-tr cl) in corner sp; repeat from *, join with sl st in beg cl. Fasten off.

Work remaining Motifs in same manner, working in colors indicated on illustration.

Edging

Rnd 1: Join white with sl st in any corner ch sp, ch 5, dc in same ch sp, *(dc, ch 2, dc) in each ch sp around with (dc, ch 2, dc, ch 2, dc) in each corner ch sp at corner of assembled piece ending with dc in first corner ch sp, ch 2, join with sl st in third ch of ch-5. Fasten off.

Rnd 2: Join pink with sc in any ch sp, (ch 5, skip next ch sp, sc in next ch sp) around ending with ch 5, join with sc in first sc. Fasten off.

Rnd 3: Join purple with sl st in same ch sp, ch 5, *drop lp from hook, skip next ch sp, insert hook in next ch sp, pick up lp, ch 6; repeat from * around, join with sl st in first sl st. Fasten off.

Rnd 4: Join teal with sl st in same ch sp, ch 6, *drop lp from hook, skip next ch sp, insert hook in next ch sp, pick up lp, ch 7; repeat from * around, join with sl st in first sl st. Fasten off.

Diagonal Cables

by Nazanin Fard

Finished Size: 48" × 66".

Materials:
- ❑ Worsted yarn:
    - 67 oz. lt. purple
    - 10 oz. dk. purple
- ❑ G hook or hook needed to obtain gauge

Gauge: 4 sts = 1"; rows 1–6 = 2"; Panel is 4" wide.

Basic Stitches: Ch, sl st, sc, hdc, dc, tr.

Special Stitches: For **front cable**, skip next 3 sts, tr in next st; working in back of tr, dc in 3 skipped sts.

For **back cable**, skip next 3 sts, tr in next st; working in front of tr, dc in 3 skipped sts.

For **scallop**, 4 dc in next st.

For **joined scallop**, 2 dc in next st, remove loop from hook, insert hook in sp between second and third dc of corresponding scallop on last Panel, return loop to hook and pull loop through sp, ch 1, 2 dc in same st on this Panel as last dc.

First Panel

Row 1: With light yarn, ch 273, sc in second ch from hook, sc in each ch across, turn. *(272 sc made)*

Row 2: Ch 1, sc in each st across, turn.

Row 3: Ch 3 *(counts as first dc)*, dc in next st, work **front cable** *(see Special Stitches)* across to last 2 sts, dc in last 2 sts, turn. *(4 dc, 67 front cable sts)*

Row 4: Ch 3, dc in next st, work **back cable** across to last 2 sts, dc in last 2 sts, turn. *(4 dc, 67 back cable sts)*

Rows 5–6: Ch 1, sc in each st across, turn. *(272 sc)*

Rnd 7: Working in rnds, ch 3, dc in each st across, skip end of row 6, dc in end of row 5, (3 dc in end of next dc row) 2 times, dc in end of row 2, skip next row; working on opposite side of starting ch on row 1, dc in each ch across, skip end of row 1, dc in end of row 2, (3 dc in end of next dc row) 2 times, dc in end of row 5, skip end of next row, join with sl st in top of ch-3. *(560 sts)*

Rnd 8: Working this rnd in **back lps** *(see Stitch Guide)*, ch 1, sc in each st around, join with sl st in first sc.

Rnd 9: Ch 1, sc in first st, skip next st, work **scallop** *(see Special Stitches)*, skip next st, (sc in next st, skip next st, scallop, skip next st) around, join with sl st in first sc. Fasten off. *(140 scallops)*

Rnd 10: Working in unworked **front lps** of rnd 7, join dark yarn with sl st in any st, **reverse sc** *(see Stitch Guide)* in each st around, join with sl st in first reverse sc. Fasten off.

Next Panel (make 8)

Row 1–Rnd 8: Work same as row 1 through rnd 8 of First Panel.

Rnd 9: Ch 1, sc in first st, *(skip next st, scallop, skip next st, sc in next st) 70 times; holding this Panel and last Panel wrong sides tog, (skip next st, work **joined scallop**—*see Special Stitches,* skip next st, sc in next st) 67 times, (skip next st, scallop, skip next st, sc in next st) 2 times, skip next st, scallop, skip last st, join. Fasten off.

Rnd 10: Working in unworked **front lps** of rnd 7, join dark yarn with sl st in any st, reverse sc in each st around, join with sl st in first reverse sc. Fasten off. ⚷

Loop & Lace

by Ruby Gates

Finished Size: 40" × 61".

Materials:
- ❏ Worsted yarn:
  - 26 oz. off-white
  - 26 oz. red
- ❏ Bobby pins *(use for markers)*
- ❏ H hook or hook needed to obtain gauge

Gauge: 7 sts = 2". Each Circle is about 2" across.

Basic Stitches: Ch, sl st, sc, dc, tr.

Special Stitch: For **popcorn**, work number of dc needed in st or lp, drop lp from hook, insert hook in first dc of dc group, pick up dropped lp with hook, pull lp through first dc of group.

Strip (make 6)
First Circle
Rnd 1: With off-white, ch 4, sl st in first ch to form ring, sc in ring, ch 2 *(counts as first dc)*, work 11 more dc in ring, join with sl st in top of ch-2. Fasten off. *(12 dc made)*

Rnd 2: Join red with sc in any dc, (ch 3, sc) in each dc around, ch 3, join with sl st in first sc. Fasten off. Mark last 3 ch lps of rnd.

Added Circle (make 26)
Rnd 1: With off-white, ch 4, sl st in first ch to form ring, sc in ring, ch 2, work 11 more dc in ring, join with sl st in top of ch-2. Fasten off.

Connecting Rnd: Hold previous Circle behind rnd 1 of this Circle with wrong sides together; join red with sc in any dc of last rnd, ch 1, sc in first marked ch lp of previous Circle, ch 1, sc in next dc of last rnd, (ch 1, sc in next marked ch lp of previous Circle, ch 1, sc in next dc of last rnd) 2 times, (ch 3, sc) in each remaining dc around, ch 3, join. Fasten off. Mark 3 ch lps directly opposite of connected ch lps.

Border
Rnd 1: Starting in second Circle from end of Strip just made, join off-white with sc in first unworked ch lp, ch 2, dc in same ch lp, work 2 dc in each of next 2 ch lps, *tr in next ch-1 lp, tr in next ch-3 lp already worked into, (work 2 dc in each of next 3 ch lps, tr in next ch-1 lp, tr in next ch-3 lp already worked into) across to end Circle, work 2 dc in each of next 3 ch lps, 3 dc in next ch lp, 5 dc in next ch lp, 3 dc in next ch lp, 2 dc in each of next 3 ch lps; repeat from * across remaining side and end, tr in next ch-1 lp, tr in next ch-3 lp already worked into, join with sl st in top of ch-2. Fasten off.

Rnd 2: Skip first st of last rnd, join red with sc in next st, ch 2, work **3-dc popcorn** *(see Special Stitch)* in same st, *(ch 2, skip next 2 sts, work 4-dc popcorn in next st) across to dc sts worked around end Circle, (ch 2, skip next st, work 4-dc popcorn in next st) 12 times; repeat from * across remaining side and end Circle, ch 2, skip last st, join with sl st in top of first popcorn. Fasten off.

Rnd 3: Join off-white with sc in any ch lp of last rnd, ch 2, 2 dc in same ch lp, work 3 dc in each ch lp around, join. Fasten off.
*Note: The ch-10 loops and ch-15 loops alternate as you work; if two of the same size loops are next to each other the lacing instructions **will not work**; so periodically check to make sure they alternate.*

Rnd 4: Join red with sc in any st of last rnd, ch 10, (sc in next st, ch 15, sc in next st, ch 10) around to last st, enlarge loop on hook and drop from hook; leaving a 15" end, cut yarn *(this will be used to make last sc and ch-15 loop later)*; to **lace** ch-10 loops around outer edge of Border, skipping over ch-15 loops as you work, reach through first ch-10 loop, pick up next ch-10 loop and pull through first loop; reaching through last loop, pick up next ch-10 loop and pull it through; repeat around Strip; to **connect** last ch-10 loop to first ch-10 loop, weave loose end of ch-10 through first and last loop as shown in illustration *(pull remaining end of yarn completely through both loops—see illustration)*; working behind laced ch-10 loops only *(do not get behind ch-15 loops)*, pick up dropped loop at loose end of ch-10 and sc in last st of rnd 3, ch 15, join with sl st in first sc of rnd 4. Fasten off. *(Always work Lacing in same direction so all Strips will match.)*

Weave Ch 10 Through Loops in Direction of Arrow

First Sc **Last Sc**

To lace ch-15 loops on side edges of Strips together, place two Strips side by side; mark center 14 loops at each end of each Strip *(these loops will be used for the outer edge lacing later)*; beginning at bottom and using ch-15 loops on sides, reach through first loop on first Strip, pick up first loop on second Strip and pull through; reaching through last loop, pick up next loop on first Strip and pull through loop on second Strip; repeat up to top of Strips, stopping at the marked loops.

Place another Strip beside the second Strip and lace edges together, always starting lacing in same manner at bottom to keep direction the same.

To lace outer edges of Strips together, beginning at bottom of Strip on right-hand side of Afghan; working in same manner as ch-10 loops, lace the remaining ch-15 loops up side and around end of Strip; *pick up remaining ch-15 loop at top of next lacing seam and continue lacing across next Strip; repeat from * across all Strips, continue lacing down side and across bottom weaving loops into bottom of seams.

To connect first and last loops, with 15" piece of red yarn, join with sl st in last sc of rnd 4 on Border, ch 15 and finish connecting in same manner as ch-10 loops. ☞

Rose Filet

by Darla Fanton

Finished Size: 46" × 74".

Materials:
- ❑ 45 oz. rose cotton worsted yarn
- ❑ F hook or hook needed to obtain gauge

Gauge: 9 dc = 2"; 2 dc rows = 1".

Basic Stitches: Ch, sl st, dc, tr.

Special Stitches: For **block**, dc in next 3 sts, **or,** 2 dc in next ch sp, dc in next st.
For **beginning block (beg block)**, ch 3, 2 dc in next ch sp, dc in next st, **or,** ch 3, dc in next 3 sts.
For **mesh**, ch 2, skip next 2 chs or sts, dc in next st.

Afghan

Row 1: Ch 312, dc in fourth ch from hook, dc in each ch across, turn. *(310 dc made). First 3 chs count as first dc. Front of row 1 is right side of work.*

Note: *See Special Stitches for working block, beg block and mesh.*

Row 2: Beg block, block 2 times, (mesh 29 times, block 5 times) 2 times, mesh 29 times, block 3 times, turn.

Row 3: Work according to graph across, turn.

Row 4: For **beginning increase (beg inc), ch 5, dc in frouth ch from hook, dc in next ch, dc in next st;** block, (mesh 33 times, block) 2 times, mesh 33 times, block; for **end increase (end inc), tr in bottom strand at side of last dc made** *(see illustration);* *tr in bottom strand at side of last tr made* *(see illustration);* repeat from *, turn.

Rows 5–19: Work according to graph across, turn.

Row 20: For **beginning decrease (beg dec), sl st in first 4 sts;** beg block, mesh 12 times, block 2 times, mesh 2 times, block, mesh 2 times, block 5 times, mesh 6 times, block 3 times, mesh 4 times, block 7 times, mesh, block 3 times, mesh, block 4 times, mesh 5 times, block 5 times, mesh 17 times, block 2 times, mesh 2 times, block, mesh 2 times, block 5 times, mesh 6 times, block 3 times, mesh 6 times, block; for **end decrease (end dec), leave last 3 sts unworked;** turn.

Rows 21–31: Work according to graph across, turn.

Row 32: Ch 3, dc in each st across, turn.

Rows 33–93: Repeat rows 2–32 consecutively, ending with row 31. At end of last row, fasten off. ⌗

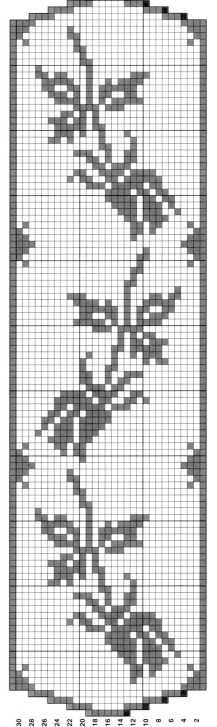

Stitch Guide

Basic Stitches

Slip stitch—sl st: Insert hook in st, yo, pull through st and lp on hook.

Chain—ch: Yo, pull through lp on hook.

Single Crochet—sc: Insert hook in st, yo, pull through st, yo, pull through both lps on hook.

Change Colors: Drop first color; with 2nd color, pull through last 2 lps of st.

Half Double Crochet—hdc: Yo, insert hook in st, yo, pull through st, yo, pull through all 3 lps on hook.

Double Crochet—dc: Yo, insert hook in st, yo, pull through st, (yo, pull through 2 lps) 2 times.

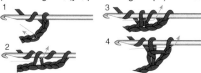

Double Treble Crochet—dtr: Yo 3 times, insert hook in st, yo, pull through st, (yo, pull through 2 lps) 4 times.

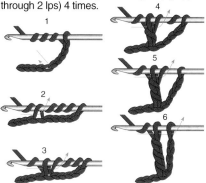

Treble Crochet—tr: Yo 2 times, insert hook in st, yo, pull through st, (yo, pull through 2 lps) 3 times.

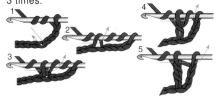

Triple Treble Crochet—ttr: Yo 4 times, insert hook in st, yo, pull through st, (yo, pull through 2 lps) 5 times.

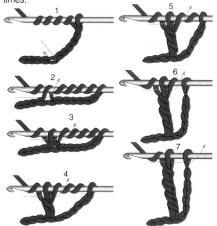

Special Stitches

Front Post Stitch—fp/Back Post Stitch—bp: Yo, insert hook from right to left around post of st on previous row, complete as dc.

Front   Back

Slip Ring

1   4" End

Working over Elastic

Reverse sc

Fringe

A.   B.   C.   D.

2

Leave ring loose until sts are made.

Front loop—front lp: Back loop—back lp:

Front Loop   Back Loop

Tassel

Tie knot.

Tighten, tie knot & tuck ends inside tassel.

Embroidery Stitches

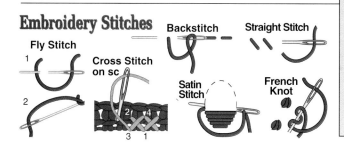

Fly Stitch

1

2

Cross Stitch on sc

2   4
3   1

Backstitch

Satin Stitch

Straight Stitch

French Knot

Standard Abbreviations

ch, chs....chain, chains
dc.........double crochet
hdc......half double crochet
lp, lps.........loop, loops
rnd, rnds..round, rounds
sc ....single crochet
sl st...............slip stitch
sp, sps ....space, spaces
st, sts ....stitch, stitches
tog ....together
tr ....treble crochet
yo ....yarn over
sc next 2 sts tog—
  (insert hook in next st, yo, pull through st) 2 times, yo, pull through all 3 lps on hook.
hdc next 2 sts tog—
  (yo, insert hook in next st), yo, pull through st) 2 times, yo, pull through all 5 lps on hook.
dc next 2 sts tog—(yo, insert hook in next st, yo, pull through st, yo, pull through 2 lps on hook) 2 times, yo, pull through 3 lps on hook.

Hook Sizes

U.S.	Metric	U.K.
14	0.60mm	
12	0.75mm	
10	1.00mm	
6	1.50mm	
5	1.75mm	
B	2.00mm	14
C	2.50mm	12
D	3.00mm	10
E	3.50mm	9
F	4.00mm	8
G	4.50mm	7
	4.75mm	
H	5.00mm	6
I	5.50mm	5
J	6.00mm	4
	6.50mm	3
K	7.00mm	2
	8.00mm	
	9.00mm	
P	10.00mm	
Q	16.00mm	

(U.S. column also: 0, 1, 2, 4, 6, 8, 9, 10, 10½, 11, 13, 15)

Ounces to Grams
1 = 28.4
2 = 56.7
3 = 85.0
4 = 113.4

Grams to Ounces
25 = $\frac{7}{8}$
40 = $1\frac{2}{5}$
50 = $1\frac{3}{4}$
100 = $3\frac{1}{2}$